Hans Fehr · Christoph Rosenberg
Wolfgang Wiegard

Welfare Effects of Value-Added Tax Harmonization in Europe

A Computable
General Equilibrium
Analysis

With 17 Figures

Springer-Verlag
Berlin Heidelberg New York
London Paris Tokyo
Hong Kong Barcelona
Budapest

Dr. Hans Fehr
University of Tübingen
Department of Economics
Mohlstraße 36
72074 Tübingen, FRG

Dr. Christoph Rosenberg
International Monetary Fund
700 19th Street NW
Washington, DC 20431, USA

Professor Dr. Wolfgang Wiegard
University of Tübingen
Department of Economics
Mohlstraße 36
72074 Tübingen, FRG

ISBN-13: 978-3-642-79495-7 e-ISBN-13: 978-3-642-79493-3
DOI: 10.1007/978-3-642-79493-3

Softcover reprint of the hardcover 1st edition 1995

42/2202-5 4 3 2 1 0 - Printed on acid-free paper

Contents

Introduction

This book uses a computable general equilibrium framework to evaluate recent value-added tax reform proposals in the European Union from a welfare point of view.

After the publication of the "White Paper" (1985) on the completion of the internal European market, an intense and heated debate about tax impediments to free trade set in. According to the original plans of the Commission of the European Union, not only physical border controls but also fiscal frontiers within the European Union would have been abolished on New Year's Day 1993. With respect to value-added taxation this amounted to replacing the destination by the origin principle. Even though the origin principle had been favored by some economists from the establishment of a common European value-added tax system, time was not yet ripe for this change. In December 1991, the ECOFIN Council could only agree on the so-called transitional system. In essence, these transitional arrangements maintain the destination principle as far as possible but shift the border tax procedure from national frontiers to firms. The transitional system is supposed to expire on December 31, 1996, with the final solution for value-added taxation in the European Union being decided upon by the ECOFIN Council until December, 1995. In the event of no decision the transitional arrangements will be continued. The most likely solution will be a switch to the origin principle combined with some clearing mechanism to prevent major revenue reallocations between member states. There are, however, some more far-reaching reform proposals that suggest not only a switch to the origin principle but, additionally, the replacement of the tax credit by the subtraction method in calculating value-added tax liabilities.

Our study aims to evaluate the welfare and revenue effects of the different tax reform proposals that followed the White Paper. Computable general equilibrium models seem to provide the appropriate methodological tool kit for the following reasons. They capture quite detailed institutional features of tax systems that are often neglected in taxation theory, but are of great practical concern; they are firmly rooted in general equilibrium theory, avoiding the excessive use of ad hoc assumptions and guaranteeing internal consistency; they combine economic theory with "the real world", i.e., data from the national accounts and other statistics; and, finally, they produce numerical estimates of welfare and revenue effects, which – when taken with the appropriate grain of salt – may yield more insight into tax policy issues than theoretical reasoning based on first-order conditions.

The structure of our book reflects this combination of institutional detail, theoretical reasoning, and policy-relevant numbers. In the first chapter we describe the evolution of the common European value-added tax system from its beginnings up to the present and explain its basic principles. This chapter may also serve as an introduction to value-added taxation. Chapter II discusses the relevant tax reform options in more detail. For each reform variant we describe its main institutional features, illustrate the mechanics of tax liability and revenue calculation by a numerical example, and present a more general mathematical formulation, which later becomes part of our computable equilibrium model. The third chapter develops the theoretical foundations necessary to evaluate and explain the welfare and revenue effects of value-added tax reforms. We discuss the efficiency properties of international taxation principles for value-added taxation, examine the validity of the exchange rate argument, and decompose welfare effects into domestic and international substitution and income effects. The following chapter contains a detailed description of our computable equilibrium model. We specify functional forms of utility and production functions and characterize public sector behavior and foreign trade relationships. Another section describes the construction of a micro-consistent data set and the calibration calculations that fit the model parameters to the base year's data set. After all these preliminaries, chapter V finally presents our simulation results and their economic explanations. The concluding chapter summarizes the basic lessons from our study and draws some policy conclusions.

Even though we feel that the fascination of computable equilibrium models lies in its unique combination of institutional detail, economic theory, and numerical computation, the various chapters of our book may be read independently of each other – perhaps occasionally at the cost of some overlap. The third chapter, for example, dealing with the efficiency properties of value-added taxes, may be of interest for its own sake. On the other hand, chapter IV may be skipped by experts from the computable equilibrium community.

Most of this book was completed while all three authors were affiliated with the University of Regensburg.* The department of economics provided a congenial atmosphere for research, which hopefully is reflected in the quality of this book. We especially thank our secretary, Christine Oel, for the beautiful job she did. For good reason, she is called the department's TEX-Queen. The technical and analytical skills of Dr. Peter Gottfried were of great help, as were the suggestions and critical remarks by Professor Clive Bell. Michelle Douglas and Rachel Hall helped to edit the manuscript. We would like to thank them all. Finally, we acknowledge generous support from the Deutsche Forschungsgemeinschaft.

Some material has previously been published in the *European Economic Review* (1993), the *Finanzarchiv* (1994) and, in German, in some other periodicals. The reader should be aware that the results presented here have been recomputed with an updated data set.

* Currently, Fehr is at Boston University, Wiegard is at the University of Tuebingen, and Rosenberg is an economist at the International Monetary Fund; however, the views expressed in this book are not necessarily those of the Fund or its member authorities.

Chapter I

An Introduction to Value-added Taxation

The debate about the use of commodity taxation as a means of protectionism is as old as the taxation of commodities itself. There were plenty of quarrels about the alleged discrimination against foreign goods and the distribution of tax revenues between different regions in medieval Europe. In 1158 a quarrel over the salt tax between bishop Otto of *Freising* and Henry the Lion resulted in the foundation of the city of Munich. Emperor Friedrich Barbarossa, himself, had to decide on a mutually acceptable distribution of salt-tax revenues, preventing a bloody battle at the very last minute. Elsewhere such tax quarrels were not settled so peacefully. The *Alcabala*, an early form of a sales tax, which was levied in Spain and its dependencies, infuriated Spain's trading partners to such an extent that Spanish tax collectors abroad were sometimes killed. Although the battle ground has largely moved to the conference table or the courts, tax discrimination between domestic and foreign goods draws just as much attention today as it did in the Middle Ages.

This question becomes particularly relevant if countries form an economic union and explicitly refrain from any (tax) discrimination between domestic and foreign goods. An early example is Germany's economic integration in the 19th century. The debate between Bavaria and other members of the German *Zollverein* (founded in 1834) on harmonizing the taxation of beer lasted for nearly 85 years. There is some evidence that the exhausting quarrels over tax harmonization in Germany in the 19th century will be repeated in the 20th century as part of the European unification process. The basic problem is the same: fiscally independent states are faced with the loss of significant parts of their tax souvereignty, abandoning fiscal traditions which may go back centuries. This conflict is reflected in the current debate on the harmonization of value-added taxes (VAT) in Europe.

In the first section of this introductory chapter we will briefly review the development of value-added taxation in Europe. The technical details of VAT accounting will be discussed in the second section. The third section contains the outline of our book and a selective literature survey, concentrating on quantitative studies of recent VAT reform proposals in Europe.

1. The Development of Value-added Taxation in the European Union

1.1. From the Beginnings to the White Book[1]

1.1.1. The Development of Turnover Taxes in Europe

The turnover tax has a long tradition in Europe, reaching back to the ἐπώνιον, which was imposed by the Greek city states of the 5th century BC, and the Roman *centesima rerum venalium*. In the Middle Ages, general fees and stamps on goods and services were particularly popular in Spain (e.g. the *Alcabala* mentioned above), France, and the German imperial towns. Even if temporarily replaced by direct taxes, turnover taxes experienced an unprecedented renaissance after World War I. In 1919, von Siemens, a German businessman, was the first to propose an early variant of modern value-added taxes, allowing for certain deductions from gross turnover. His idea of a tax on *net* turnover, however, was not realized for more than thirty years. All European turnover taxes of the interwar period were levied on *gross* turnover. Due to its serious disadvantages – for example, the tax burden on a commodity depended on the number of production stages through which it passed – the von Siemens proposal of a tax on *net* turnover was reconsidered. In 1949, the Shoup-Mission had already recommended

[1] Hahn (1988) gives a very detailed description of the VAT reform debate.

introducing a value-added tax system in post-war Japan. After successive postponements, the proposal was completely abrogated in 1954.[2] In the same year, France became the first European country to introduce a *net* turnover tax (*"taxe sur la valeur ajoutée"*), applying the tax to revenues less certain deductions.

Certain conventions also emerged with respect to the taxation of international trade. It became common practice between countries to levy a compensating tax on imports and to rebate taxes on exports. While the exact determination of these tax rebates and import taxes may have been disputed, the general principle of some border tax adjustments was commonly accepted. This was legalized by the regulations of the General Agreement on Tariffs and Trade (GATT) of 1947, which explicitly permitted border tax adjustments for indirect taxes. These GATT regulations, however, were quite vague on some points and open to divergent interpretations. The "correct" use of border tax adjustments as well as the legitimacy of the system itself remained hotly disputed. Moreover, new questions arose in connection with European unification. The harmonization of turnover taxes, that is of tax types, tax bases and tax rates, was put on the European agenda.

The nucleus of tax harmonization, as so often in the history of European integration, was the Benelux region. During the German occupation of World War II the exiled governments of the Netherlands, Belgium and Luxembourg signed a treaty of close political and economic cooperation. This treaty explicitly referred to the removal of border tax adjustments. This plan was specified more precisely by a committee of fiscal experts that was established in 1946. The resulting tax policy draft for the Benelux Union proposed a complete switch to the origin principle (OP) while maintaining the destination principle (DP) with respect to all other countries.[3] A far-reaching harmonization of tax structures and tax rates was also envisaged. This first attempt to draw up a plan for an extensive fiscal integration failed, however, because it left unresolved the question of how tax revenues would be distributed, a failure that was to plague its many successors. Hence,

---

[2] See Sullivan (1965) for a detailed discussion of VAT legislation in France and Japan.

[3] The destination principle and the origin principle will be defined in the next section. For the moment, let the DP be a system where taxes on exports are refunded and imports are taxed when crossing the border. The OP is a system without such border tax adjustments.

the actual treaty, which became effective January 1, 1948, confined the Benelux Union to a pure tariff union (Scailteur, 1974, pp. 476-478).

The first step towards the European Union as we know it was the formation of the European Coal and Steel Community (ECSC), which came into being on April 18, 1951, and whose members were the Benelux states, the Federal Republic of Germany, France, and Italy. The treaty excluded the question of border taxes and only vaguely talked about the removal of distorting trade barriers. Very soon it became obvious, however, that this could not be seen independently of the border tax adjustment procedure. The German *"Wirtschaftsvereinigung Eisen- und Stahlindustrie"* (steel industry federation) filed a complaint to the High Authority[4] concerning the 19 percent French import tax, the rate being only four percent in Germany. To German industry, this boiled down to discrimination against German and in favor of French steel. The argument was based on the heavier direct tax burden on German products (for which border tax adjustments were not permitted) and on the higher effective tax burden in Germany, which was due to the cascading effect of the gross turnover tax. Consequently, the plaintiffs demanded the abolition of border tax adjustments, i.e. a switch to the origin principle, for steel products. France, on the other hand, argued that only a system of border tax adjustments could ensure a trade-neutral tax system, because it gave countries the possibility of balancing price differentials due to differing tax rates.

The Franco-German tax quarrel raised the very fundamental problem of an appropriate international taxation principle for cross-border trade. The High Authority did not consider itself competent enough to give an immediate answer to this question and appointed a committee under the chairmanship of the Dutch economist Jan Tinbergen. In a mere three weeks this group of experts prepared a "Report on the problems raised by the different turnover tax systems applied within the common market", henceforth referred to as the Tinbergen Report (1953). In a simple model framework the committee came to the somewhat surprising conclusion, that "so far as long-term static equilibrium is concerned, the only difference between systems *a* and *b* would be in the exchange rate" (1953, p. 24).[5] Provided that all commodities were

---

[4] The High Authority was a decision-taking body of the ECSC, whose members were designated by the governments of the member states.

[5] Here, system *a* refers to the destination principle and system *b* to the origin principle.

taxed at the same rate within any country, the switch from one international taxation principle to the other would have no real effects at all.

This is the first time that the so-called "exchange rate argument" appeared in the literature. The idea that the destination and the origin principle were equivalent under certain conditions merely provided the theoretical background for the committee's conclusions. With regard to the tax quarrel between Germany and France, two important qualifications were made. First, it was argued, the tax in question was a special tax on steel products, not a general turnover tax. Second, the destination principle (system *a*) was not applied correctly in Germany since the border tax adjustment procedure could not fully reflect the effective tax burden on German products. Abolishing the border tax adjustment procedure would therefore result in economic distortions. Since exchange rates were not flexible, and Germany was not likely to adopt a French-type *net* turnover tax, the Tinbergen Report was reluctant to recommend removing border tax adjustments for the steel sector only. When applying the destination principle, the Report noted that one should take care that the compensating tax rate on steel imports should not exceed the domestic rate. The High Authority decided to maintain the system as it was, and Germany had to surrender. The economic insights presented in the Tinbergen Report, however, caused a lively political and academic debate. Public attention was now directed towards questions relating to a common tax base and to international taxation principles in an economic union.

1.1.2. The Treaty of Rome[6]

The Treaty of Rome, which was signed on March 25, 1957 in Rome, was the next and most important step in the process of European unification. Its signatories, the Benelux countries, France, Germany, and Italy, founded the European Economic Community (EEC). Their aim was to create a legal framework for a common European market for factors and goods, in which cross-border trade was not distorted by any kind of government intervention. With respect to indirect taxation, the old question of how border tax adjustments should be designed to guarantee trade neutrality arose once more. Government

[6] The historical development and the institutions (Council of Ministers, Commission and so on) of the European Community are described in Nicoll and Salmon (1994).

officials could not, however, come to an agreement on this question. As so often in the history of European integration, they postponed this problem and decided to leave its solution to a future council of ministers. Nevertheless, the Treaty of Rome contains some important tax rules, which played a decisive role in the harmonization debates of the following years. The contents of Articles 95 to 97 and 99 to 101, which refer to indirect taxes, will therefore be sketched briefly.

The first three articles in the part of the Treaty of Rome devoted to taxation issues, were supposed to prevent discrimination against goods from EEC partner countries, i.e. to eliminate the disputed border tax adjustment procedure as a means of protectionist trade policy. Article 95 (1) of the Treaty therefore states: "No Member State shall impose, directly or indirectly, on the products of other Member States any internal taxation of any kind in excess of that imposed directly or indirectly on similar domestic products". This is thought to confine import levies to the level of domestic tax rates. Regarding exports to EEC partner countries, Article 96 states that "...any repayment of internal taxation [on goods] shall not exceed the internal taxation imposed on them". Finally, the problem of determining the correct rate if a gross (i.e., cascade type) turnover tax is in place is addressed in Article 97. Flat import levies are permitted, "provided that there is no infringement of the principles laid down in Articles 95 and 96", i.e. as long as they do not exceed the nominal domestic rates. To summarize, Articles 95 to 97 implicitly accept the destination principle as the international taxation principle; the respective provisions are thought to ensure the correct application of the border tax adjustment procedure.

In Article 99 of the Treaty of Rome, the Community goes a step further in explicitly laying out a harmonization requirement. This implies not only an adjustment of tax rates and tax structures, but also the possibility of a switch in the taxation principle. Some authors, such as Andel (1985, p. 13), even see a commitment to the origin principle. According to his interpretation, the wording that indirect taxes "can be harmonized in the interest of the common market" (Article 99 (1)) requires a complete abolition of tax barriers and hence of border tax adjustments. Looking at the 35 years following the Treaty of Rome, one may indeed note a slow but steady move towards this goal.

Articles 95 to 97 attempt to restrict the protectionist manoeuvers of member states within the destination principle, while Article 99 opens the possibility for the Council to promote the goal of tax harmonization. The route is laid out in Article 99 (2) in connection with Articles 100 and 101. These articles regulate the formal procedure for dealing with harmonization proposals, including the Commission's draft and its course through various EEC institutions (Council of Economic and Social Affairs, European Parliament, Council of Ministers) until its final adoption as an official tax directive by the EEC Council. According to Article 189 of the Treaty of Rome, such directives are binding upon all member states, i.e. they must be transformed into national legislation. Within this legal framework the EEC has meanwhile prepared over twenty turnover tax draft proposals, most of which have been adopted. Most of them deal with details; only the first, the second, and the sixth Council Directive, which we will discuss in the next section, are of a more general interest.

1.1.3. Creating a European Value-added Tax

The immediate effects of the Treaty of Rome were rather modest. Due to the intentionally vague formulations in the legal text, many questions were left unanswered. For example, the rather arbitrary determination of the flat border tax adjustment rate in countries with cascade (gross) turnover taxes opened ample possibilities for discrimination; a true tax content on a commodity below this rate caused an export subsidy or import discrimination. In the years following the Treaty of Rome, some countries, especially Italy and Belgium, made extensive use of such manipulation possibilities. Almost inevitably, the question of a common turnover tax system became the focus of interest.

Persistent quarrels about the turnover tax at the end of the 1950s made the EEC Commission think seriously about a final solution to the problem. The commissioner responsible for trade issues, von der Groeben, appointed a "Fiscal and Financial Affairs Committee", which was chaired by the German economist Fritz Neumark. This group of academics was supposed to clarify the basic economic questions of a unified turnover tax law for Europe. In addition to the committee, a task-force of three subgroups (A, B and C), with experts and practitioners from national administrations, was established.

The Fiscal and Financial Affairs Committee's report (henceforth referred to as the Neumark Report) is a landmark in European tax harmonization history. It established the idea that European tax integration should be understood as a continuous process in accordance with the general coalescence of the member states, i.e. should not be a one-time undertaking. Consequently, the Neumark Report developed a step-by-step plan in which the necessary measures were ranked in order of priority. The first and most important step was "...that none of the Member States of the EEC maintains a cascade system of gross turnover tax" (Neumark Report, 1963, p. 124). All EEC members should introduce a net turnover (or value-added) tax, as already existed in France.

There was broad agreement in favor of an all-stage, non-cumulative turnover tax. Possible alternatives, such as a one-stage retail tax or a wholesale tax, were unanimously rejected by the members of the Neumark Committee. A much more controversial discussion arose about which was the most practicable and theoretically superior method of calculating tax liabilities. The basic choice was between the credit or invoice method on the one hand, and the subtraction method on the other. Under the former, each taxable firm may deduct the taxes paid on its purchases of intermediate and investment goods from the tax that is due on its sales. Under the subtraction method, the firm deducts its outlays from its sales and applies the tax rate to the difference. In the second section of this chapter and in Chapter II this will be explained in more detail.

The Neumark Committee itself, consisting almost exclusively of academics, favored the subtraction method. It was argued that only this method would lead neither to tax revenue shifts nor to trade distortions once the origin principle had been introduced (Neumark Report, 1963, p. 130). Task-force subgroup C, however, composed of tax experts from member states and the Commission, was in favor of the credit method.

The proponents of the subtraction method in the Neumark Committee built their arguments on two fairly unrealistic assumptions. First, they presupposed a far-reaching harmonization of tax rates within the EEC. Second, they believed the origin principle would be realized shortly. Rate harmonization as well as a switch to the origin principle have not, however, come about until today. The practitioners in subgroup C may have realized that an immediate transition to the origin principle was not a very realistic prospect in view of the strong prevailing national interests (especially the fear of revenue losses). Moreover, they were well aware of the reservations about rate harmonization between member states. In their view, the credit method was the superior method of tax calculation under the destination principle, especially because correct border tax adjustments were possible even if tax rates were differentiated within and between countries. As is well-known, the EEC Commission decided in favor of the credit method. With hindsight, this decision was a very prudent and farsighted one.

Based on the findings of the Neumark Report (1963) and a joint report of the ABC subgroups, the EEC Commission in November 1962 proposed a three-stage procedure for harmonizing turnover taxes. During the first stage, member states would replace their *gross* turnover taxes with a non-cumulative system. During the second stage (ending on December 31, 1969), a common value-added tax would be introduced. Finally, in the third stage, the abolition of fiscal frontiers was at stake. After intensive discussion in the European Parliament and the Council of Ministers, the latter adopted the First and the Second VAT Directive, both dated April 11, 1967. The First Directive required all member states, except for France, to replace their turnover taxes with a common value-added tax not later than January 1, 1970. The Second Directive was more precise, specifying the technical details of a European VAT system, utilizing the credit method and the destination principle.

For good reasons, the introduction of these two VAT Directives was celebrated as a great success of European integration. The first countries to comply with the Directives were France (1968) and Germany (1968). In the case of France, the change in taxation was less dramatic and required little adjustment. Although Luxembourg and the Netherlands introduced their VAT regulations in 1969, i.e. within the appointed time, Belgium and Italy were rather reluctant to introduce the new tax. They complied only after several postponements. By 1973, however, all EEC member states, including the new entrants Denmark, Ireland, and the United Kingdom, had introduced a consumption type value-added tax.[7]

Although all member states of the EEC had introduced value-added taxes by 1973, the national tax laws differed considerably with respect to some important details. The VAT treatment of agriculture, the deduction of import taxes, the existence of exemptions, and the taxation of services across frontiers were the most obvious problem areas, requiring further harmonization efforts. But there was another, perhaps more pressing reason to achieve closer harmonization of national VAT laws. In April 1970 the Council of Ministers decided to fund the

[7] The difference between consumption and income type value-added taxes will be explained in the second section.

Community's budget with its own resources. From 1975 on, the EEC budget would comprise agricultural levies, customs duties, and a one per cent levy on a VAT tax basis, determined in a uniform manner for all member states. A uniform basis of assessment in all member states was required in order to eliminate the influence of differences in national VAT rates on national contributions to the EEC budget.

Against this background, the Sixth VAT Directive of May 17, 1977 was a further landmark on Europe's way to a universal value-added tax system. Its general aim was a common basis of assessment in all member states through the adoption of more precise definitions concerning taxable transactions, place of taxable transactions, taxable persons, territorial application and so on. Furthermore, the Sixth Directive contained special provisions for farmers, travel agencies, and secondhand sales and listed the allowable exemptions including postal, medical, social, educational and cultural services, and certain insurance, banking and financial transactions.[8]

The years following the Sixth VAT Directive were full of discussions about the correct interpretation of its 38 articles. Since then, fifteen or more directives have been submitted to the Council of Ministers, ten of which have been approved by the Council. Most of them struggled with minor details. In some respect, there were even relapses, as in the case of the Twentieth Directive, authorizing Germany to compensate its farmers by way of higher VAT tax credits for income losses from agricultural policy. The Commission and the Council increasingly seemed to have lost sight of the previously established goal of abolishing tax barriers.

1.2. The VAT Harmonization Debate Since 1985

1.2.1. The White Paper

The 1980s marked the beginning of a new pro-European era within the continental part of the European Community (EC). It was the time when truckers blocked the frontiers between Italy, France and Germany for days and weeks, making it obvious to everybody that border controls were still considerably impeding trade within the Community. The European Parliament, which was now directly elected, demanded

---

[8] See Terra and Kajus (1992, pp. 9-17) for more details.

a clear signal in favor of a truly integrated market. As a consequence, the European Council committed itself to the completion of the internal market until 1992. Shortly thereafter the EC Commission under its new president Jacques Delors published the "White Paper" (COM (85) 310 final), which lays out the consequences of this commitment. This blueprint for economic integration presented a detailed program for the creation of the European internal market and a timetable for implementing the necessary measures. The White Paper is divided into three parts: the removal of physical barriers (part 1); the removal of technical barriers (part 2); and the removal of tax barriers (part 3). Taken together, 279 separate measures are listed, all of which were to have been adopted by the Council and enacted by the national parliaments.[9]

The necessary legal basis was created by the Single European Act, which became effective on July 1, 1987 and considerably revised the Treaty of Rome. With regard to the internal market, the Treaty of Rome was supplemented by Article 8a, which bound the Community gradually to implement the Single Market, with completion planned for December 1992. The internal market was defined as "...an area without internal frontiers in which the free movement of goods, persons, services and capital is ensured in accordance with the provisions of this Treaty". The harmonization of laws concerning indirect taxation was seen as a prerequisite for the functioning of the Single Market. The legal basis was created by the revised Article 99, which directly refers to the time limit laid down in Article 8a. While the unanimity principle was generally replaced by a qualified majority principle, it was retained for taxation questions.

The Commission considered the harmonization of indirect taxes to be one of the keys to the completion of the internal market and the White Paper made clear what remained to be done in this field. The general aim was to fully abolish intra-community border controls and fiscal frontiers by January 1, 1993. Twenty more VAT Directives were thought to be necessary to realize the complete harmonization of value-added taxes.

With its courageous program for the Single Market, the Commission had added monumentum to European integration. The setting of a deadline for the elimination of all border controls meant that

[9] A brief review of the third part of the White Book can be found in van der Zanden and Terra (1987).

member states had to tackle the VAT harmonization issue seriously. In the next sections we will describe the tough negotiations between the Commission and the Council for Economic and Financial Affairs (ECOFIN) that led to the present compromise, and the (possible) future solution. Our presentation is confined to the broad policy lines; the details of the different reform proposals are explained in the next chapter.

1.2.2. The 1987/89 Harmonization Proposals

Many questions concerning the technical and administrative details of VAT were left open in the White Paper. In its global communication, "Completion of the Internal Market: Approximation of Indirect Tax Rates and Harmonization of Indirect Tax Structure" (COM (87), 320 final), the Commission became more specific. In August 1987 it presented a number of detailed VAT proposals (COM (87) 321 final, COM (87) 322 final, COM (87) 324 final) and a working document (COM (87) 323 final/2) to the Council. In essence, the EC Commission's aim was to treat cross-border trade within the Community in the same way as trade within a member state. This would mean the abolition of the existing system of relieving goods from tax at exportation and of imposing tax at importation. VAT on foreign goods is fully credited by domestic fiscal authorities.

The abolition of fiscal frontiers would lead to VAT revenue shifts between EC member states. Therefore, a clearing system had to be installed to ensure that the same revenue distribution prevailed as under the destination principle. Basically, this is a central account through which member states draw or pay money periodically, depending on the extent to which they are net exporters and net importers. The respective amounts are calculated on the basis of information supplied in the traders' VAT returns. According to the Commission, this system had to be supplemented by a standardization of the number and range of VAT rates as well as by a reduction in the spread of tax rates. Without such additional measures intolerable competitive distortions, trade deflections, and tax evasion were feared.

The 1987 harmonization proposal turned out to be too ambitious. Even supporters of the clearing idea, such as Germany, considered the envisaged clearing system too complicated, too bureaucratic, and too expensive. Other countries did not even agree to abolish fiscal frontiers. It became obvious that the Commission's harmonization plans were politically infeasible. At an informal meeting of the European ministers of finance in September 1988, the Commission was advised to revise its concepts and to present a new, more moderate proposal.

The Commission did its homework quickly. Only a year later it presented a revised draft to the Council and the European Parliament (COM (89) 260 final). Basically, this proposal attempted to rescue the original harmonization strategy by providing far-reaching concessions to the member states. Numerous special provisions with respect to purchases of tax-exempt firms in other member states were added; traveller's allowances were quadrupled; and mail order and direct car imports were supposed to be administered according to the destination principle. With regard to intra-community trade between taxable firms, however, the Commission stuck to the abolition of border tax adjustments. The Commission was also generous regarding tax rate adjustments. With regard to the standard rate only a minimum rate, not lower than 14 per cent, was suggested. Even zero rates were allowed for a limited number of products. Finally, the clearing mechanism was redesigned. Tax claims and liabilities were now to be calculated on the basis of inter-country trade statistics. This would make it possible to do the accounting on a purely bilateral basis, making a central clearing institution obsolete. A prerequisite for such a system is, of course, the existence of reliable trade statistics, even after border controls had been abolished. According to the Commission this was supposed to be accomplished by making EC firms file regular reports on their intra-community transactions (COM (88) 810 final).

All these concessions, however, were in vain. An ad-hoc group was appointed by the Council to examine the latest Commission proposals and it soon turned out that most member states were not willing to accept this compromise. Instead, the majority wanted to stick to some sort of destination principle – at least for a transitional period.

1.2.3. A Tough Compromise: The Transitional System

On October 9, 1989 the ECOFIN Council finally decided to abandon the idea of immediately switching, fully or partly, to the origin principle. At least for a transitional period, border tax adjustments were to be maintained, although not necessarily at the national border. Quite obviously, the political intention of such a purely cosmetic operation (after all, tax borders remain effective) was to abolish turnpikes with great pomp, while maintaining the destination principle of VAT at large. There remained, however, an increased danger of tax evasion.

This was supposed to be mitigated by stricter controls, an obligation on firms for extensive VAT reporting, and improved cooperation among national fiscal authorities. In addition, special provisions concerning distance selling (especially mail order and vehicle purchases) were thought to ensure the destination principle even in this sensitive area. The Commission was required to work out the legal and administrative details of such a transitional system.

Now that its original harmonization plan had been fully abandoned, the Commission had to swallow a bitter pill and work on a transitional system, meeting the Council's objectives. The revised harmonization plan was completed in May 1990 and consisted of two parts: the proposal for a transitional system (COM (90) 182 final) and a proposal for improved cooperation by national administrations in the field of indirect taxation (COM (90) 183 final).[10] Following the Council's recommendations, the transitional system amounts to the following:

- no more controls at the (national) border;
- destination principle for cross-border trade between firms;
- origin principle for non-commercial cross-border shopping within the Community;
- special provisions for distance sales to final consumers.

The transitional system was supposed to apply only until December 31, 1996. It was simply added to the original proposal of August 1987. Thus, by adopting the transitional system, the Council would automatically acknowledge its ultimate replacement by a "definite system for the taxation of trade between Member States based in principle on taxation in the Member State of origin of the goods or services supplied" (Aujean and Vis, 1992, p. 118).

While the transitional system may seem straightforward, its details are somewhat tricky. The Commission spent considerable effort on designing accurate control mechanisms that would keep the administrative burden for firms as small as possible. At first, the computerized information exchange system to be used by fiscal authorities was not accepted by the Council, supposedly because it was not accurate enough. The ECOFIN Council's ad-hoc group modified the system, making firms report their intra-community turnovers on a quarterly basis. These proposals were finally adopted on December 3, 1990.

---

[10] Additionally, an amended proposal concerning trade statistic (COM(90)177 final) was presented.

Further problems arose in connection with the legal construction of a European VAT system. Maintaining the destination principle without frontier controls required the creation of a new taxable event which would be applicable only to transactions between taxable entities in the Community. Other legal questions to be resolved included the chargeability of the tax, the place of supply of goods, and triangular transactions. Among the experts consensus could, however, be reached without major discussion.

The most troublesome question was the treatment of distance sales to final consumers. The original Commission proposals were not regarded as sufficient to prevent competitive distortions and revenue shifts between member states. The ECOFIN Council devised two special provisions to deal with cross-border sales to private households. First, for cross-border acquisitions of new vehicles, which were believed to be particularily sensitive to intra-community tax rate differentials, the decision was made to levy the tax in the member state where the first (permanent) registration took place. Second, all distance sales to final consumers were to be taxed in the country of destination, provided the vendor had an annual turnover of more than 100,000 ECU (in some special cases 35,000 ECU) with the respective partner country. Distance sales are defined as all supplies of goods for which the transport of the goods is by or on behalf of the vendor. Thus this provision is not, as originally intended by the Commission, confined to mail order firms.

Particularily this last feature of the transitional system was heavily disputed. Some countries, such as Germany, favored a much broader definition of turnovers to be treated according to the origin principle. Most countries, however, were extremely fearful of losing VAT revenues. Since fairly generous travel allowances were already in place before 1993, not much was expected to change compared to the present destination principle. This prospect led the ECOFIN Council to adopt the transitional system at its December 16, 1991 meeting. In the meantime, it has been largely transformed into national laws.

Several months earlier, on June 24, 1991, the ECOFIN Council had already decided on the appropriate VAT rate structure and level in the Community. Here, too, the Commission had to give up some of its original goals. According to the Council's compromise, member states have to apply a minimum standard rate of at least 15 per cent. They may, however, apply a minimum reduced rate of 5 per cent to a limited list of goods and services. Countries with lower reduced rates (including zero rates) may retain these. This tax rate diversity seemed tolerable because the transitional system largely maintained the DP. Rate adjustments in order to prevent trade distortions were not considered to be as urgent as under the origin principle.

1.2.4. What Comes After 1996?

The transitional system is supposed to expire on December 31, 1996. Specific proposals for the definitive VAT system in the EU have to be accepted by the Council before December 31, 1995. Otherwise, the transitional arrangements are automatically continued, and introduction of the definitive system will be postponed. The first possibility for value-added taxation after 1996 therefore is that the transitional system will be the final one, at least for this century. The second option is that the Council will adopt an amended version of the Commission's 1989 proposal as presented in COM (89) 260 final. At present, the Commission is working on an improved version of that proposal.

There is, however, a third, more radical alternative. Some prominent economists in Germany have launched a proposal not only to switch to the origin principle in 1997 but also to replace the tax credit method with the subtraction method in calculating tax liabilities. This stirs up the old debate from the 1960s about the appropriate VAT system when tax frontiers have been abolished. The main argument of its advocates is that such a system would make a harmonization of tax rate levels unnecessary. If tax rates were uniform within each country, distortions in competition due to differing tax rate levels in the member states could be compensated for by a one time adjustment of exchange rates. Three variations of this proposal were put forward.

The first goes back to the Council of Economic Advisors to the German Ministry of Economics (1986). This group of eminent economists proposed retaining the credit method for domestic transactions, but switching to the subtraction method for cross-border transactions between taxable entities. Even if uniform VAT rates within each country were considered to be the ulitmate aspiration, differing rates could be maintained provided a common definition of low-taxed goods could be agreed upon. A similar proposal, although developed in a somewhat different model framework, was suggested by Sinn (1990).

A second variation was proposed by the Kiel Institute for World Economics (Siebert, 1989a, 1989b; Boss, 1989; Donges, 1989). This calls for a complete transition to the subtraction method in all member states. It was pointed out that reduced tax rates would apply mainly to non-traded goods and would therefore not be problematic.

A final variation was proposed by Terra (1988, pp. 105-106), Krause-Junk (1990), and was discussed much earlier by Shoup (1969, pp. 263-264). It attempts to maintain the advantage of the subtraction method, namely, the equalization of different tax levels through the exchange rate, while still retaining the credit method. A fictive tax credit would be allowed for at the first stage through which the commodity passed after importation. Firms in the importing country would not deduct the amount actually paid in the exporting country but rather the amount they would have paid according to domestic rates on the value of the (net) import. The VAT rate used for this tax credit is always the rate applicable to the importing firm.

In the literature[11] it has been shown that the first and the third variant, i.e. the simultaneous application of the credit and the subtraction method, raise considerable technical and administrative difficulties. Only the second variant, the complete transition to the subtraction method, can be considered as a serious alternative to the credit method.

2. Principles of Value-added Taxation

In the last section we referred to several features of value-added taxation; we will now try to be more precise in characterizing those features of VAT that are of central importance for our study. Other features are dealt with only cursorily.

When considering the enactment or reform of value-added taxes the following choices have to be made:[12]

- the broad type of tax: consumption versus income versus gross product type;
- the rate structure: uniform versus differentiated rate structure;
- the method of calculating tax liabilities: credit versus subtraction method;
- the international taxation principle: destination versus origin principle or variants thereof;

[11] See, especially, Andel (1986) or Spahn and Kaiser (1991).

[12] Similar classification schemes may be found in Shoup (1990), Tait (1988), McLure (1987) and U.S. Treasury Department (1984).

- other issues: exemption versus zero rating; tax treatment of special industries.

In our context, the third and the fourth topic are of special importance.

2.1. Types of Value-added Taxes

Even if the term "value-added tax" (VAT) is quite common now, it is highly misleading. Generally, a value-added tax need not be a tax on value-added, neither in the aggregate nor at the single firm's level. In principle, there are three broad types of value-added taxes differing in their treatment of capital goods that have been purchased from other firms.

To illustrate the differences, consider the following example of a three-staged production process, where succeeding stages may be interpreted as manufacturing, wholesaling, and retailing.

Each firm employs a given capital stock at the beginning of the production process (which depreciates linearly at a rate of 5 per cent) and hires primary factors of production. For each firm, the value of its capital stock as well as its factor payments and profits are given in lines 3 and 4 of Table 1. Firm 1 produces intermediate goods using only primary factors and sells its product to firm 2. This firm employs intermediates as well as primary factors to produce a commodity that is sold to firm 3 and is used as both an intermediate input and as a capital good. Firm 3, finally, produces a consumption good. Sales of goods and purchases of inputs are listed in lines 1 and 2 of Table 1. The last lines illustrate the tax bases for the three types of value-added taxes.

The three possible types of value-added taxes are: consumption, income and gross product type, where each refers to the *aggregate* tax base.

Consider the consumption type VAT first. Each individual firm determines its tax base by deducting all its input purchases of intermediate goods and capital goods (including additions to inventories) from its total sales. Purchases of capital goods are equal to gross investment expenditures. On an aggregate level, total sales minus outlays for intermediate inputs in a closed economy yields gross national product. Deducting gross investment (net investment and depreciation) one obtains aggregate consumption as the aggregate tax base. Hence, a multi-stage consumption type VAT is equivalent to an ideal retail tax: a single-stage tax on sales to final consumers.

Table 1. Illustrating different types of VAT by a three stage production process

Items (in ECU)	Stage of production 1	2	3	Aggregate
1. Sales of ...				
a. intermediate goods	110	120		230
b. capital goods		50		50
c. consumer goods			185	185
2. Input purchases of ...				
a. intermediate goods		110	120	230
b. capital goods			50	50
3. Capital stock ...				
a. initial value	200	200	300	700
b. depreciation	10	10	15	35
c. purchases of capital	-	-	50	50
d. terminal value	190	190	335	715
e. net investment	−10	−10	35	15
4. Factor payments and profits (net value added)	100	50	50	200
5. Tax base for ...				
a. consumption type VAT	110	60	15	185
b. income type VAT	100	50	50	200
c. gross product type VAT	110	60	65	235

Under the income variant of the value-added tax, purchases of intermediate inputs and depreciation of the capital stock are deductible from total sales. In this case, the aggregate tax base corresponds to national product or aggregate net value added. Of course, the base of an income type VAT will exceed that of a consumption type VAT by the amount of net investment expenditure.

Finally, the tax base for a gross product type VAT is determined by deducting purchases of intermediate inputs from a firm's sales. Deducting purchases of capital goods, or even depreciation, is not allowed. The aggregate tax base, therefore, equals gross national product.

We will not discuss the pros and cons of these different types of VAT. Most countries, and all member states of the EU, employ the consumption type VAT. Virtually no one proposes a switch to one of the other two types of VAT. Note that from a taxation point of view, investment expenditure is treated in exactly the same manner as outlays for intermediate inputs under a consumption type VAT. Without much loss of generality, we can therefore neglect investment in the following.

2.2. The Rate Structure of a Value-added Tax

Value-added taxes may be operated with a uniform or with differentiated tax rates. Table 2 illustrates that except for Denmark all member states of the EU employ a differentiated rate structure. In addition to the standard rate, some countries apply a "luxury" rate to commodities such as automobiles, jewelry, furs, and cosmetics. On the other hand, there is a reduced rate in most member states applying to items regarded as necessities, such as food, books, newspapers and public transport. Some countries, particularly Ireland and the United Kingdom make extensive use of a zero rate.

The 1993 tax rates are in accordance with the ECOFIN Council's decision of June 24, 1991 regarding the rate structure in the EU after 1992. The list of goods and services which may be subject to reduced VAT rates is specified in a proposal of December 16, 1991, presented by the Commission to the Council.

Table 2 illustrates that VAT rates continue to vary widely among member states, and that the speed of tax rate convergence is very slow. Optimal taxation theory teaches us that a differentiated rate structure may be necessary for efficiency and equity reasons, whereas administrative and compliance costs point to a unified rate. This is not the place, however, to discuss the possible advantages of multiple VAT rates over a single tax rate.[13]

[13] Optimal tax calculations for value-added taxes in Germany are presented in Kaiser, Wiegard and Zimmermann (1992); Cnossen (1982) and Tait (1988, pp. 42-44) discuss reasons for a uniform VAT rate.

Table 2. Value-added tax rates in the EU 1987, 1991 and 1993 (in per cent)

	April 1, 1987			June 1, 1991			February 1, 1993		
Countries	Reduced	Standard	Higher	Reduced	Standard	Higher	Reduced	Standard	Higher
Belgium	6; 17	19	25; 33	1; 6; 17	19	25; 33	1;6; 12	19,5	-
Denmark	-	22	-	-	22	-	-	25	-
France	5.5; 7	18.6	33.3	2.1 to 13	18.6	22	2.1; 5.5	18.6	-
Germany	7	14	-	7	14	-	7	15	-
Greece	6	18	36	4; 8	18	36	4;8	18	36
Ireland	0; 2; 6; 10	25	-	0; 2 to 12.5	21	-	0; 2.7 to 16	21	-
Italy	2; 9	18	38	4; 9; 12	19	38	4; 9; 12	19	38
Luxembourg	3; 6	12	-	3; 6	12	-	3; 6; 12	15	-
Netherlands	6	20	-	6	18.5	-	6	17.5	-
Portugal[a]	8	16	30	8	17	30	5	16	30
Spain	6	12	33	6	12	33	3; 6	15	28
United Kingdom	0	15	-	0	17.5	-	0	17.5	-

[a] mainland only; different rates apply in the Azores and Madeira

Source: German Ministry of Finance

2.3. Calculating Tax Liabilities

In Table 1 above we calculated the tax bases for different types of value-added taxes by subtracting purchased inputs from sales. The simplest method of calculating tax liabilities would be to apply the statutory VAT rate to these bases. This, however, is not the manner in which tax liabilities are actually calculated. Concentrating on the different methods of calculating tax liabilities, we will neglect the existence of capital stock and of investment expenditures. With these assumptions, consumption, income, and gross product type value-added taxes coincide. In the presence of value-added taxes, the most general presentation of a single firm's budget identity is then

$$\text{gross-of-tax sales} = \text{value added} + \text{gross-of-tax input purchases} + \text{tax liability}, \quad (1)$$

where value added includes wages, rent, interest, and net profit, and sales and purchases are made at tax-inclusive (gross-of-tax) prices. Equation (1) is a convenient way to illustrate the different methods of calculating tax liabilities.

2.3.1. The Credit or Invoice Method

Whenever the credit method is in use, each purchase invoice must identify, separately, the gross-of-tax price and the value-added tax amount. This amount is calculated by applying the relevant statutory VAT rate to the net-of-tax price. From the viewpoint of a seller, this tax amount is called his gross tax liability, whereas for the buyer it constitutes an input tax. Under the tax credit method each taxable firm or person calculates the actual tax liability by first computing the gross tax liability and then deducting all input VAT on purchases of intermediate (and capital) goods, i.e.

$$\text{tax liability} = \text{gross tax liability} - \text{input VAT on purchases}. \quad (2)$$

Splitting gross-of-tax sales (purchases) up into its components, net-of-tax sales (purchases) and gross tax liability (input VAT on purchases), and considering the calculation of tax liability according to (2), equation (1) reduces to

$$\text{net-of-tax sales} = \text{value added} + \text{net-of-tax input purchases}. \quad (3)$$

Table 3 illustrates the credit method in our three stage production example for a uniform as well as for a differentiated structure of tax rates. It is clear that our example fulfills equations (1) to (3).

Table 3. Illustration of the credit method

Items (in ECU)	uniform tax rate[a]				differentiated tax rates[b]			
	1	2	3	Total	1	2	3	Total
1. Input purchases								
a. gross-of-tax	-	110	165	275	-	110	157.5	267.5
b. VAT included	-	10	15	25	-	10	7.5	17.5
2. Value added (factor payments and profits)	100	50	50	200	100	50	50	200
3. Net-of-tax sales of ...								
a. intermediate goods	100	150	-	250	100	150	-	250
b. consumer goods	-	-	200	200	-	-	200	200
4. Gross tax liability	10	15	20	45	10	7.5	20	37.5
5. Tax liability (4.-1b.)	10	5	5	20	10	−2.5	12.5	20

[a] The tax rate is assumed to be 10 per cent.

[b] We assume a standard tax rate of 10 per cent for firms 1 and 3 and a reduced tax rate of 5 per cent for firm 2.

An important point to note is that in our example total tax revenue is independent of whether a uniform or a differentiated rate structure is applied. In a staged production process only the tax rate at the last production stage, the retail stage, matters. A multi-stage value-added tax with a 10 per cent tax rate at the retail stage is equivalent to a 10 per cent taxation on final consumption. Lower tax rates at any pre-retail stage are fully offset by higher taxes at the retail stage. In our example, firm 2 even receives a tax rebate. In an input-output framework, i.e. a non-staged production process, matters are somewhat different as we will see in the next chapter.

It should now be clear where the term credit or invoice method comes from. "Credit" method points to the fact that a credit is allowed for all VAT paid on purchased inputs against gross tax liability. The term "invoice" method reminds us that each invoice must separately identify gross-of-tax sales and VAT included.

2.3.2. The Addition and the Subtraction Method

In addition to the credit method there are two other methods of calculating tax liabilities. Consider the so-called addition method first. Tax liability is calculated by simply applying the relevant tax rate, τ, directly to a firm's value added:

$$\textsf{tax liability} = \tau \times (\textsf{value added}). \tag{4}$$

This method is called the addition method because the tax base is determined in an additive manner by summing up wages, rent, interest, net profit, and depreciation (which, however, is neglected in our examples). One of the main problems of this method is that is requires the auditing of net profits. Note that the addition method is best suited for an income type VAT. To realize a consumption type VAT, value added would have to be calculated under the assumption of full expensing or immediate deductibility for all capital purchases.

Turning to the subtraction method, each taxable firm calculates its tax liability by first subtracting its input (and capital) purchases from its sales, and then applying the VAT rate to this difference. This, at least, is the description that can be found in the current literature.[14] In our view, however, it needs some important qualifications. To derive the tax base under the subtraction method, substitute for value added in equation (4) from (1), to obtain

$$\begin{aligned}\textsf{tax liability} = \tau \times (&\textsf{gross-of-tax sales} - \textsf{tax liability}\\ &- \textsf{gross-of-tax input purchases}).\end{aligned}$$

Solving for tax liability, one obtains

$$\begin{aligned}\textsf{tax liability} = \frac{\tau}{1+\tau} \times (&\textsf{gross-of-tax sales}\\ &- \textsf{gross-of-tax input purchases}).\end{aligned} \tag{5}$$

Two points merit attention. First, to derive the tax base, gross-of-tax purchases have to be subtracted from gross-of-tax sales. Hence, there is no need to separately identify the VAT amount on a purchase invoice. Second, statutory VAT rates should be expressed as tax-inclusive rates, and not, as under both the credit as well as the

[14] See, for example, Sullivan (1965, p. 7), U.S. Treasury Department (1984, p. 7), McLure (1987, p. 16), and Shoup (1990, p. 8).

addition method, as tax-exclusive rates.[15] Finally the reader should note that calculating tax liability according to (5) deviates from the illustrations of the subtraction method as contained, for example, in McLure (1972, p. 16; 1987, p. 82) or the U.S. Treasury Department (1984, p. 9).[16] There, the tax-exclusive tax rate is applied to the difference between net-of-tax sales and net-of-tax purchases. This requires easy identification of gross tax liability and of input VAT on purchases of intermediate goods. Generally, this information is available only under the credit method. In Table 4 we illustrate tax liability calculation according the addition method, equation (4), or the subtraction method, equation (5).

Table 4. Illustration of addition/subtraction method

Items (in ECU)	uniform tax rate[a]				differentiated tax rates[b]			
	1	2	3	Total	1	2	3	Total
1. Input purchases at gross-of-tax prices	-	110	165	275	-	110	162.5	272.5
2. Value added (factor payments and profits)	100	50	50	200	100	50	50	200
3. Tax liability	10	5	5	20	10	2.5	5	17.5
4. Gross-of-tax sales								
a. intermediate goods	110	165	-	265	110	162.5	-	272.5
b. consumer goods	-	-	220	220	-	-	217.5	217.5

[a] 10 per cent under the addition method; $({}^{0.1}/_{1.1}) \times 100$ per cent under the subtraction method.

[b] Standard rate for 1 and 3: 10 per cent addition method; $({}^{0.1}/_{1.1}) \times 100$ per cent subtraction method; reduced rate for 2: 5 per cent addition method; $({}^{0.05}/_{1.05}) \times 100$ per cent subtraction method.

If tax rates are uniform, all three methods of calculating tax liabilities will give the same result. In a world with multiple VAT rates,

[15] If τ^I denotes the tax-inclusive and τ, as before, the tax exclusive rate $\tau^I = {}^{\tau}/(1+\tau)$ must hold, if tax revenues have to be the same in both cases; see Shoup (1990, p. 13) for a detailed exposition.

[16] This, of course, is not a mere coincidence. McLure directed the preparation of the Treasury Department's VAT reform proposal as a deputy assistant secretary for tax policy.

however, firm-specific tax liabilities as well as aggregate VAT revenues diverge. Whereas under the credit method VAT is equivalent to a tax on final consumption, under the subtraction or the addition method it is a tax on a firm's value added. Hence, under the latter there exist strong incentives to minimize tax liabilities by adopting production and distribution techniques that shift as much of value added as possible to the low-taxed sector. If the aim of value-added taxation is to burden final consumption, the credit method clearly is the superior choice. Under the subtraction method, the implicit tax rate on final consumption is far less obvious, even if it can be computed with some effort. In our staged production example it can be obtained as a weighted average of VAT rates where the weights are value added shares.[17] As we will see in Chapter V, matters become much more complicated in an input-output framework.

Hence, it is no wonder that the credit method is the preferred method of calculating tax liabilities whenever tax rates are differentiated. As far as we know, only Finland and Japan employ the subtraction method.[18] Not surprisingly, both countries employ a uniform rate structure.

2.4. International Taxation Principles for VAT

So far, our discussion of value-added taxes has referred only to a closed economy. In the context of an open economy the most intriguing question is how cross-border commodity transactions should be treated under VAT. In accordance with the mainstream literature, we distinguish between two international taxation principles, the destination principle (DP) and the origin principle (OP).

The destination principle is characterized by a system of border tax adjustments that guarantees that exports leave a country free of any VAT, while imported commodities are subject to (import) VAT at the rate applied to comparable domestic goods. The destination

---

[17] From our example in Table 4, the tax-exclusive consumption tax rate has to be calculated as the weighted average of tax-exclusive VAT rates, i.e.

$$0.1\frac{100}{200} + 0.05\frac{50}{200} + 0.1\frac{50}{200} = 0.0875.$$

Applying this tax rate to net-of-tax consumption expenditures of ECU 200, yields ECU 17.5 as total tax revenue.

[18] See Shoup (1990, p. 8) and Ishi (1993, p. 325).

principle ensures that commodities are taxed in the country where they are consumed (the country of destination), regardless of the country where they are produced. VAT revenue accrues to the country where consumption takes place. Border tax adjustments are equivalent to maintaining fiscal frontiers between countries. Border controls for taxation purposes, however, are not necessary for the application of border tax adjustments. Under the transitional system, effective in the EU since January 1, 1993, border controls have been removed while border tax adjustments have been maintained.

The alternative international taxation principle for indirect taxes is the origin principle. This taxation principle is characterized by the absence of any border tax adjustments and, hence, fiscal frontiers. There is no rebate for VAT on exports, and imports are not taxed in the importing country. If the origin principle is applied, commodities are taxed in the country where they are produced, regardless of the country where they are consumed. The revenue distribution between countries, however, is less clear under the origin principle. It partly depends on which method is used in calculating tax liabilities.

Whenever countries form a tax union, both taxation principles may be applied simultaneously. Trade between tax union countries may be taxed according to the origin principle, whereas the destination principle may be applied to trade with the rest of the world. This geographically limited application of the origin principle has been named restricted origin principle by Shibata (1967).

The choice between the destination and the origin principle is usually based on reasoning about trade neutrality. We will extensively elaborate on this question in later chapters. Here we will concentrate on another issue. With the help of some examples we will try to find out which method of calculating tax liabilities is compatible with which international taxation principle. This is of considerable importance for our analysis of different VAT reform proposals in the European Union.

Table 5 illustrates the operation of border taxes under the destination principle for both the credit as well as the subtraction method. We consider two countries, D and F, and two industries in each country. Industry 2 in country F produces consumer goods only, whereas all other industries produce and sell intermediate products to the next production stage. In each country, VAT rates are differentiated.

Under the destination principle, exports are zero rated. This means that no VAT is charged on export sales, and that VAT on all inputs used in the production of export goods is rebated. Zero rating of

Table 5. Border tax adjustments under the destination principle

Country D: Reduced rate for 1: 5 per cent; Standard rate for 2: 10 per cent — Industry	1	2	Border tax adjustments	1	2	Country F: Reduced rate for 1: 20 per cent; Standard rate for 2: 30 per cent — Industry
			Credit method			
1. Gross-of-tax purchases		73.5	*Import* →	130	180	Gross-of-tax purchases
a. Net-of-tax purchases		70	*VAT:* 30	100	150	a. Net-of-tax purchases
b. VAT on inputs		3.5		30	30	b. VAT on inputs
2. Value added	70	30	*Export value:* 100	50	50	Value added
3. Gross-of-tax-sales	73.5	110		180	260	Gross-of-tax sales
a. Net-of-tax sales	70	100	*Tax rebate:* −10	150	200	a. Net-of-tax sales
b. Gross tax liability	3.5	10		30	60	b. Gross tax liability
c. Tax rebate for exports		−10 ←				
4. Tax liability	3.5	−3.5				Tax liability
					30	a. Tax payments
				30		b. Import VAT
			Subtraction/addition method[a]			
1. Gross-of-tax purchases		73.5	*Import* →	130	190	Gross-of-tax purchases
2. Value added	70	30	*VAT:* 30	50	50	Value added
3. Tax liability						Tax liability
a. Tax payments	3.5	3	*Export value:* 100	10	15	a. Tax payments
b. Tax rebate for exports		−6.5 ←		30		b. Import VAT
4. Gross-of-tax sales	73.5	106.5	*Tax rebate:* −6.5	190	255	Gross-of-tax sales

[a] If the subtraction method is used, the tax-exclusive tax rates have to be transformed into tax-inclusive rates.

exports requires some documentary evidence that the goods have, indeed, left the country. Until December 31, 1992 this evidence was mainly based on border controls and frontier formalities. If the credit method is used, zero rating of exports may be achieved as follows. Just as in our earlier examples, the second industry in country D calculates its gross tax liability and deducts all input VAT. At the border, however, there is a rebate for the VAT on export sales, i.e. exports leave the country at a net-of-tax price of ECU 100. Hence, there is no VAT on export sales, whereas all input VAT is refunded by the domestic Treasury. In our example, the exporting industry receives a tax rebate of ECU 3.5. Total tax revenue in country D is zero.

Under the subtraction method, the zero rating of exports is much more difficult to achieve, as is illustrated in the lower part of Table 5. To determine the correct tax rebate for exports, one has to know the number of previous stages of production, the value added at each of them, and the VAT rate applied at each stage. All this information is unlikely to be available. As a consequence, whenever VAT rates are differentiated within a country, the subtraction method and the destination principle are considered to be incompatible. Only in the case of a uniform tax structure within each country is the subtraction method feasible.

Turning to the import side of the ledger, the customs authorities of the importing country calculate the import VAT that has to be paid by the importer. In our example it is assumed that the imported good is subject to country F's standard rate. Within country F, tax liabilities and gross-of-tax prices are calculated as in Tables 3 and 4. The border tax adjustment procedure ensures that all VAT revenue accrues to the country where final consumption takes place. Under the credit method total tax revenue in country F amounts to ECU 60, corresponding to a 30 per cent tax on consumption expenditures. Under the subtraction method, the tax burden on final consumption is ECU 55, and the implicit tax rate on final consumption may be calculated as a weighted average of all VAT rates involved in the different stages of the production process, including tax rebates for exports and VAT on imports.[19]

[19] More precisely, the implicit consumption tax rate (tax-exclusive) has to be calculated as

$$0.05\frac{70}{200}+0.1\frac{30}{200}-\frac{6.5}{200}+\frac{30}{200}+0.2\frac{50}{200}+0.3\frac{50}{200}=\frac{55}{200}=0.275.$$

Let us now assume that border controls and fiscal frontiers have been abolished between countries *D* and *F*. On the one hand, exports are no longer zero rated but bear the exporting country's VAT when crossing the border. On the other hand, the importing country does not levy VAT on imports. Input purchases from abroad are treated in exactly the same manner as domestic input purchases. This is illustrated in Table 6. Note that the origin principle can be administered with both the credit method and the subtraction method, even if tax rates are differentiated within as well as across countries. The revenue distribution, however, as well as the effective tax burden on final consumption expenditures, differs between the credit and the subtraction method. The credit method ensures that under the origin principle consumption is taxed according to the rates of the country where consumption takes place. The VAT revenue, however, no longer accrues to that country but is split between the countries involved in the production of the consumption good. The exact revenue distribution depends on export volumes and on statutory VAT rates on exporting industries. Under the subtraction/addition method, the revenue distribution between countries is calculated according to the value added shares weighted with the respective VAT rates.

Turning to the restricted origin principle, it is clear that the correct tax rebate for exports from tax union countries to the rest of the world is very difficult to calculate whenever tax union countries apply the subtraction method. Border tax adjustments between tax union members and other countries are, however, easy to handle if the credit method is used.

In summary, international taxation principles and methods of calculating tax liabilities may be combined as follows:

- If the destination principle is applied by all countries, the credit method seems to be the natural method of calculating tax liabilities.
- If tax union countries switch to the origin principle but retain the destination principle for trade with other countries, the credit method again seems to be the only feasible choice.
- The subtraction method seems to be feasible only if *all* countries switch to the origin principle.
- Any combination of the subtraction and the credit method within a country seems to be infeasible.

Table 6. The origin principle

Country D Reduced rate for 1: 5 per cent Standard rate for 2: 10 per cent				Country F Reduced rate for 1: 20 per cent Standard rate for 2: 30 per cent		
Industry	1	2		1	2	Industry
			Credit method			
1. Gross-of-tax purchases		73.5		→ 110	180	Gross-of-tax purchases
a. Net-of-tax purchases		70		100	150	a. Net-of-tax purchases
b. VAT on inputs		3.5		10	30	b. VAT on inputs
2. Value added	70	30		50	50	Value added
3. Gross-of-tax-sales	73.5	110 —		180	260	Gross-of-tax sales
a. Net-of-tax sales	70	100		150	200	a. Net-of-tax sales
b. Gross tax liability	3.5	10		30	60	b. Gross tax liability
4. Tax liability	3.5	6.5		20	35	Tax liability
			Subtraction/addition method[a]			
1. Gross-of-tax purchases		73.5		→ 106.5	165.5	Gross-of-tax purchases
2. Value added	70	30		50	50	Value added
3. Tax liability	3.5	3		10	15	Tax liability
4. Gross-of-tax sales	73.5	106.5 —		165.5	231.5	Gross-of-tax sales

[a] If the subtraction method is used, the tax-exclusive tax rates have to be transformed into tax-inclusive rates.

2.5. One Further Issue in Value-added Taxation: Exemption Versus Zero Rating

So far our characterization of basic VAT principles has been conducted in very general terms. Hopefully, the non-specialized reader will have a more precise idea of different VAT tax bases, international taxation principles, and methods of calculating tax liabilities. These are important ingredients in understanding the results presented in later chapters, but only scratch the surface of problems which appear when designing a practicable VAT system. In this section we will mention one further problem: exemption versus zero rating.

As an introduction, consider a destination-based consumption type VAT which is administered by the credit method. Under ideal circumstances, the VAT tax base is equivalent to domestic consumption expenditures. Unfortunately, matters are not that simple. In most countries there are considerable exclusions from the consumption tax base, rendering VAT a kind of hybrid consumption-investment tax. This is due to the preferential tax treatment of certain industries or goods, as for example, small businesses, farming, housing, medical care, and the services of financial institutions and life insurance companies. The latter are excluded for administrative reasons, the former for distributive ones.

Exclusion from VAT may appear in two different forms. First, goods or industries may be zero rated. In this case, a firm selling zero-rated items is still a registered tax payer (it is "in the system") and has to file VAT returns. It is still allowed to receive credits for taxes paid on its purchases of intermediate and investment goods and it is liable to a VAT rate, which, however, happens to be zero (hence: zero rating). This method is heavily relied upon in the United Kingdom and Ireland. Under zero rating, a consumption type VAT is still equivalent to a consumption tax, the only qualification being that part of consumption expenditures is subject to a zero rate. This does not hold under the second form of exclusion, namely exemption, which is used in Germany, France and most other countries.[20] Here, firms selling exempt items are not registered tax payers (they are "outside the system"). Consequently, an exempt trader does not pay VAT on his purchases, but at the same time cannot obtain a credit for its input taxes. In our staged production example, there will be a break in the

[20] Tait (1988, p. 52) gives a summary overview of exemptions and zero rates in different countries.

chain of credits, when exemption is granted at a lower than the retail stage. As a consequence, the VAT burden on a commodity may be increased rather than reduced. Because exempt firms are not entitled to deduct VAT on inputs, taxes remain on their use of intermediate products and investment goods. When selling exempt items to taxable firms, double taxation occurs, increasing total revenue. In this case, even a consumption type VAT no longer equals a consumption tax. To illustrate the quantitive significance of exemptions, consider Germany as an example. Here, approximately 65 per cent of total VAT revenues fall on consumption expenditures, whereas 20 per cent remain on intermediate products and around 15 per cent fall on investment.

In the following chapters we do not deal with exemptions and, hence, there is no need to elaborate on this point. Instead, we refer to Gottfried and Wiegard (1991), which deals with the efficiency effects of exemption versus zero rating, and to a considerable body of literature dealing with the VAT treatment of special industries.[21]

3. Questions and Answers: The Plan of the Book

3.1. The Questions

This book is about value-added taxation in the European Union. More precisely, we shall focus on the welfare effects of alternative VAT reform proposals, including the current transitional system as well as different reform options that could be adopted after January 1, 1997. We bring out the main determinants of these welfare effects and elaborate on their quantitative significance. Evaluating and measuring welfare effects of tax policies is one of the major challenges for an economist. From the exchequer's point of view, however, welfare considerations seem to be less important than concerns about tax revenue. At least one is left with this impression after observing the recent debate about the harmonization of value-added taxes in Europe. The economist's and the exchequer's point of view do not necessarily present a contradiction. We will determine and compute both welfare and revenue effects of different VAT reform proposals in

[21] For example: Tait (1988, chapters 4 to 7), McLure (1987, chapter 8), U.S. Treasury Department (1984, chapter 6) and the papers by Due, Kay and Davis, Gillis and Conrad in a volume, edited by Gillis, Shoup and Sicat (1990).

order to establish the precise connection between changes in economic welfare, tax revenues, and relative prices.

The discussion about harmonizing VAT in the European Union centers on the following three topics:

- The removal of tax barriers. This amounts to the choice of an appropriate international taxation principle after border controls have been abolished in the EU. This question is the focus of our book. We will determine the welfare and revenue effects of the current transitional system and of a possible switch to the origin principle after 1997, if either the credit method is retained or the subtraction method introduced.
- The approximation of VAT rates. The Commission of the EU has always recognized that a shift of tax bases (or international taxation principles) is closely related to the harmonization of tax rates. As mentioned above, the 1987/89 harmonization proposals included a switch to a two rate system and a permitted range for the reduced and the standard tax rate. The latter proposal was replaced by some minimum requirements for the reduced and the standard rate when the transitional system came into force at the beginning of 1993. A cursory glance at Table 2, however, reveals that not too much happened with regard to the approximation of tax rates. In the following chapters we will more or less neglect possible changes in VAT rates. This reflects our feeling that tax rate harmonization will be more difficult to achieve and less important than tax base adjustments. This may be considered a serious restriction and we will comment on it in a later subsection.
- Administrative features. Concerns about the practicability of VAT harmonization proposals constitute an important part of the story. They contributed to the failure of the Commission's original taxation proposals and they plague the current transitional system. All too often, tax reform recommendations favored by the scientific community were put aside because of practical objections, and in tax policy hearings the advice of tax administrators and accounting professionals seems to carry more weight than scientific advice. Our comparative advantage is definitely not in the more practical matters of VAT administration. Therefore, we will only comment on some of the most serious administrative difficulties but otherwise concentrate upon the computation and explanation of the economic effects of VAT policy options.

In summary, this book primarily deals with the welfare and revenue effects of a change in international taxation principles for VAT, the rate structure being given. Besides theoretical insights, we are mainly interested in quantifying the most important determinants of welfare changes.

3.2. The Methodology: Computable General Equilibrium Analysis

Having outlined the main questions, a suitable theoretical model to answer these questions has to be chosen. In his appraisal of the incidence effects of value-added taxation, Charles McLure, one of the leading VAT experts in the U.S., established the following requirements for an adequate model framework (1990, p. 38):

> "A partial equilibrium analysis that focuses only on sales to ultimate consumers, with ad hoc adjustments for taxes paid at prior stages, is unlikely to capture the [incidence of VAT]. Clearly a general equilibrium framework that allows for input-output relations is required. Such a framework can take explicit account of taxes paid at the preretail as well as at retail stages of production and distribution. The analysis would ideally reflect the mechanics of the credit method of collecting VAT .... In all cases net liabilities at all stages of production would be aggregated through input-output relations".

He adds: "No study is known that actually follows this methodology". Our endeavor will be to meet these demands. We will construct a multi-country, multi-commodity and multi-factor general equilibrium model with full-fledged input-output relationships between domestic and foreign production sectors. However, analytic solutions of complex general equilibrium models are hard to obtain or provide only a limited degree of information. Furthermore, there is a widespread feeling in the profession that general equilibrium theory is too remote from real world issues. Computable general equilibrium (CGE) models respond to these objections by attempting to link theory and application by combining equilibrium theory with data from national accounts.

The principal strength of computable general equilibrium analysis is that it allows quantitative policy conclusions while being firmly rooted in the accepted body of microeconomic theory. Hence, CGE models avoid excessive use of ad hoc assumptions and enforce internal consistency of the model. When analyzing tax policy questions or other economy-wide issues, CGE analysis allows all feedback effects to be taken into account, quite detailed institutional features of the tax system to be captured and discrete and "large" policy changes to be considered. Particularly when dealing with efficiency or welfare effects of tax policy, there seems to be no real alternative to this kind of model – despite its many limitations. Here we will not discuss the weaknesses and strengths of CGE models. In a later chapter there is a short description of the CGE methodology; the reader is referred to the relevant literature for a detailed discussion.

3.3. The Chapters to Come

The remainder of this book is organized as follows. In Chapter II we discuss and develop the VAT reform options which are currently under discussion: the transitional system, the origin principle with the credit method, and the origin principle combined with the subtraction method. The discussion of each of these reform proposals follows the same pattern. First, we summarize the main institutional features of the respective proposals. Based on a small-dimensional interregional input-output table we then illustrate the determination of tax liabilities and aggregate VAT revenues. These numerical examples reflect one essential feature of our general equilibrium model as developed in later chapters. Third, we generalize the examples and formulate the mechanics of VAT revenue calculation in mathematical terms. The accounting identities used to describe the formal structure of VAT will later become part of the general equilibrium model.

The third chapter develops the theoretical foundations as well as the basic economic intuition used in evaluating the welfare effects of value-added taxation in open economies. As a point of reference, we first derive the necessary conditions for an efficient worldwide allocation of resources in a first-best framework. We then consider the distortive features of taxes and tariffs, with special emphasis on different international taxation principles of VAT. The following section deals with the exchange rate argument that has played a prominent role in international taxation theory since the Tinbergen Report. By distinguishing between Paretian trade neutrality on the one hand, and physical trade neutrality on the other, we hope to contribute to a better understanding of the implications and assumptions underlying the exchange rate argument. In the final section of this chapter we explore how national and worldwide welfare depend on substitution and income effects induced by a change in international taxation principles for VAT. In open economies there are two of both effects, domestic and international income effects as well as domestic and international substitution effects. This decomposition proves to be indispensable for the economic explanation of our numerical results.

In Chapter IV we present the full specification of our computable general equilibrium model. We start with some general remarks on the structure and relevance of the CGE methodology. This is followed by a complete description of our theoretical model. We specify the functional forms of utility and production functions and develop in considerable detail the full set of equations characterizing our model. The next section is devoted to the construction of a microconsistent data set, which has to match the consistency requirements of Walrasian equilibrium theory. The chapter closes with a discussion of "calibration". This involves determining the free parameters of the model so that the numerical solution replicates the observed data set.

Finally, Chapter V contains our numerical results of the welfare and revenue effects of the VAT reform proposals considered. We do not only present the numbers but endeavor to explain the results in economic terms. We develop the concept of effective consumption tax rates, which proves extremely helpful in isolating income and substitution effects.

The last chapter summarizes our main results. We hesitate to anticipate our main conclusions. Suffice to say that some results were unexpected. Had we known them beforehand, we would have written a different book.

3.4. Related Work

This book intends to add one further element to the complex puzzle concerning the welfare effects of commodity tax harmonization. Concentrating on the welfare effects of a change in international VAT principles allows us to treat this question more thoroughly than most other studies. The obvious opportunity cost is the neglect of a number of closely related problems.

Probably the most critical assumption made, is that the structure of tax rates remains unchanged. This is particularly disturbing because a switch in tax bases may induce strategic incentives for an adjustment of tax rates. An increasing number of theoretical contributions deals with non-cooperative tax rate competition when fiscal frontiers are abolished, notably Mintz and Tulkens (1986), de Crombrugghe and Tulkens (1990), Kanbur and Keen (1993), and Lockwood (1993). Another strand in the literature deals with optimal taxation or Pareto-improving tax reform issues in a tax union. Key references are Rose (1987), Keen (1987, 1989), Abe and Okamura (1989), Turunen-Red and Woodland (1990), and Haufler (1993).

Without a doubt, all these papers yield considerable insight into the possibilities of a welfare-increasing tax rate setting in open economies. In our view, however, they are too remote from the current policy debate and do not capture the essentials of the Commission's tax reform proposals. There is a choice between the following alternatives. On the one hand, there are complex theoretical and small-dimensional numerical models dealing with both tax base changes and tax rate adjustments, but neglecting essential institutional details. On the other hand, one could concentrate on a limited number of problems and try to thoroughly model the more important institutional features, without, of course, being able to capture each and every detail of the problem. Both research lines are complementary. A good economist and policy maker will draw his insights and conclusions from both approaches.

We shall close this chapter by cursorily commenting on some of the *quantitative* studies on commodity tax harmonization. Three different kinds of simulation studies may be distinguished. The first class of models is characterized by the exclusion of any behavioral reactions, relying on so-called first round calculations only. These studies usually incorporate considerable insitutional detail and may be appropriate if distributional issues are the center of interest, but they are definitely not suited to dealing with efficiency problems. The EC Commission used such a model when computing the transfers to and from a central clearing institution in COM (87) 323 final/2, appendix A. Another example is a study by the German "ifo-institute" on the revenue effects of the harmonization of tax rates in the EU (Parsche et al., 1988, chapter 3).

The second class of models includes behavioral reactions but is restricted to partial equilibrium considerations. These studies usually allow for a disaggregated household sector in a single country and rely on econometric estimates of demand parameters by using the linear expenditure system, the almost ideal demand system or some other functional form. This approach can deal with distributional as well as efficiency effects of tax harmonization issues. A disadvantage is the partial equilibrium nature of these models and their restriction to a single country. Typical representatives of these models are Lee, Pearson and Smith (1988) and Symons and Walker (1988) for the UK, and Brugiavini and Weber (1988) and Patrizi and Rossi (1991) for Italy.

The final class of models comprises all macroeconomic simulation models dealing with VAT harmonization problems. These studies may be divided into two broad subgroups. The first includes all macroeconometric simulation studies such as "Hermes-Italia" (Bosi et al., 1988), the German "DIW-ifo-model" (Parsche et al., 1988, pp. 339-363), and the OECD's Interlink-model (Cornilleau, 1988). These studies focus on the inflation, employment, and GNP effects of VAT harmonization. Because of their weak microeconomic foundations, welfare effects of tax reforms cannot be dealt with adequately. Computable general equilibrium models constitute the second subgroup of macroeconomic models. Here, welfare effects come to the fore, whereas inflation and employment problems usually are neglected. Whalley (1976) and Hamilton and Whalley (1986) are two of the classics in this field. More recently, Haufler (1993) presented a small-dimensional CGE model for VAT harmonization issues in Europe. Whereas these models are essentially static in nature, Perraudin and Pujol (1990) and Frenkel, Razin and Symansky (1991) present intertemporal CGE models.

All these different approaches have advantages and disadvantages. Our initial intuition was that general equilibrium effects were important and that static welfare effects were more significant than intertemporal welfare considerations, because investment expenditures are deductible under a consumption type VAT. Hence we decided on a medium sized, static CGE model in the Shoven-Whalley tradition. Note that the first class of models mentioned above may be treated as a special kind of CGE model. In our simulations we experimented with first round calculations in order to assess the importance of behavioral reactions for overall welfare effects. At least to us, the results turned out to be quite surprising.

Chapter II

VAT Policy Options for an Integrated Europe

In this chapter we discuss the VAT policy options that are applicable in an integrated Europe. We distinguish between three broad policy options. The first presupposes that border controls have been abolished but that international tax barriers have been retained as far as possible. The current transitional VAT system, effective since January 1, 1993, operates in this way. Compliance costs aside, the economic effects of the transitional system depend heavily on the tax treatment of cross-border sales to final consumers. Our preferred interpretation is that either the destination or the origin principle be applied to intra-community sales to private persons whatever taxation principle is of mutual advantage for the vendor and the purchaser in different EU member states. We will call this the "switching option". In contrast to this, the relevant literature seems to assume that *all* cross-border sales to final consumers are taxed according to the origin principle under the transitional system. According to this interpretation, the current situation is described as a "mixed system", taxing trade between registered taxpayers by the DP but applying the OP to cross-border sales to non-registered taxpayers.

The second broad reform option is to abolish border controls as well as tax frontiers, but retain the credit method with respect to both national and international transactions. Two different VAT variants would then evolve. The first is the so-called "common market principle", the second the "clearing system", which was favored by the EC Commission in its proposal COM (87) 323 final/2. Although the efficiency properties of both schemes are more or less the same, they differ with respect to the revenue distribution between member states.

The third and final policy option is the most far-reaching. It not only abolishes border controls and tax frontiers, but also replaces the credit method with the subtraction method. Although this variant is favored by some members of the scientific community, the EC Commission has not even mentioned it.

In the following sections each of these reform options is discussed more thoroughly. We illustrate each variant with a numerical example, thereby capturing an essential feature of our CGE model and subsequently translate it into a more general mathematical representation. Behavioural assumptions and a comparative static analysis are postponed to later chapters.

1. Some Basic Elements of our Model

Translating VAT policy options into a model-equivalent form requires a brief sketch of the basic structure of our theoretical model.

On an aggregate level we distinguish between two trading blocs, the European Union (EU) and the rest of the world (ROW). The EU is disaggregated into its member states or blocs of member states. Let EU denote the index set of these member states, i.e.

$$EU = \{F, I, D, \ldots\},$$

where F stands for France, I for Italy, D for Germany, etc. W is the index set for all the countries in the world, i.e. $W = \{EU, ROW\}$. In general, we denote by h an element of EU or W. Finally, W_h or EU_h are, respectively, the sets W or EU with country h deleted. Let R be the total number of countries or blocs of countries.

Each country (or region) produces a given number J of commodities. We define N to be the index set of the identical number of commodities in all countries. For tax purposes it may be important to distinguish services from (physical) goods. Let commodity s be services and let N_s denote the index set for commodities other than services.

An important feature of our model is the so-called Armington (1969) assumption, according to which products are distinguished by their place of origin. This means that, for example, commodity $i \in N$ in Germany is different from but possibly a close substitute for commodity i produced in France, Italy or elsewhere. Think of French wine which is different from but may be similar to German or Italian wine. The Armington assumption is a convenient device, widely used in empirical trade literature (Whalley, 1985, pp. 36-39). Its principal advantage is that it allows cross-hauling to be included in empirical trade models. By cross-hauling we mean that a country is both importing and exporting the same commodity. A further advantage of the Armington assumption is that import demand functions are well-defined and can be used for empirically estimating trade elasticities. In Chapter IV we will see how these trade elasticities fit into our CGE model. We will not conceal, however, that the use of the Armington assumption in empirical trade models is debatable.[22] In our context, probably the most serious restriction is that it precludes examining trade deflections caused by tax arbitrage considerations. Trade deflection cannot be adequately dealt with because the Armington assumption implies complete specialization in production: German products are produced only in Germany and have to be imported directly from Germany.

Use of the Armington assumption requires a somewhat cumbersome notation. We will use subscripts to refer to commodities or industries[23] and superscripts to refer to countries. If we use two subscripts or two superscripts the first indicates the place of origin, the second the place of destination. For example, the symbol V_{ij}^{kh} stands for the intermediate use of commodity i, originating from country k, in the production of commodity j in country h. The other symbols used in this chapter are:

τ_j^h: VAT rate levied in country h on sales of commodity j;

q_j^h, p_j^h: producer, consumer price of commodity j in country h;

w^h, r^h: wage rate, rental price of capital in country h;

Q_j^h: output of commodity j, produced in country h;

$X_j^{hk}; X_j^h$: export of commodity j from country h to country k, with

$$X_j^h = \sum_{k \in W_h} X_j^{hk};$$

as country h's total export of commodity j;

---

[22] See Norman (1990) for a critical assessment.

[23] It is assumed that each industry produces only one homogeneous commodity.

M_j^{kh}, M_j^h: import of commodity j by country h from country k, with

$$M_j^h = \sum_{k \in W_h} M_j^{kh}$$

as country h's total import of commodity j;

C_j^{kh}: quantity of commodity j produced in country k and consumed in country h; if $k \neq h$: cross-border sales of commodity j from country k to final consumers in country h.

In the following sections our description of VAT accounting refers to an arbitrary country h. In order to avoid excessive notation we suppress index h or replace it by a dot whenever possible. For instance, we write V_{ij} and $V_{ij}^{k\cdot}$ instead of V_{ij}^{hh} and V_{ij}^{kh}.

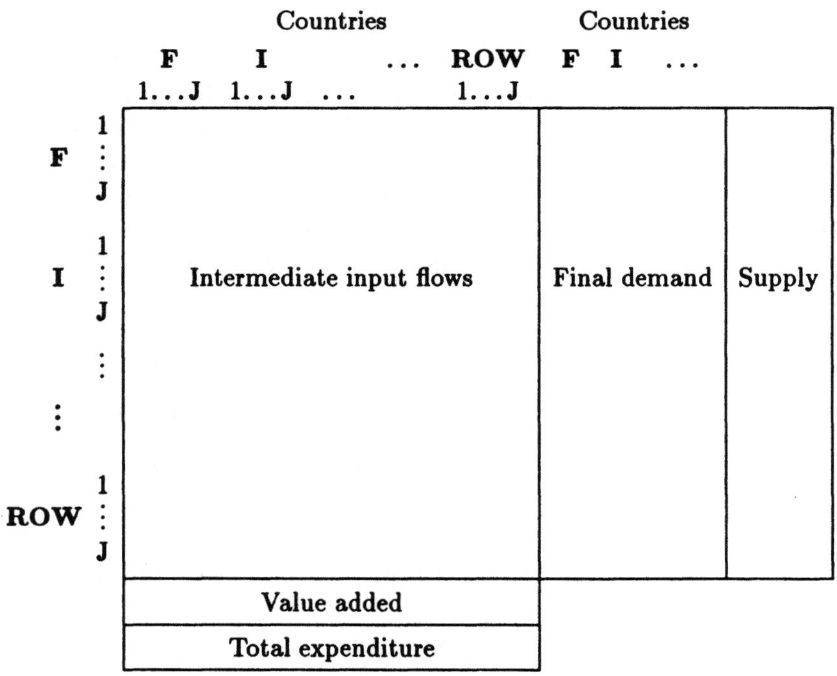

Figure 1. Illustration of an interregional input-output table

As a final prerequisite we will introduce the general structure of an interregional input-output table (Figure 1). Such a table is an essential feature of our micro-consistent data base (Chapter IV) and is particularly well suited to illustrate the mechanics of VAT revenue calculation. For the moment, however, we will neglect VAT or any other taxes.

Each entry in the table represents the flow of commodities (in value terms) from the row sector/country to the column sector/country. Consistency requires that each row sum is equal to the respective column sum. Furthermore, total value added has to be equal to total final demand. Throughout in the following, we neglect investment as a final demand category. The important point to note is that interregional input-output tables require exports and imports to be disaggregated by commodity *and* country. In national input-output tables as provided by EUROSTAT, OECD or national statistical offices, exports and imports are disaggregated by commodity but usually not by country.

In the next sections we will illustrate the different VAT reform options by considering a drastically simplified interregional input-output table. We consider two countries, D and F, each producing two commodities that may be used for consumption or for intermediate production. Government activities are neglected. Figure 2 presents our example.

		D		**F**		**D**	**F**	Total
		1	2	1	2			
D	1	20	40	*10*	*10*	80	*10*	170
	2	30	20	*20*	*10*	60	*30*	170
F	1	*10*	*20*	40	50	*10*	70	200
	2	*20*	*20*	30	30	*10*	50	160
Value added		90	70	100	60			
Total		170	170	200	160			

Figure 2. Numerical example for an interregional input-output table

The slanted numbers present the trade figures for intermediate products and cross-border sales to final consumers: the trade accounts are balanced.

We can now proceed to a detailed consideration of VAT reform options. To simplify matters, we neglect travellers' allowances and ignore all other taxes, such as excises, income taxes or tariffs. These taxes will be introduced in later chapters.

2. The Destination Principle

2.1. Some Institutional Features

In order to assess the welfare and revenue effects of different VAT reforms, each option has to be compared with a common benchmark: the destination principle, that was effective until January 1, 1993. According to this principle, exports leave a country free of any tax and VAT on inputs is refunded. This zero-rating of exports follows from Articles 15(1) and 17(3) of the Sixth Council Directive in the version *before* 1993. While Article 15(1) exempted "the supply of goods dispatched or transported to a destination outside the territory" of a member state, Article 17(3) allowed a deduction or refund of VAT on inputs used in the production of export goods. The counterpart of zero-rating exports is the taxation of imports under the destination principle. Article 8(2) of the Sixth Directive, in force until December 31, 1992, specified that the place of supply of imported goods "shall be deemed to be within the country of import of the goods".[24] As a consequence, the importation of goods is a taxable event and subject to (import) VAT. The VAT rate levied on imported goods has to be the same as that which applies to comparable domestic goods. The taxation of imports under the DP is independent of whether the good is imported by a registered taxpayer or by a non-taxable person. There are, however, allowances for cross-border shopping.

Registered taxpayers may deduct import VAT when filing their tax returns in the same way as for VAT on domestic purchases. The import VAT is usually payable together with the customs duty. Border controls represent an essential part of the administration of border tax adjustments under the destination principle.

So far, we have only dealt with the tax treatment of *goods* under the destination principle. The VAT treatment of *services* is a little

[24] This is in derogation of Article 8(1)(a), which defines the place of supply of goods being dispatched or transported as the place where the transportation *commences*.

more difficult. Here we concentrate on the regulations concerning international trade in services. Kay and Davis (1990) and Gillis (1990) present a more general discussion.

The distinctive feature of the VAT treatment of services is an agreement on the place of supply of services. Article 9 of the Sixth Council Directive contains the details. According to Article 9(1) the place of supply is deemed to be the place where the *supplier* has established his business or has his permanent address. There are, however, a large number of exceptions to this general principle. In our context, probably the most important exception is that a number of services[25] are taxable in the country where the *customer* is established, provided that these services are supplied by a taxable person registered in a member state and the recepient is a taxable person in another country. As a net result of these provisions, we will model the international VAT treatment of services as follows. Trade in services between registered taxpayers is taxed according to the DP; exports of services are zero rated, whereas imports of services are subject to import VAT. With respect to intra-community sales of services to private persons, we assume the OP will be applied. For example, tourist expenditures on lodging abroad clearly include foreign VAT and border tax adjustments are not permitted.

We can now turn to the calculation of tax revenues under the destination principle. The tax credit method, which was explained in detail in the preceding chapter, is applied.

2.2. A Numerical Example

The calculation of tax liabilities under the DP will be illustrated for two different cases. In the first case, both countries impose uniform VAT rates, which are assumed to be 10 per cent in $D\,(\tau^D = 0.1)$ and 20 per cent in $F\,(\tau^F = 0.2)$. The second case considers a differentiated rate structure in both countries. The reduced rates are 5 per cent in D and 10 per cent in F, and the standard rates are 10 per cent and 20 per cent, respectively.

Figure 3 summarizes the calculation of VAT liabilities. When calculating gross tax liabilities one has to consider that the use of a commodity in the production of the same commodity does not constitute

[25] These services are listed in Article 9(e) of the Sixth Directive.

a taxable event.[26] Total VAT revenue, shown in the last line, is the sum of domestic firms' tax liabilities and import VAT. Our example illustrates that a multi-stage consumption type VAT is equivalent to a single-stage consumption tax on retail sales. Under the latter, tax revenues in country D with a differentiated rate structure would be given by

$$0.05(80 + 10) + 0.1(60 + 10) = 11.5,$$

as in Table 1.

Table 1. Calculating tax revenues under the destination principle

	Uniform tax rates				Differentiated tax rates			
Country	D		F		D		F	
Industry	1	2	1	2	1	2	1	2
Tax rates	*0.1*		*0.2*		*0.05*	*0.1*	*0.1*	*0.2*
1. Gross tax liability	15.0	15.0	32.0	26.0	7.5	15.0	16.0	26.0
2. Tax rebate for exports	3.0	6.0	8.0	10.0	1.5	6.0	4.0	10.0
3. Tax rebate for domestic inputs	3.0	4.0	6.0	10.0	3.0	2.0	6.0	5.0
4. Tax rebate for imported inputs	3.0	4.0	6.0	4.0	2.5	3.0	5.0	3.0
5. Tax liability (1. − 2. − 3. − 4.)	6.0	1.0	12.0	2.0	0.5	4.0	1.0	8.0
6. Import VAT	4.0	5.0	6.0	12.0	2.0	5.0	3.0	12.0
7. Total VAT revenue	16.0		32.0		11.5		24.0	

2.3. A More General Formulation

In this section we will present VAT revenue accounting in a more general context. We will use a precise mathematical representation, which generalizes our example in an obvious manner and which will later become part of our general equilibrium model.

[26] According to Article 5(1) of the Sixth Directive 'supply of goods' is defined as the *transfer* of the right to dispose of tangible property as owner.

Consider a firm $i \in N_s$ in country $h \in EU$. Under the credit method, its tax liability, T_i, is calculated according to (index h being omitted)

$$T_i = \overbrace{\tau_i q_i (Q_i - V_{ii})}^{\text{Gross tax liability}} - \overbrace{\tau_i q_i X_i}^{\text{Tax rebate for exports}} - \overbrace{\sum_{j \in N_i} \tau_j q_j V_{ji}}^{\text{Tax rebate for domestic inputs}}$$
$$- \underbrace{\sum_{k \in W_h} \sum_{j \in N} \tau_j q_j^k V_{ji}^{k\cdot}}_{\text{Tax rebate for imported inputs}} \qquad i \in N_s. \tag{1a}$$

Following our discussion in the preceeding section, a firm supplying services calculates its tax liability as follows:

$$T_s = \tau_s q_s (Q_s - V_{ss}) - \sum_{k \in W_h} \sum_{j \in N} \tau_s q_s V_{sj}^{\cdot k} - \sum_{j \in N_s} \tau_j q_j V_{js}$$
$$- \sum_{k \in W_h} \sum_{j \in N} \tau_j q_j^k V_{js}^{k\cdot}. \tag{1b}$$

Remember that we assumed the origin principle would be applied to the taxation of direct consumption exports and imports of services. As a consequence, there will be a tax rebate only for service exports to registered VAT traders rather than for total exports of services. On the other hand, import VAT is levied on all imported goods, but only on imported services in so far as they are used in intermediate production.

Country h's total VAT revenue, obtained by aggregating individual tax liabilities over all firms and adding the import VAT, is therefore given by

$$T = \sum_{i \in N} \tau_i q_i (Q_i - V_{ii}) - \sum_{i \in N_s} \tau_i q_i X_i - \sum_{k \in W_h} \sum_{j \in N} \tau_s q_s V_{sj}^{\cdot k}$$
$$- \sum_{i \in N} \sum_{j \in N_i} \tau_j q_j V_{ji} - \sum_{k \in W_h} \sum_{i \in N} \sum_{j \in N} \tau_j q_j^k V_{ji}^{k\cdot}$$
$$+ \underbrace{\sum_{k \in W_h} \sum_{i \in N_s} \tau_i q_i^k M_i^{k\cdot} + \sum_{k \in W_h} \sum_{j \in N} \tau_s q_s^k V_{sj}^{k\cdot}}_{\text{Import VAT revenue}}. \tag{2}$$

After some manipulation involving the domestic market equilibrium conditions

$$Q_i = C_i + \sum_{j \in N} V_{ij} + X_i, \qquad i \in N \tag{3}$$

the national tax revenue equation may be written as

$$T = \sum_{i \in N} \tau_i q_i C_i + \sum_{k \in W_h} \sum_{i \in N_s} \tau_i q_i^k C_i^{k\cdot} + \sum_{k \in W_h} \tau_s q_s C_s^{\cdot k}. \tag{4}$$

Neglecting the last term on the right-hand side, equation (4) supports the widespread view that VAT essentially is a tax on consumption (from domestic or foreign sources). With respect to (physical) goods, revenue accrues to the country where the goods are consumed. This is an immediate consequence of the destination principle. Note, however, that the origin principle applies to exports of services to private persons; the respective tax revenue accrues to the country of origin or production. In the presence of exemptions, matters become much more complicated; see Gottfried und Wiegard (1991) for a detailed analysis in a similar model framework.

For later reference we will also specify the zero profit condition for a firm $i \in N_s$ and the current account for a country h.

Assuming perfect competition in goods and factor markets the zero profit condition for the i-th firm in country h reads

$$\underbrace{rK_i + wL_i}_{\text{Value added}} = \underbrace{(1+\tau_i)q_i(Q_i - V_{ii})}_{\text{Gross turnover}} - \underbrace{\tau_i q_i X_i}_{\text{Tax exemptions of exports}} - \underbrace{\sum_{j \in N_i} (1+\tau_j) q_j V_{ji}}_{\text{Expenditure on domestic inputs}}$$

$$- \underbrace{\sum_{k \in W_h} \sum_{j \in N} (1+\tau_j) q_j^k V_{ji}^k}_{\text{Expenditure on imported inputs}} - \underbrace{T_i}_{\text{VAT liability}}$$

$$\overset{(1a)}{=} q_i Q_i - \sum_{j \in N} q_j V_{ji} - \sum_{k \in W_h} \sum_{j \in N} q_j^k V_{ji}^{k\cdot}. \tag{5}$$

This equation illustrates that, in our framework, production decisions are not directly affected by VAT.

In our model we assume labor to be internationally immobile, but allow for international capital movements in a worldwide homogeneous capital market. Even if the first assumption is not entirely realistic, capital surely is the more mobile factor in an international context. Let $\bar{K}$ denote country h's fixed supply of capital (again, we omit index h for simplification). Then $(\sum_{i \in N} K_i - \bar{K})$ represents inflows or outflows of capital services depending on whether the difference between domestic capital demand (by firms) and domestic capital supply (by households) is positive or negative. Due to our homogeneity assumption, there is a uniform world rental price of capital, r. In the absence of international transfer payments, country h's current account is then given by

$$0 = \overbrace{\sum_{i \in N_s} \Big(q_i X_i - \sum_{k \in W_h} q_i^k M_i^{k\cdot}\Big)}^{\text{Foreign trade balance for goods}} + \overbrace{r\Big(\bar{K} - \sum_{i \in N} K_i\Big)}^{\text{Net inflow of capital income}}$$

$$\underbrace{+ \sum_{k \in W_h} \sum_{j \in N} \Big(q_s V_{sj}^{\cdot k} - q_s^k V_{sj}^{k\cdot}\Big) + \sum_{k \in W_h} \Big(q_s(1+\tau_s) C_s^{\cdot k} - q_s^k (1+\tau_s^k) C_s^{k\cdot}\Big)}_{\text{Foreign trade balance for services}} \qquad (6)$$

In our static context, there is no capital account and the balance of payments is equivalent to the current account. In the absence of international transfers, a possible deficit (surplus) in the balance on goods and services has to be matched by an inflow (outflow) of capital income from abroad. Note that cross border purchases of services by, and sales to, private persons are valued at consumer (tax inclusive) prices, whereas all other exports and imports are traded at producer prices. According to Walras' Law, the balance of payments condition is automatically fulfilled if all markets clear and all domestic agents meet their budget constraints.

3. The Transitional System[27]

On December 16, 1991, the ECOFIN Council agreed on Directive 91/680/EEC, supplementing the common system of VAT and amending the Sixth Council Directive with a view to the abolition of fiscal

[27] Terra and Kajus (1992) and Ernst & Young (1993), amongst others, offer a more detailed introduction to the transitional system.

frontiers. As a consequence, on New Year's Day 1993, physical border controls within the European Union were abolished. This required a number of changes in the VAT system that had been in force until 1993. As a general rule, the transitional system is designed to maintain the destination principle as far as possible, in spite of the removal of border controls. This requires special provisions concerning intra-community sales to final consumers of new means of transportation and with regard to distance sales. The VAT treatment of services roughly remains the same under the transitional system. There are some changes for services relating to the transportation of goods between member states that, however, are too detailed to be considered in our theoretical model. The transitional system's most important features will be described in the next section. The following two sections resume our numerical example and contain the model-equivalent presentation of the transitional system. In this context, two alternative interpretations of the transitional system are offered.

3.1. Main Institutional Features

The transitional system is concerned only with intra-community trade. The VAT treatment of trade with third countries (i.e. the rest of the world) is not affected. The most important changes introduced by the transitional system are the following:

3.1.1. Intra-community Supplies and Acquisitions

In a true common market without frontiers the concepts of exportation and importation no longer make sense. Therefore the transitional system introduces two new taxable events, namely intra-community supply and intra-community acquisition of goods. These terms refer to a movement of goods from a VAT registered business in one member state to a taxable person or a non-taxable legal person in another member state. The vendor in the member state of dispatch makes an 'intra-community supply for acquisition', the recipient in the member state of arrival is making the 'acquisition'. According to the newly introduced Article 28a(1) of the amended Sixth Directive, intra-community acquisitions are subject to VAT.[28] The place of supply of such acquisitions is deemed to be the place where the goods are at the time when dispatch or transportation to the purchaser ends. The tax

[28] There are a number of exceptions which, however, will be neglected in our presentation.

rate applicable shall be that applied to the supply of like goods within the territory of the country where the acquisition is taxable (i.e., the destination country). The person liable to pay VAT is the person effecting an intra-community acquisition of goods. If this person is established abroad, a tax representative (or another person) within the member state of destination becomes liable for paying the tax. The VAT due on acquisitions is deductible, provided a right to deduction exists. On the other hand, supplies of goods by a taxable person to a taxable person or a non-taxable legal person in another member state are exempt from VAT.

As far as trade between VAT-registered traders is concerned, these rules amount to re-establishing border tax adjustments, i.e. the destination principle, even in the absence of border controls.

Hence, the main effect of the transitional system is to shift the border tax adjustment procedure from the border to the books of firms. This requires considerable control mechanisms for intra-community trade, with administration and compliance costs far exceeding those of the previous VAT system. Some new administrative obligations under the transitional system are: registration for VAT in another member state if taxable supplies to that country are in excess of certain thresholds; the introduction of VAT identification numbers; an obligation for taxable persons to keep a register of certain goods which are not deemed to be supplies for acquisitions; an obligation for taxpayers to submit a recapitulative statement of the persons to whom intra-community supplies of goods were made.

Finally, we note that the transitional system contains some regulations concerning triangulation.[29] Due to the Armington assumption, we cannot consider these rules in our equilibrium model.

3.1.2. Means of Transport

Whereas intra-community supplies of goods to another member state are tax exempt only if the purchaser is a taxable person (or a non-taxable legal person), intra-community supplies of *new* private vehicles and other *new* means of transportation – for example, boats or aircraft – are exempt, regardless of the status of the acquirer or the vendor.

[29] Triangulation occurs if, for example, a German supplier sells goods to a taxable person in France and that customer sells the same goods to a business in Spain. The delivery of goods, however, is directly from the German vendor to the customer in Spain.

For new means of transportation, tax exemption of supplies to another member state is granted even if the purchaser is a private person. VAT will be levied in the country where the acquisition occurs, i.e. in the country of destination. For a private person, the tax may become payable when the vehicle is registered in the country of acquisition; the details are set out by the customs authority.

The reason for these special provisions with respect to purchases of new means of transportation is the sensitivity of purchases to intra-community tax rate differentials, given the high value of these items. If sales of new automobiles or other new means of transportation to private persons in other member states were taxed according to the origin principle, significant distortions and tax revenue re-allocations between member states could be expected. To prevent high-tax countries from revenue losses, border tax adjustments have been maintained with respect to all intra-community transactions concerning new means of transportation. 'Old' means of transport[30] are treated just like other goods supplied and dispatched to customers in other member states. There is, however, some debate between tax experts concerning possible changes in the VAT treatment of secondhand goods.

3.1.3. Distance Sales

Distance selling occurs when a supplier in one member state sells goods to final consumers or to non-registered persons in another member state *and* when the supplier is responsible for the delivery of goods. Distance sales do *not* include goods where the purchaser takes delivery in the member state of dispatch and arranges the transport of goods to his home country. The most obvious examples for distance sales are purchases made by intra-community mail order or by tele-shopping.

The VAT treatment of distance sales depends on whether or not the value of a supplier's sales to another member state in a calendar year exceeds a certain threshold. If it does, the place of supply of goods in cases of distance sales is the place where the dispatch or transport ends, i.e. in the country of destination. In this case, the supplier has to register for VAT in the country of destination and to account for VAT at that country's rate on the goods concerned. Suppliers with no place of business in the member state of arrival may appoint a

[30] A means of transport is regarded to be 'old', if more than three months have passed since its first entry into service, or if it has travelled more than 3,000 kilometers in the case of land vehicles (similar conditions apply for boats and aircraft).

tax representative responsible for paying VAT. If the value of distance sales falls below the threshold level, the above rules are not applicable, and the supplier accounts for VAT on the goods concerned according to the origin principle.

The threshold amounts to the equivalent of 100,000 ECU in national currency. The member state where the distance selling ends may limit this threshold to 35,000 ECU.[31] In this case, the public authorities in the member state of dispatch have to be informed. There are further complications due to the additional provision that suppliers may opt for taxation in the country of destination, even if the value of their distance sales has not exceeded the threshold for that country.[32] The following figure illustrates the VAT treatment of distance sales.

Figure 3 illustrates that with respect to distance sales to final consumers, there is a choice between applying the destination or the origin principle. Our presumption is that this possibility to choose is made use of whenever it is of mutual advantage for the vendor and purchaser located in different member states. For example, one can easily imagine that many legally independent enterprises may be founded, in order to keep their sales below the threshold level. Likewise, purchase contracts may designate either the vendor or the purchaser as responsible for the delivery and transport of the goods to the country of destination. After all, the efficiency of a market economy depends on such an exploitation of the gains from trade. There is some empirical evidence that suppliers in low-tax member states in fact make arrangements to settle distance sales to high-tax member states according to the origin principle. According to a recent poll (Clemens and Paulini, 1991, pp. 106-124), half of all German mail order firms were already active across Europe before 1993 and were expecting a clear increase in intra-community sales after 1993. As a consequence, low-tax countries will gain and high-tax countries lose in VAT revenue. It is this fear of revenue losses which induces high-tax countries such as Denmark or Ireland to keep the sales threshold at its lower limit.

We will call this choice between the DP and the OP with respect to distance sales the *switching option*. Consumers in low-tax countries

---

[31] This lower limit was adopted by Belgium, Denmark, Greece, Ireland, Italy, Portugal and Spain, whereas France, Germany, Luxemburg, the Netherlands and the UK apply the regular limit of 100,000 ECU.

[32] Matters are even more complicated by the fact that distance sales which are subject to excise duties (such as alcoholic drinks or tobacco) will always be taxed in the country of destination. To simplify our presentation, we will neglect this provision.

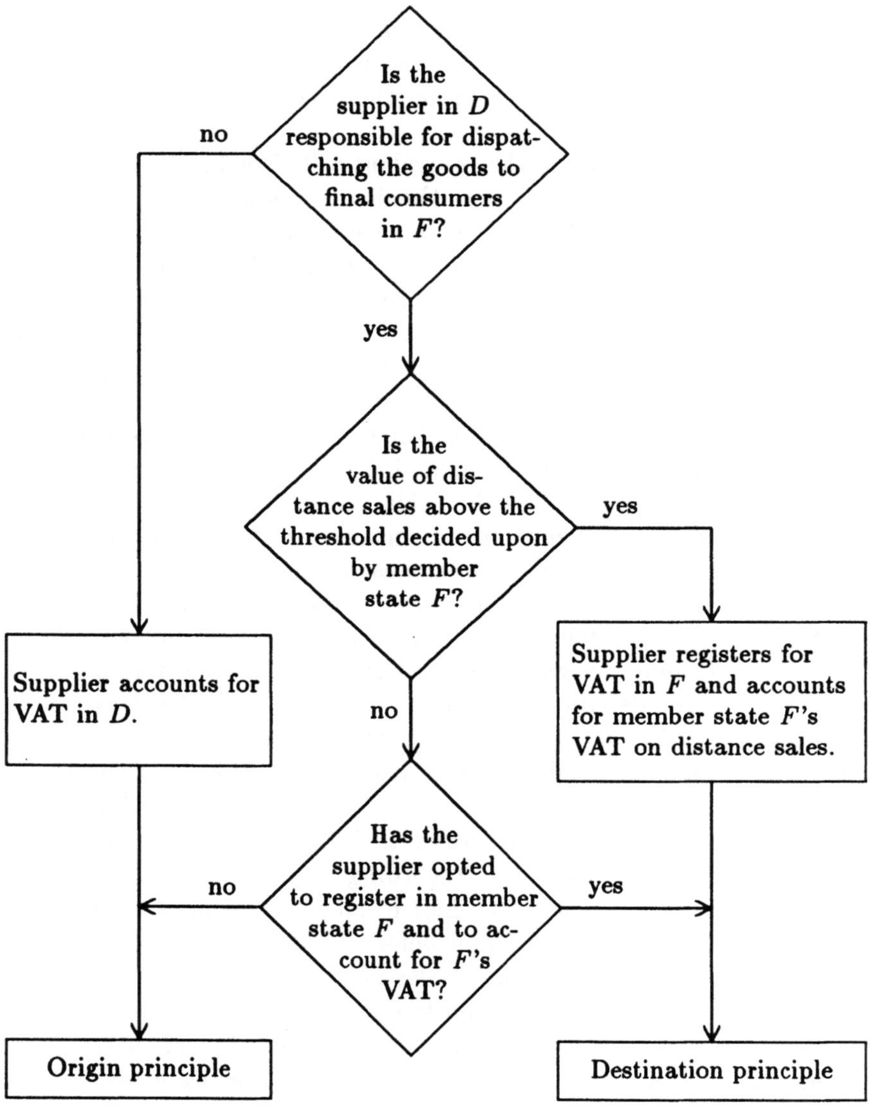

Figure 3. VAT treatment of sales from member state D to final consumers in member state F

will purchase from suppliers in high-tax countries by making use of the destination principle. Conversely, consumers in high-tax countries face an incentive to settle their distance sales from suppliers in low-tax countries according to the origin principle. In both cases, the VAT revenue on distance sales accrues to the country of origin.

In the literature, there is another interpretation of the transitional system. Sinn (1990), Krause-Junk (1990) or Haufler (1993), for example, seem to assume that, under the transitional system, trade between VAT registered persons follows the destination principle, whereas *all* distance sales to final consumers are taxed according to the origin principle. Following Krause-Junk, we will speak of a *mixed system*. We do not share this view, but nevertheless will deal with this interpretation in the following sections and chapters.

There is, of course, a third possibility in addition to the switching option and the mixed system. This is that the special provisions with respect to distance sales guarantee taxation according to the destination principle. In this case, everything remains as it was before 1993 (except for an increase in compliance costs).

3.2. A Numerical Example

In this section we will resume our numerical example to illustrate the calculation of tax liabilities and tax revenues under the different interpretations of the transitional system. We exclude distance sales to final consumers in other member states when calculating gross tax liability in the first line of Table 2. The various forms of VAT treatment of distance sales are described in the lower part of the table.

Under the switching option, consumers may choose to purchase goods in another member state either according to the destination or the origin principle. In our example, consumers in the low-tax country D will choose the destination principle whereas consumers in the high-tax country F will use the origin principle for distance sales. Under the mixed system, all distance sales are settled according to the OP. Finally, if the threshold for distance sales is exceeded, the destination principle applies. The interesting point to note is that the VAT revenue distribution between member states differs considerably between the three alternatives considered.

Table 2. Calculating tax revenues under the transitional system

	Uniform tax rates				Differentiated tax rates			
Country	D		F		D		F	
Industry	1	2	1	2	1	2	1	2
Tax rates	*0.1*		*0.2*		*0.05*	*0.1*	*0.1*	*0.2*
1. Gross tax liability (excluding distance sales to final consumers)	14.0	12.0	30.0	24.0	7.0	12.0	15.0	24.0
2. Tax rebate for exemption of intra-community supplies for acquisition	2.0	3.0	6.0	8.0	1.0	3.0	3.0	8.0
3. Tax rebate for domestic inputs	3.0	4.0	6.0	10.0	3.0	2.0	6.0	5.0
4. VAT on intra-community acquisitions	3.0	4.0	6.0	4.0	2.5	3.0	5.0	3.0
5. Tax rebate for VAT on intra-community acquisitions	3.0	4.0	6.0	4.0	2.5	3.0	5.0	3.0
6. Tax liability (1. – 2. – 3. + 4. – 5.)	9.0	5.0	18.0	6.0	3.0	7.0	6.0	11.0
	Tax revenues from taxation of distance sales							
7a. Switching option:								
Dist. sales from D to F	1.0	3.0	-	-	0.5	3.0	-	-
Dist. sales from F to D	1.0	1.0	-	-	0.5	1.0	-	-
8a. Total VAT revenue under switching option	20.0		24.0		15.0		17.0	
7b. Mixed system	1.0	3.0	2.0	2.0	0.5	3.0	1.0	2.0
8b. Total VAT revenue under mixed system	18.0		28.0		13.5		20.0	
7c. Value of distance sales above threshold	1.0	1.0	2.0	6.0	0.5	1.0	1.0	6.0
8c. Total VAT revenue	16.0		32.0		11.5		24.0	

3.3. A More General Formulation

3.3.1. The Switching Option

The switching option implies that consumers in country h will buy directly from suppliers in country $k \in EU_h$ according to the destination or origin principle, depending on whether k is a high- or low-tax country as compared to h. To formalize this we have to introduce some additional notational complexities. Let us partition the set EU_h into the two (disjoint) subsets EU_h^L and EU_h^H where the first comprises the low- and the second the high-tax countries from the viewpoint of country h. Note that whether country k is a low- or a high-tax country may differ from commodity to commodity.

Assuming that the present system of border tax adjustments is maintained for trade with ROW, i.e., exports from the EU to ROW are zero rated, whereas imports from ROW are subject to import VAT, we can now restate the relevant equations from the first section. Under the transitional system, the tax liability of firm $i \in N_s$ (in country h) is calculated by[33]

$$T_i = \overbrace{\tau_i q_i (Q_i - \sum_{k \in EU_h^L} C_i^{\cdot k})}^{\text{Gross tax liability excluding distance sales to final consumers}} + \overbrace{\sum_{k \in EU_h} \sum_{j \in N} \tau_j q_j^k V_{ji}^{k\cdot}}^{\text{Tax liability on the acquisition of intermediate inputs from EU member countries}} - \overbrace{\tau_i q_i X_i^{\cdot ROW}}^{\text{Tax rebate for exports to ROW}}$$

$$- \underbrace{\sum_{k \in EU_h} \sum_{j \in N} \tau_i q_i V_{ij}^{\cdot k}}_{\text{Tax exemption of intra-community supplies of intermediate inputs}} - \underbrace{\sum_{k \in W} \sum_{j \in N} \tau_j q_j^k V_{ji}^{k\cdot}}_{\text{Tax rebate for the acquisition of intermediate inputs}} . \qquad (7)$$

Note that under the transitional system, firm i is liable to pay VAT on the acquisition of inputs from other EU countries. At the same time, however, the acquiring firm is given a credit for this tax. Hence, in fact, such acquisitions bear no tax burden at all in the country of destination.

---

[33] The VAT treatment of the service sector remains as described in Section 2.3. above.

As an additional refinement, the above-mentioned special provisions for intra-community trade in new vehicles have to be taken into account. Here we would generally have to apply the DP. In order to keep our representation at least somewhat transparent, this is not considered in the equations of this section, but will be taken into account in the simulations described in later chapters.

Country h will receive some additional VAT revenue from the following sources:

$$\underbrace{\sum_{i \in N_*} \tau_i q_i^{ROW} M_i^{ROW \cdot} + \sum_{j \in N} \tau_s q_s^{ROW} V_{sj}^{ROW \cdot}}_{\text{Import VAT from ROW}} + \underbrace{\sum_{k \in EU_h^H} \sum_{i \in N_*} \tau_i q_i^k C_i^{k \cdot}}_{\text{VAT from distance sales in high-tax member states}}.$$

Aggregating the tax liabilities of domestic firms (including the service sector) and adding the additional revenue from trade relations, total tax revenue (after some manipulations) is given as

$$T = \sum_{i \in N} \tau_i q_i C_i + \sum_{i \in N_*} \tau_i q_i^{ROW} C_i^{ROW \cdot} + \sum_{i \in EU_h^H} \sum_{i \in N_*} \tau_i q_i^k C_i^{k \cdot} + \sum_{k \in EU_h^H} \sum_{i \in N_*} \tau_i q_i C_i^{\cdot k} + \sum_{k \in W_h} \tau_s q_s C_s^{\cdot k}. \qquad (8)$$

When compared with equation (4), the basic difference in national tax revenue between DP and the switching option under the transitional system is as follows: country h does not collect any VAT revenue from direct consumption purchases from low-tax EU countries but instead keeps VAT on its supplies to high-tax member states.

The last equation may look somewhat complicated. It is, however, only the explicit (mathematical) formulation of our interpretation of the transitional system. Note also that the equation for the balance of payments will change because under the transitional system direct consumption sales to high-tax as well as direct consumption purchases from low-tax member states have to be valued at consumer prices rather than at producer prices as in (6).

3.3.2. The Mixed System

Under the mixed system, all distance sales are taxed according to the origin principle. Hence, there is no longer any need to differentiate between low- and high-tax member states. For the sake of simplicity it may suffice to present the equation for country h's VAT revenue as:

$$T = \sum_{i \in N} \tau_i q_i C_i + \sum_{i \in N_s} \tau_i q_i^{ROW} C_i^{ROW \cdot} + \sum_{k \in EU_h} \sum_{i \in N_s} \tau_i q_i C_i^{\cdot k} + \sum_{k \in W_h} \tau_s q_s C_s^{\cdot k}. \quad (9)$$

The difference between revenue equations (8) and (9) should be self-explanatory.

4. The Origin Principle and the Credit Method

Not surprisingly, the transitional system is considered to be transitional in nature. In 1997, the final VAT system shall become effective. Even if the details are not yet settled, the EU Commission and the ECOFIN Council seem to agree that not only border controls but fiscal frontiers as well, i.e. border tax adjustments, should be abolished. In the first chapter, a situation without any border tax adjustments was defined as the origin principle. According to the plans of the Commission, the origin principle will be applied only with respect to trade between member states of the EU. Trade with third countries will be treated as before, i.e. according to the destination principle. Even if the international taxation principle for VAT should change in 1997, it is most probable that the credit method for calculating tax liabilities will be retained. In any case there is no hint at all in the official documents released by the Commission that the subtraction method is being seriously considered for adoption.

4.1. Some Institutional Features

A situation where the origin principle is administered with the tax credit method is called the "common market principle" (CMP) in the literature. Biehl (1969, 1982, 1988) is one of its main proponents. Under the CMP all intra-community sales and purchases are treated in the same manner as corresponding domestic transactions. As a general rule the place of supply for goods is deemed to be the place where the transportion commences, independent of whether the goods concerned are delivered from, say, Munich to Regensburg or from Munich to Paris. In both cases, the VAT revenue accrues to the country of origin. On the other hand, if the purchaser is a taxable person he may deduct input taxes in the member state in which he is a registered taxpayer. Hence, whenever imports from other member states pass through at least one domestic production stage, the credit method ensures that all sales to consumers within any country are taxed according to that country's VAT rates. Only intra-community sales to final consumers bear the full tax burden of the country of production or origin. Whereas consumption is still the tax base under the CMP, the VAT revenue no longer accrues to the country where consumption takes place, as is the case under the destination principle. This, of course, is due to the possibility of deducting foreign VAT as input taxes. Adopting the CMP may therefore result in considerable revenue shifts between member states, depending on intra-community tax rate differentials and on bilateral trade balances. Of course, those member states which apply high (low) tax rates and have large trade surpluses (deficits) will gain (lose) in VAT revenue. Due to these shifts in revenue, there is no chance at all – at least as long as the unanimity principle for taxation issues holds – that the CMP will ever be realized.

The Commission's original idea, as outlined in the working document COM (87) 323 final/2, was to supplement the CMP[34] with a special redistributional measure, namely the VAT "clearing mechanism". The clearing procedure would ensure that VAT revenues "continue to accrue to the country of final consumption (for budgetary reasons and in accordance with the principles of VAT as a general consumption tax)".[35] Hence, VAT collected in one member state on sales to other member states should be reimbursed to the latter where input taxes are deducted and final consumption takes place. The obvious problem is to design a clearing system

- which *correctly* attributes to the appropriate member states the VAT revenue on intra-community sales to it, which has been collected in the member states of origin, and
- which imposes minimal compliance and administrative costs.

---

[34] Quite astonishingly, the term "common market principle" has never been used in any official EU document.

[35] COM(87) 323 final/2 (1).

Four basic problems have to be solved concerning the *operation* of the clearing mechanism. Firstly, a decision has to be made on whether the equalization payments should be calculated on the basis of *macro*economic or *micro*economic data. The second problem is whether or not the clearing payments should be made on a bilateral basis or handled centrally by some supra-national institution, a redistributional agency or a bank for VAT purposes. The third problem deals with the question of whether clearing payments between member states should be made on a gross or a net basis. Under the former, each member state of origin calculates the VAT revenues on its export sales to other member states and remits this amount directly to the respective member state of destination or indirectly, through a central clearing institution. Alternatively, each member state could calculate its net position vis-à-vis other member states or the Community as whole by subtracting input taxes on intra-community sales.

The final problem concerns the fact that input taxes on intra-community purchases and VAT revenues on intra-community sales do not exactly match. This is due to the fact that sales to other member states include supplies made to customers not entitled to deduct input taxes. These are unregistered and tax-exempt traders on the one hand, and final consumers on the other. As a consequence, the central clearing institution would run a surplus which has to be distributed to the member states. If, instead, VAT compensation payments were made on a bilateral basis, the transfers from the member state of origin to the one of destination would exceed the input taxes on sales from that member state.

Beginning with the problem of equalization payments, one is faced with a trade-off between accuracy and simplicity. A microeconomic clearing procedure is based on monthly or quarterly reports of taxable persons in each member state, indicating the VAT figures on input purchases and/or output sales for intra-community trade. On the basis of this information, the member state of origin calculates the aggregate gross or net VAT payments due to other member states, either bilaterally or through a central clearing institution. The advantage of this procedure is its high degree of accuracy, its disadvantage the costly controls and checks which are necessary to validate the claims put forward by member states. Detailed audit trials and a regular program of verification checks are vital elements of each microeconomic clearing procedure. A macroeconomic clearing system, on the other hand, relies on aggregate data on intra-community trade. The German "ifo-institute" favors this concept and has made several detailed proposals for a macroeconomic clearing procedure.[36] Although this approach minimizes compliance and administrative costs, it is unlikely to provide an acceptable degree of accuracy. With the abolition of frontier controls, statistics on intra-community trade are no longer based on information provided by customs. Instead, entrepreneurs have to report trade volumes with other member states directly to national statistical offices for compilation into intra-community trade statistics. These statistics, however, are not geared to the requirements of a VAT clearing mechanism. First, services are excluded from these statistics; second, the volume of trade in goods is not completely registered because intra-community sales under a certain threshold do not have to be reported. Hence, there seems to be widespread agreement that the macroeconomic data presently available are full of uncertainties and not suited to serve as the basis for a functioning clearing system.

With respect to the other problems mentioned above, the EU Commission in 1987 proposed a central clearing institution, operating under the supervision of the Commission, with monthly payments to and from this institution based on *net* revenue figures. The Commission made no precise proposals regarding the surplus of the central clearing institution due to the lack of reliable data on intra-community sales to VAT exempt business and to private individuals. As is well-known, this proposal was not accepted by the ECOFIN Council. Currently, the Commission and expert groups in member states are working on an improved version of the clearing mechanism.

Germany's Country of Origin Commission (1994) recently presented its proposal for a definitive European value-added taxation scheme and for a functioning clearing procedure. In essence, the suggestions amount to *bilateral* clearing based on *gross* revenue figures. The member state of origin calculates the VAT compensation payments separately for each other member state on the basis of microeconomic data for all supplies of goods and services and remits this amount to the countries of destination at monthly intervals. In addition, taxable persons in each member state report the amount of VAT charged to them by business partners in other member states, and this is deducted as input taxes. This allows the country of destination to verify, at least to some degree, whether the payments by the country of origin are correct. Actually, the payments received must exceed the input taxes

[36] See, for example, Parsche, Seidel and Teichmann (1988, pp. 430-445) or Parsche (1991).

deducted from intra-community trade. A deviation of 10 per cent is considered to be realistic and tolerable. In other words, the German Country of Origin Commission presupposes that, on average, 10 per cent of intra-community sales are made to non-taxable entities and that there should be no compensation payments for VAT revenues on these sales. Only if this deviation limit between VAT retained and input taxes deducted is exceeded, must bilateral corrections be made.[37] The proposal is to divide these correction payments equally between the member states concerned. We will illustrate the exact determination of these correction payments in our numerical example and in our mathematical formulation of the clearing system.

At present, it is hard to say whether or not the proposals of Germany's Country of Origin Commission have a greater chance of being accepted by member states than the EU Commission's original plans. The solution proposed is certainly less centralized and more concrete than the previous proposal. On the other hand, some VAT revenue shifts between member states seem to be unavoidable. In view of the intense quarrels following the presentation of COM(87)323 final/2 some scepticism about the adoption of the more recent proposals seems to be appropriate.

4.2. A Numerical Example

Let us now illustrate the CMP as well as the clearing system by recourse to our numerical example. Table 3 contains the relevant numbers. In the upper part, tax liabilities and revenues are calculated when countries D and F switch to the CMP. From line 5 it is obvious that country F would realize considerable gains in VAT revenue. The reasons are that country F is not only the high-tax country, but in addition has a surplus in trade in intermediate inputs. Note that total VAT revenues of the two member states taken together are lower under the CMP than under the DP. This is due to the fact that, under the CMP, distance sales are taxed according to the VAT rate of the country of origin.

In the middle part of Table 3 we illustrate the clearing mechanism as designed by the German Country of Origin Commission. Line 6 shows the uncorrected clearing payments from the country of origin (−) to

[37] The exact deviation limit may be negotiated on a bilateral basis. We will assume that a 10 per cent limit is generally agreed upon.

Table 3. Calculating tax revenues under the origin principle and the credit method

	Uniform tax rates				Differentiated tax rates			
Country	D		F		D		F	
Industry	1	2	1	2	1	2	1	2
Tax rates	*0.1*		*0.2*		*0.05*	*0.1*	*0.1*	*0.2*
1. Gross tax liability	15.0	15.0	32.0	26.0	7.5	15.0	16.0	26.0
2. Tax rebate for domestic inputs	3.0	4.0	6.0	10.0	3.0	2.0	6.0	5.0
3. Tax rebate for intra-community purchases of inputs	6.0	8.0	3.0	2.0	5.0	6.0	2.5	1.5
4. Tax liability (1. – 2. – 3.)	6.0	3.0	23.0	14.0	–0.5	7.0	7.5	19.5
5. Total VAT revenue under the CMP	9.0		37.0		6.5		27.0	

	Clearing procedure according to Germany's Country of Origin Commission					
6. Uncorrected clearing payments (–) from country of origin to country of destination	+18.0	⟵	–18.0	+14.0	⟵	–14.0
	–9.0	⟶	+9.0	–7.5	⟶	+7.5
7. Uncorrected net clearing payments (–) and receipts (+)	+9.0	⟵	–9.0	+7.5	⟵	–7.5
8. Calculation of correction payments:						
a. Input taxes on purchases from other member states	14.0		5.0	11.0		4.0
b. Tolerable deviation limit: 10 per cent of clearing receipts	1.8		0.9	1.4		0.75

c. Actual deviation between clearing payments from country of origin and input taxes deducted in country of destination	4.0		4.0	3.0		3.5
d. Correction payments (–) ((8c. – 8b.) : 2)	–1.1 +1.55	⟶ ⟵	+1.1 –1.55	–0.8 +1.375	⟶ ⟵	+0.8 –1.375
9. Net correction payments (–)	+0.45	⟵	–0.45	+0.575	⟵	–0.575
10. Total clearing payments (–) and receipts (+) after correction (7. + 9.)	+9.45	⟵	–9.45	+8.075	⟵	–8.075
11. Total VAT revenues after clearing (5. + 10.)	18.45		27.55	14.575		18.925
	Clearing procedure according to the EU-Commission (COM(87) 323 final/2)					
12. VAT on sales to other member states	9.0		18.0	7.5		14.0
13. Input taxes on purchases from other member states	14.0		5.0	11.0		4.0
14. Net position vis-à-vis central clearing institution (claims +; liabilities –)	5.0		–13.0	3.5		–10.0
15. Total VAT revenues before distribution of clearing surplus	14.0		24.0	10.0		17.0
16. Surplus of central clearing institution		8.0			6.5	
17. Correct disposition of surplus	4.0		4.0	3.0		3.5
18. Total VAT revenues after an ideal clearing mechanism	18.0		28.0	13.0		20.5

the country of destination (+). These payments correspond to the VAT collected by the country of origin on its supplies of goods and services to the country of destination. Netting out payments and receipts yields the uncorrected net clearing amounts. Line 8 examines and, if necessary, determines bilateral correction payments. The suggested procedure works as follows. The two member states concerned first compare the (uncorrected) clearing payment from the country of origin to the country of destination (line 6) and the input taxes deducted in the latter country on purchases from the former (line 8a). If the difference (line 8c) does not exceed the tolerable deviation limit of 10 per cent of the uncorrected clearing payment (line 8b), no further adjustments are considered to be necessary. On the other hand, if the tolerable deviation limit is exceeded the difference is split up between the two countries concerned. The country of destination has to reimburse part of the received clearing payment to the country of origin (line 8d). Total clearing payments (line 10) result from adding the net correction terms (line 9) to the initial clearing payments (line 7). A mathematical presentation of this correction procedure is given in the following subsection.

The final part of Table 3 contains the clearing procedure as suggested by the Commission of the EU in 1987. Net claims and liabilities against the central clearing institution (line 14) are calculated by subtracting VAT on all sales to the other member states from the input taxes on purchases from partner countries. The surplus on the clearing account (line 17) corresponds to VAT on all intra-community sales to non-taxable or tax-exempt persons. In line 18 we have assumed that these sales can be monitored accurately and that the surplus can be correctly distributed to the member states.

4.3. A More General Formulation

4.3.1. The Common Market Principle

Assuming that fiscal frontiers and, hence, border tax adjustments have been abolished within the EU but maintained with ROW, a taxable firm $i \in N_s$ in an EU member state h calculates its tax liability as follows:

$$T_i = \overbrace{\tau_i q_i (Q_i - V_{ii})}^{\text{Gross tax liability}} - \overbrace{\sum_{j \in N_i} \tau_j q_j V_{ji}}^{\text{Tax rebate for use of domestic inputs}} - \overbrace{\sum_{k \in EU_h} \sum_{j \in N} \tau_j^k q_j^k V_{ji}^{k\cdot}}^{\text{Tax rebate for use of intermediate inputs from EU countries}}$$

$$- \underbrace{\tau_i q_i X_i^{\cdot ROW}}_{\text{Tax rebate for exports to ROW}} - \underbrace{\sum_{j \in N} \tau_j q_j^{ROW} V_{ji}^{ROW\cdot}}_{\text{Tax rebate for use of intermediate inputs from ROW}} \qquad (10)$$

Consider the tax rebates, each taxable entity can offset against its gross tax liability. The first two terms describe the rebate for VAT paid on intermediate inputs from EU member states. Since there are no border tax adjustments within the EU, intermediate imports from these countries bear the full burden of foreign VAT; these are refunded by the domestic treasury. On the other hand, the DP still applies to trade with ROW. Therefore, firm i receives a tax rebate for its exports to ROW. Imports from ROW are subject to domestic VAT. As far as intermediate imports are concerned, this import VAT may be deducted from gross tax liability.

Note that with respect to services ($i = s$) we assume the origin principle to be applied for all trade with EU member states as well as for sales to final consumers from ROW. Only when services are used as intermediate inputs, is trade between the EU member states and ROW taxed according to the destination principle.

Total tax revenue under the CMP is obtained by aggregating individual tax liabilities according to (10) and adding the import VAT collected on imports from ROW:

$$T = \sum_{i \in N} T_i + \sum_{i \in N_s} \tau_i q_i^{ROW} M_i^{ROW\cdot} + \sum_{j \in N} \tau_s q_s^{ROW} V_{sj}^{ROW\cdot}.$$

After some manipulation, this last equation may also be written as follows:

$$T = \sum_{i \in N} \tau_i q_i C_i + \sum_{i \in N_s} \tau_i q_i^{ROW} C_i^{ROW \cdot} + \sum_{k \in EU_k} \sum_{i \in N_s} \tau_i q_i C_i^{\cdot k}$$

$$+ \sum_{k \in W_k} \tau_s q_s C_s^{\cdot k} + \sum_{k \in EU_k} \sum_{i \in N} \sum_{j \in N} (\tau_i q_i V_{ij}^{\cdot k} - \tau_i^k q_i^k V_{ij}^{k \cdot}). \quad (11)$$

This equation may best be interpreted by comparing it with the corresponding expression (4) for the DP.

Assuming for a moment that tax rates, producer prices and quantities are the same under both tax regimes, a switch from DP to CMP results in the revenue difference

$$\sum_{k \in EU_k} \Big(\sum_{i \in N_s} \tau_i q_i C_i^{\cdot k} + \sum_{i \in N} \sum_{j \in N} \tau_i q_i V_{ij}^{\cdot k} \Big) -$$

$$- \sum_{k \in EU_k} \Big(\sum_{i \in N_s} \tau_i q_i^k C_i^{k \cdot} + \sum_{i \in N} \sum_{j \in N} \tau_i^k q_i^k V_{ij}^{k \cdot} \Big). \quad (12)$$

Two countervailing effects can be identified. On the one hand, there is a revenue gain for the home country because exports to EU member states are no longer zero-rated. On the other hand, there is a loss of import VAT on direct consumption imports by domestic consumers from other EU states, and, moreover, a tax rebate for foreign taxes on intermediate imports must be paid. Which effect dominates depends on tax rate differentials within the EU and on bilateral trade balances. High-tax countries with a positive intra-EU trade balance will presumably realize a considerable increase in VAT revenue at the expense of their EU trading partners. The contrary holds for low-tax member states with a trade deficit.

This revenue re-allocation between the EU member states makes the CMP politically infeasible. This is why the Commission of the EU proposed that the CMP be supplemented by a clearing mechanism. Before describing the mechanics of the clearing procedure, we note that, whereas the zero-profit condition remains the same for the CMP as for the DP, the current account equation changes in so far as trade between EU member states is valued at consumer prices under the CMP.

4.3.2. The Clearing System

The 1987 Proposal of the EU Commission

A member state's net position against the central clearing institution is determined by the difference

$$\overbrace{\sum_{k\in EU_h}\sum_{i\in N}\sum_{j\in N}\tau_i^k q_i^k V_{ij}^{k\cdot}}^{\text{Input taxes on purchases from other EU member states}} - \overbrace{\sum_{k\in EU_h}\sum_{i\in N}\sum_{j\in N}\tau_i q_i V_{ij}^{\cdot k}}^{\text{VAT on total sales to registered traders in other member states}}$$
$$- \underbrace{\sum_{k\in EU_h}\sum_{i\in N_s}\tau_i q_i C_i^{\cdot k}}_{\text{VAT on sales of goods to final consumers in other member states}}. \qquad (13)$$

A positive difference constitutes a claim, a negative one a liability against the clearing institution.

The surplus realized by this institution corresponds to VAT on all intra-community sales of goods to non-taxable persons:[38]

$$\sum_{h\in EU}\sum_{k\in EU_h}\sum_{i\in N_s}\tau_i^k q_i^k C_i^{kh}.$$

Under an ideal clearing mechanism each member state would receive an amount S^h of this surplus, being equal to the VAT on intra-community supplies to final consumers in the member state concerned. We therefore have

$$S^h = \sum_{k\in EU_h}\sum_{i\in N_s}\tau_i^k q_i^k C_i^{kh}. \qquad (14)$$

Adding this to the claims or liabilities against the clearing account yields total revenues under an ideal clearing mechanism:

$$T = \sum_{i\in N}\tau_i q_i C_i + \sum_{i\in N_s}\tau_i q_i^{ROW} C_i^{ROW\cdot} + \sum_{k\in W_h}\tau_s q_s C_s^{\cdot k}$$
$$+ \sum_{k\in EU_h}\sum_{i\in N_s}\tau_i^k q_i^k C_i^{k\cdot}. \qquad (15)$$

---

[38] Remember that we have neglected tax-exempt firms in our model.

Even in this 'ideal' case, national tax revenues under the DP and the clearing system do not exactly coincide. Assuming prices and quantities remain unchanged, the revenue difference is given by

$$\sum_{k \in EU_h} \sum_{i \in N_*} (\tau_i^k - \tau_i) q_i^k C_i^{k\cdot}. \tag{16}$$

The reason for this difference is that after abolishing border tax adjustments the clearing mechanism ensures that whereas intra-community purchases by final consumers bear the foreign countries tax burden, the corresponding VAT revenue accrues to the country where the consumption takes place. Therefore, the clearing system can be thought of as the DP supplemented by an additional tax or subsidy on direct consumption imports according to the tax rate differential $(\tau_i^k - \tau_i)$. Equation (16) indicates that low tax countries will gain and high tax countries will lose revenue.

The Proposal of the German Country of Origin Commission

The clearing procedure proposed works on a bilateral basis. Let country $h \in EU$ be the country of origin and country $k \in EU_h$ be the country of destination. For country h the uncorrected net clearing payments[39] to and receipts from member state k are given by

$$\sum_{i \in N} \sum_{j \in N} \tau_i q_i V_{ij}^{\cdot k} + \sum_{i \in N_*} \tau_i q_i C_i^{\cdot k} - \sum_{i \in N} \sum_{j \in N} \tau_i^k q_i^k V_{ij}^{k\cdot} - \sum_{i \in N_*} \tau_i^k q_i^k C_i^{k\cdot}. \tag{17}$$

Note again that service exports to final consumers are excluded from these clearing payments.

Let S^{kh} be the correction payment from country k to h. Given a deviation limit of 10 per cent, S^{kh} is determined by

$$S^{kh} = 0 \quad \text{if} \sum_{i \in N_*} \tau_i q_i C_i^{\cdot k} \le 0.1 \Big(\sum_{j \in N} \sum_{i \in N} \tau_i q_i V_{ij}^{\cdot k} + \sum_{i \in N_*} \tau_i q_i C_i^{\cdot k} \Big) \tag{18a}$$

or otherwise by

$$S^{kh} = \Big(0.9 \sum_{i \in N_*} \tau_i q_i C_i^{\cdot k} - 0.1 \sum_{j \in N} \sum_{i \in N} \tau_i q_i V_{ij}^{\cdot k} \Big) : 2. \tag{18b}$$

[39] Note that in our numerical example we have defined clearing payments as negative numbers, whereas in this section payments are defined by positive numbers.

Consider the case (18a) that no correction payments are necessary. To obtain the bilateral net clearing payments between country h and all other member states, one has to aggregate (17) for all $k \in EU_h$. Subtracting this sum from (11) yields national VAT revenues after the clearing procedure as

$$T = \sum_{i \in N} \tau_i q_i C_i + \sum_{i \in N_s} \tau_i q_i^{ROW} C_i^{ROW \cdot} + \sum_{k \in W_h} \tau_s q_s C_s^{\cdot k} + \sum_{k \in EU_h} \sum_{i \in N_s} \tau_i^k q_i^k C_i^{k \cdot}, \tag{19}$$

which is exactly the same as total revenue (15) under an ideal clearing system as proposed by the Commission of the EU.

Turning to case (18b) where correction payments are required, matters become more complicated. First, one has to correct (17) by subtracting S^{kh} and adding S^{hk}.[40] This yields the corrected total clearing payments or receipts, which, after collecting terms, may be written as

$$1.05 \sum_{i \in N} \sum_{j \in N} (\tau_i q_i V_{ij}^{\cdot k} - \tau_i^k q_i^k V_{ij}^{k \cdot}) + 0.55 \sum_{i \in N_s} (\tau_i q_i C_i^{\cdot k} - \tau_i^k q_i^k C_i^{k \cdot}).$$

Aggregating over all partner countries in the EU ($k \in EU_h$) and subtracting from (11) finally gives us total VAT revenues of country h after the clearing mechanism:

$$\begin{aligned} T = {} & \sum_{i \in N} \tau_i q_i C_i + \sum_{i \in N_s} \tau_i q_i^{ROW} C_i^{ROW \cdot} + \sum_{k \in W_h} \tau_s q_s C_s^{\cdot k} \\ & + \sum_{k \in EU_h} \sum_{i \in N_s} \tau_i^k q_i^k C_i^{k \cdot} \\ & + 0.45 \sum_{k \in EU_h} \sum_{i \in N_s} (\tau_i q_i C_i^{\cdot k} - \tau_i^k q_i^k C_i^{k \cdot}) \\ & + 0.05 \sum_{k \in EU_h} \sum_{i \in N} \sum_{j \in N} (\tau_i q_i V_{ij}^{\cdot k} - \tau_i^k q_i^k V_{ij}^{k \cdot}). \end{aligned} \tag{20}$$

This equation may look complicated, but it is merely the exact mathematical representation of the (corrected) clearing mechanism as designed by the German Country of Origin Commission.

---

[40] Here, S^{hk} has to be determined in obvious analogy to (18b).

As a final remark we note that the current account now includes the balance of unilateral transfers, which contains net clearing payments and receipts.

5. The Origin Principle and the Subtraction Method

In this final section we will deal with the most radical variant for reforming VAT after 1996. This amounts to not only abolishing border tax adjustments but additionally to replacing the tax credit by the subtraction method. Proponents of this proposal[41] generally refer to the exchange rate argument according to which a change in VAT principles has no real effects when accompanied by a one time exchange rate realignment. In the next chapter we are concerned with these and related theoretical considerations. Here, our interest is restricted to a description of the proposal.

As already mentioned in the previous chapter, several variants of introducing the origin principle and the subtraction method have been proposed. We will focus on the most radical one: *all* countries, the member states of the EU as well as all third countries, are assumed to switch from the DP to the OP and from the credit to the subtraction method. Admittedly this is a rather unrealistic reform option. Nevertheless, it may be of interest to gain some insight into the allocational and international redistributional effects of this proposal. The other two variants – a fictive tax credit for intra-community purchases of intermediate products on the one hand, and a combination of the subtraction and the credit method on the other hand – are more difficult to administer and do not possess any superior efficiency properties.

Unfortunately, resuming our numerical example is no easy matter. The reason is that our input-output data are valued at producer (or tax-exclusive) prices, whereas determination of the tax base under the subtraction method requires knowledge of market (or tax-inclusive) prices. One could try to infer market prices from producer prices, but this would require some rather sophisticated arguments as will become obvious in the following chapters. Hence, in this section dealing with the mathematical presentation first is preferable.

If market prices are known, computing tax liability under the subtraction method is straightforward. To obtain the tax base, the in-

[41] In Section 1.2.4. of the first chapter we have named the more prominent supporters of this proposal.

dividual firm simply deducts all input expenses from its gross sales, where all prices are tax-inclusive market prices. Consequently, a tax-inclusive VAT rate has to be applied to this tax base. Denoting, as before, τ_i as the tax-exclusive rate, the former can be expressed by $\tau_i/(1+\tau_i)$. Hence, firm-specific tax liability is calculated according to

$$T_i = \frac{\tau_i}{1+\tau_i}[p_i Q_i - \sum_{k \in W} \sum_{j \in N} p_j^k V_{ij}^{k\cdot}]. \tag{21}$$

This equation corresponds exactly to equation (5) of the previous chapter.

Instead of calculating tax liability in a subtractive manner, one could equally well use the addition method

$$T_i = \tau_i \underbrace{(wL_i + rK_i)}_{\text{Value added}}. \tag{22}$$

The equivalence of (21) and (22) becomes apparent when considering the zero profit condition

$$wL_i + rK_i = p_i Q_i - \sum_{k \in W} \sum_{j \in N} p_j^k V_{ji}^{k\cdot} - T_i. \tag{23}$$

Aggregating tax liabilities yields national tax revenue in country h as

$$T = \sum_{i \in N} \tau_i [wL_i + rK_i]. \tag{24}$$

The equations would become slightly more complicated if investment expenditures were considered.

Using equation (24), national tax revenues may now be easily calculated for our numerical example. To conclude, we note that all exports and imports have to be valued at market prices when considering the current account of any country h.

Chapter III

Theoretical Foundations

In the preceding chapters the main institutional features of various VAT reform options were described and translated into a model-equivalent form. Our ultimate aim is the computation of price, revenue and especially welfare effects when switching from a reference VAT system – which was effective until 1992 – to one of the reform proposals discussed in the preceeding chapter. This corresponds to performing some numerical comparative static experiments. Our main interest, however, is not in the computation but in the economic explanation of the resulting welfare effects. This requires some understanding of the economic mechanisms at work in an equilibrium model. After all, one of the main virtues of CGE modelling is its firm embedment in traditional general equilibrium theory, now the dominant theoretical framework for taxation problems. We therefore have to extend the accounting identities and market equilibrium conditions as outlined in the preceding chapter to a complete general equilibrium model. The reader is assumed to be sufficiently familiar with general equilibrium theory so that the following remarks should suffice.

On the consumer side of each country, we assume a representative agent maximizing his utility subject to a budget constraint. Each utility function is well-behaved and depends on consumption from domestic or foreign production and on leisure. The consumer derives income from his supply of labor and capital services and from government transfers. On the production side we assume production functions to depend on the primary production factors, labor and capital, as well as on intermediate products. Producers maximize profits or minimize costs. In this chapter, all commodities are assumed to be tradable. Capital is mobile between production sectors *and* countries, whereas labor is assumed to be internationally immobile. All markets are perfectly competitive.

This chapter aims to provide some of the more important theoretical foundations as well as the basic economic intuition used in evaluating the numerical results presented in Chapter V. We start by deriving the first-order conditions for a worldwide first-best allocation of resources and then inquire into the distortive features of taxes and tariffs. The final two sections explore the validity (or fallacy) of the so-called exchange rate argument and the welfare effects of indirect taxes in open economies due to income and substitution effects.

1. The Command Optimum

The distortive features of taxes can only meaningfully be discussed with reference to an efficient, non-distorted state of the economy. The marginal conditions characterizing such an efficient allocation of resources may be obtained by solving the optimization problem of a benevolent (worldwide) planner. Using the general forms of utility and production functions the planner maximizes the utility of the representative consumer in country h

$$\max U^h(C_i^{hh}, C_i^{kh}, \ell^h \,|\, i \in N, k \in W_h)$$

subject to

$$U^k(C_i^{kk}, C_i^{lk}, \ell^k \,|\, i \in N, l \in W_k) - \bar{U}^k = 0 \qquad k \in W_h$$

$$Q_i^k - f_i^k(K_i^k, L_i^k, V_{ji}^{lk} \,|\, j \in N, l \in W) = 0 \qquad i \in N; k \in W$$

$$Q_i^k - \sum_{l \in W} C_i^{kl} - \sum_{l \in W} \sum_{j \in N} V_{ij}^{kl} = 0 \qquad i \in N; k \in W$$

$$\bar{E}^k - \ell^k - \sum_{i \in N} L_i^k = 0 \qquad k \in W$$

$$\sum_{k \in W} \bar{K}^k - \sum_{i \in N} \sum_{k \in W} K_i^k = 0.$$

The constraints are the utility levels in all other countries, the production technologies, and full employment conditions. The control variables are the consumption quantities $(C_i^{kh} \,|\, i \in N; h, k \in W)$, leisure $(\ell^h \,|\, h \in W)$, output quantities $(Q_i^k \,|\, i \in N; k \in W)$, factor demands $(L_i^h, K_i^h \,|\, i \in N; h \in W)$ and intermediate inputs $(V_{ji}^{kh} \,|\, i, j \in N; k, h \in W)$. Taken together there are $3JR + JR^2 + R^2J^2 + R$ endogenous variables, where R is the number of countries and J the number of commodities.

After routine manipulations the first-order conditions as represented in Table 1 are obtained. In total we have $JR + JR^2 + J^2R^2 - R$ equations, which, together with the $2JR + 2R$ constraints, are assumed to have a unique solution. In Table 1, equations (1a)-(1e) describe the optimal resource allocation within country h, whereas the set of equations (1f)-(1i) refers to the international dimension of the allocation problem.

The first-order conditions (1a)-(1e) are well-known from closed economy models and can be readily explained. According to equation (1a) the use of commodity i as an input in its own production should be extended up to the point where an increase in input use produces an identical increase in output. Equations (1b) and (1c) require the equality of marginal rates of technical substitution between factors of production in different industries. Whereas (1b) refers to the efficient allocation of the primary factors labor and capital, (1c) refers to the factor allocation between intermediate inputs and primary factors. Equation (1d) calls for the equality of the marginal rates of substitution and the marginal rates of transformation between commodities j and i in country h. The next condition characterizes the efficient allocation of labor (or leisure) between consumption and production activities.

A link between countries is established by the remaining set of equations. In an international exchange optimum, domestic and foreign marginal rates of substitution between comparable goods should be equal. Equation (1f) represents marginal rates of substitution between two different goods that are produced in country h but consumed in countries h and $k \in W_h$, whereas equation (1g) refers to marginal rates of substitution between similar goods, produced in different countries. Finally, equation (1h) is the necessary condition for an efficient international coordination of consumption and production decisions, requiring that international marginal rates of substitution and transformation be equalized. Lastly, first-order condition (1i) describes the efficient

Table 1. First-order conditions in a CGE trade model

		Domestic allocation		
(1a)	$\frac{\partial f_i^h}{\partial V_{ii}^{hh}}$	$=$	1	$i \in N; h \in W$
(1b)	$\frac{\partial f_i^h/\partial L_i^h}{\partial f_i^h/\partial K_i^h}$	$=$	$\frac{\partial f_j^h/\partial L_j^h}{\partial f_j^h/\partial K_j^h}$	$j \in N_i; h \in W$
(1c)	$\frac{\partial f_i^h/\partial L_i^h}{\partial f_i^h/\partial V_{mi}^{lh}}$	$=$	$\frac{\partial f_j^h/\partial L_j^h}{\partial f_j^h/\partial V_{mj}^{lh}}$	$j \in N_i; m \in N; h, l \in W$
(1d)	$\frac{\partial U^h/\partial C_i^{hh}}{\partial U^h/\partial C_j^{hh}}$	$=$	$\frac{\partial f_j^h/\partial L_j^h}{\partial f_i^h/\partial L_i^h}$	$j \in N_i; h \in W$
(1e)	$\frac{\partial U^h/\partial \ell^h}{\partial U^h/\partial C_j^{hh}}$	$=$	$\frac{\partial f_j^h}{\partial L_j^h}$	$h \in W$
		International allocation		
(1f)	$\frac{\partial U^h/\partial C_i^{hh}}{\partial U^h/\partial C_j^{hh}}$	$=$	$\frac{\partial U^k/\partial C_i^{hk}}{\partial U^k/\partial C_j^{hk}}$	$j \in N_i; k \in W_h; h \in W$
(1g)	$\frac{\partial U^h/\partial C_i^{hh}}{\partial U^h/\partial C_i^{lh}}$	$=$	$\frac{\partial U^k/\partial C_i^{hk}}{\partial U^k/\partial C_i^{lk}}$	$l, k \in W_h$
(1h)	$\frac{\partial U^h/\partial C_i^{hh}}{\partial U^h/\partial C_i^{kh}}$	$=$	$\frac{\partial f_i^k/\partial K_i^k}{\partial f_i^h/\partial K_i^h}$	$k \in W_h$
(1i)	$\frac{\partial f_i^h/\partial K_i^h}{\partial f_i^h/\partial V_{mi}^{lh}}$	$=$	$\frac{\partial f_i^k/\partial K_i^k}{\partial f_i^k/\partial V_{mi}^{lk}}$	$m \in N; k \in W_h; l \in W$

allocation of tradable factors of production, requiring marginal rates of technical substitution to be equal in the production of similar goods in different countries. Due to the Armington assumption our international efficiency conditions deviate from those of traditional Heckscher-Ohlin models. One can, however, generate these latter conditions from ours by assuming commodities to be internationally homogeneous. In this case one would obtain, for example,

$$\frac{\partial U^h}{\partial C_i^{hh}} = \frac{\partial U^h}{\partial C_i^{kh}} \qquad \text{and, therefore,} \qquad \frac{\partial f_i^k}{\partial K_i^k} = \frac{\partial f_i^h}{\partial K_i^h},$$

which is the familiar condition for an efficient allocation of world capital. The other equations would have to be similarly adjusted.

A Pareto-efficient allocation as characterized by Table 1 may be decentralized by introducing a system of prices and competitive national and international markets, resulting in a free trade equilibrium.

2. Tax Distortions

Taxes, unless imposed in a lump-sum manner, distort the efficient allocation of resources by driving wedges between the respective marginal rates of substitution and marginal rates of transformation or between consumer and producer prices. In this section we identify these different tax wedges. Our interest focuses on the distortive features of alternative VAT schemes. We shall briefly sketch the allocative distortions of other taxes. If taxes only distort the marginal conditions (1a)-(1e), we will speak of domestic distortions. International distortions arise whenever the remaining first-order conditions are affected.

2.1. Tariffs, Income Taxes, and Production Taxes

By driving a wedge between domestic and international transactions, tariffs distort the international allocation of resources. In general, they interfere with the equality between the marginal rates of substitution in (1f) and (1g), and create a gap between marginal rates of transformation and marginal rates of substitution in equation (1h) as well as between the international rates of technical substitution in (1i). Not all of these equations need to be involved. For example, if country k levies a uniform tariff against imports from country h, equation (1f) will remain undistorted. Similarly, the formation of a tariff union will leave some marginal conditions unchanged.

Wage taxes drive a wedge between the marginal productivity of labor and the marginal rate of substitution between consumption and leisure as given in equation (1e). Because labor is assumed to be internationally immobile, wage taxes do not directly interfere with the international allocation of goods and factors. If labor supply is completely inelastic, equation (1e) vanishes and the wage tax becomes a lump-sum tax. The treatment of the taxation of interest income depends on whether the residence or the source principle is applied on border-crossing interest income flows.[42] In our model we assume the residence principle to be in force, as is the rule between OECD countries. In this case, residents of a given country are taxed uniformly on their worldwide interest income, regardless of the source of that income. Market forces will then equate gross, i.e. tax-inclusive interest rates. Because marginal products of capital are adjusted to the common world interest rate, the taxation of interest income according to the residence principle does not distort the efficient international allocation of capital as characterized by equation (1h). It would, however, distort the equilibrium allocation of world savings. In our model, however, saving decisions are neglected and, hence, interest income taxation creates no efficiency losses at all.

Production taxes are levied on domestic production values. Because primary factors of production as well as intermediate inputs are equally included in the tax base, equations (1b) and (1c) remain undistorted, whereas tax wedges are driven between equations (1d) and (1e). As to the international allocation of resources, production taxes distort the coordination between international consumption and production decisions in first-order condition (1h). Because VAT under the origin principle will have the same effect, some of the implications of this are given later.

When discussing value-added taxes in the following subsections we ignore all other taxes. Our analysis can be confined to the destination principle and the origin principle, using either the credit or the subtraction method. The efficiency properties of the transitional system as well as of the clearing system are simply combinations of the two basic international taxation principles, depending on the treatment of direct consumption imports. Similarly, the restricted origin principle is a combination of the destination and the origin principle, when applied to different countries.

---

[42] For a thorough discussion of these basic principles of international income taxation see, for example, Sinn (1987, pp. 195-200) or Frenkel, Razin and Sadka (1991, pp. 22-31).

2.2. Destination-based VAT

In order to examine the distortive effects of VAT in more detail we consider the decision problems of consumers and producers in country h. From the previous chapter's equation (5) it should be clear that value-added tax rates do not affect a firm's production decisions if the credit method is used. Profit maximization yields the familiar conditions that marginal rates of technical substitution are equated to factor prices and marginal rates of transformation to producer prices:

$$\frac{\partial f_i^h/\partial L_i^h}{\partial f_i^h/\partial K_i^h} = \frac{\partial f_j^h/\partial L_j^h}{\partial f_j^h/\partial K_j^h} = \frac{w^h}{r} \qquad j \in N_i \qquad \text{(2a)}$$

$$\frac{\partial f_j^h/\partial L_j^h}{\partial f_i^h/\partial L_i^h} = \frac{\partial f_j^h/\partial V_{mj}^{lh}}{\partial f_i^h/\partial V_{mi}^{lh}} = \frac{q_i^h}{q_j^h}. \qquad j \in N_i; m \in N; \; l \in W \qquad \text{(2b)}$$

Consumer decisions, on the other hand, are based on consumer prices $p_i^h = q_i^h(1+\tau_i^h)$ and factor prices w^h and r.[43] The representative consumer in any country h chooses his consumption-leisure-bundle according to the marginal conditions:

$$\frac{\partial U^h/\partial \ell^h}{\partial U^h/\partial C_i^{hh}} = \frac{w^h}{q_i^h(1+\tau_i^h)} = \frac{w^h}{p_i^h} \qquad i \in N \qquad \text{(3a)}$$

$$\frac{\partial U^h/\partial C_i^{kh}}{\partial U^h/\partial C_j^{kh}} = \frac{q_i^k(1+\tau_i^h)}{q_j^k(1+\tau_j^h)} \qquad j \in N_i; k \in W \qquad \text{(3b)}$$

$$\frac{\partial U^h/\partial C_i^{hh}}{\partial U^h/\partial C_i^{kh}} = \frac{q_i^h}{q_i^k}. \qquad i \in N; k \in W_h \qquad \text{(3c)}$$

If one combines these equations in order to make them comparable with the first-best allocation, one obtains:

$$\frac{(1+\tau_j^h)\,\partial U^h/\partial C_i^{hh}}{(1+\tau_i^h)\,\partial U^h/\partial C_j^{hh}} = \frac{\partial f_j^h/\partial L_j^h}{\partial f_i^h/\partial L_i^h} = \frac{q_i^h}{q_j^h} \qquad j \in N_i; \; h \in W \qquad \text{(1d')}$$

$$(1+\tau_j^h)\frac{\partial U^h/\partial \ell^h}{\partial U^h/\partial C_j^{hh}} = \frac{\partial f_j^h}{\partial L_j^h} = \frac{w^h}{q_j^h} \qquad h \in W \qquad \text{(1e')}$$

$$\frac{(1+\tau_j^h)\,\partial U^h/\partial C_i^{hh}}{(1+\tau_i^h)\,\partial U^h/\partial C_j^{hh}} = \frac{(1+\tau_j^k)\,\partial U^k/\partial C_i^{hk}}{(1+\tau_i^k)\,\partial U^k/\partial C_j^{hk}} = \frac{q_i^h}{q_j^h}. \qquad j \in N_i; \; k \in W_h; \; h \in W \qquad \text{(1f')}$$

---

[43] Because capital is assumed to be internationally mobile, the rental price of capital, r, will be uniform throughout the world. Wage rates, however, will be country-specific because labor is internationally immobile.

As far as domestic resource allocation is concerned, value-added taxes drive wedges between the marginal rates of substitution and marginal rates of transformation between any two consumption goods and between consumption and leisure. In addition, the international allocation of consumption goods is distorted. This is illustrated in Figure 1 (point B), which depicts an Edgeworth box for a two-country, two-commodity world with a fixed endowment of commodities i and j produced in country h, but consumed in countries h and k.

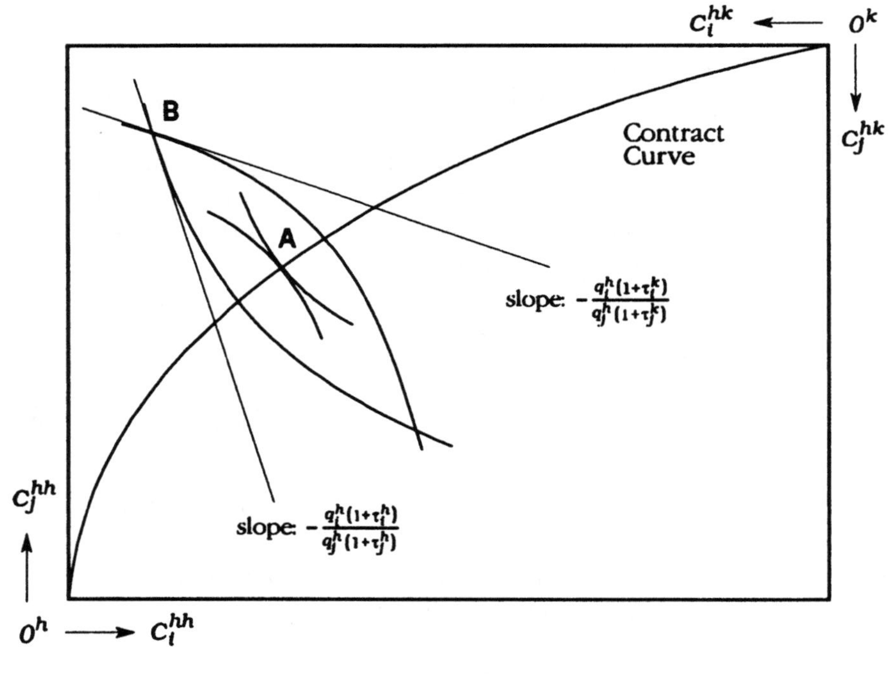

Figure 1. Allocation of world consumption under a destination-based VAT

All other marginal conditions of equation set (1) remain unaffected. Note that international capital allocation remains efficient under a destination-based VAT. Furthermore, the allocation of tradable factors across countries remains undistorted. This means that world production is on the aggregate world production possibility frontier.

If each country levies a uniform VAT within its borders, first-order conditions (1d) and (1f) are restored (point A in Figure 1). All international distortions disappear, and, in a domestic context, only the leisure-consumption choice is distorted. In essence, VAT then is equivalent to a wage tax. Even with differentiated tax rates within and across countries the international allocation of consumption is efficient if the tax rate differentiation obeys

$$\frac{1+\tau_j^h}{1+\tau_i^h} = \frac{1+\tau_j^k}{1+\tau_i^k}.$$

If, for example, countries h and k apply standard rates of 17 and 20 percent and reduced rates of 5.3 and 8, respectively, trade will be efficient between these two countries.[44]

2.3. Origin-based VAT under the Credit Method

Now suppose that all countries switch from the destination to the origin principle, but retain the credit method when calculating tax liabilities. In the case of a tax union this switch would be confined to union member states whereas trade with other countries would be taxed according to the destination principle. In this case the following remarks apply to tax union countries only. To simplify matters we consider a universal switch to the origin principle when the credit method is used. With respect to the first-order conditions, it does not matter whether or not the OP is supplemented by a clearing mechanism. This would involve an international redistribution of tax revenues, but does not concern efficiency considerations.

As before, marginal production decisions are unaffected by value-added taxes and the first-order conditions (1a), (2a), (2b) remain valid. There is, however, one decisive change in the consumer's decision problem. Direct consumption purchases from abroad now bear the full tax burden of the country of origin, whereas consumption of domestically produced goods is subject to national tax rates. The first-order conditions for the consumer's optimum in country h now become (3a), (3b') and (3c'), with the latter two being given by

$$\frac{\partial U^h/\partial C_i^{kh}}{\partial U^h/C_j^{kh}} = \frac{q_i^k(1+\tau_i^k)}{q_j^k(1+\tau_j^k)} = \frac{p_i^k}{p_j^k} \qquad j \in N_i; k \in W \qquad \text{(3b')}$$

$$\frac{\partial U^h/\partial C_i^{hh}}{\partial U^h/C_i^{kh}} = \frac{q_i^h(1+\tau_i^h)}{q_i^k(1+\tau_i^k)} = \frac{p_i^h}{p_i^k}. \qquad i \in N; k \in W_h \qquad \text{(3c')}$$

[44] The same point is made by Fratianni and Christie (1981, p. 415), amongst others.

This has the following consequences for resource allocation when compared with the DP. The marginal conditions for domestic resource allocation are the same under the DP and the OP combined with the credit method, only the international efficiency conditions change. On the one hand, the international allocation of consumption goods as characterized by equation (1f) will no longer be distorted. On the other hand tax wedges are introduced, distorting the international coordination of consumption and production decisions. Instead of equation (1h) one now obtains

$$\frac{\partial U^h/\partial C_i^{hh}}{\partial U^h/\partial C_i^{kh}} = \frac{(1+\tau_i^h)\partial f_i^k/\partial K_i^k}{(1+\tau_i^k)\partial f_i^h/\partial K_i^h}. \qquad k \in W_h \qquad \text{(1h')}$$

This suggests the following interpretations: firstly, international marginal rates of substitution deviate from the respective marginal rates of transformation; secondly, marginal rates of transformation between similar goods in different countries are no longer equal, implying a loss in aggregate world output; and, thirdly, according to (1i), the marginal rates of technical substitution between capital and any intermediate input in the international production of comparable goods continue to coincide. The international distortions evoked by a VAT under the origin principle and the credit method may be illustrated by Figures 2 and 3. We consider two countries, two commodities, and capital as the only factor of production. In the first quadrant of Figure 2 domestic indifference curves as well as an international transformation curve are depicted, the latter being derived from the national production functions as shown in the second and fourth quadrants. The efficient allocation of resources is given by points A, O^k, C and D. O^k indicates the quantities produced in countries h and k, using capital inputs given by points C and D. Consumption, exports, and imports are then determined by point A together with points O^h and O^k. The international marginal rate of transformation at O^k coincides with the marginal rates of substitution at point A, according to equations (1g) and (1b). Whenever the foreign tax rate exceeds the domestic one, the distorted allocation under the OP combined with the credit method may be represented by points such as $O^{k'}$ and B. The marginal rates of substitution still coincide according to equation (1g), but VAT introduces a tax wedge between the international marginal rates of transformation and the marginal rates of substitution, implying that the domestic economy produces too much of commodity i and employs more than the efficient quantity of capital.

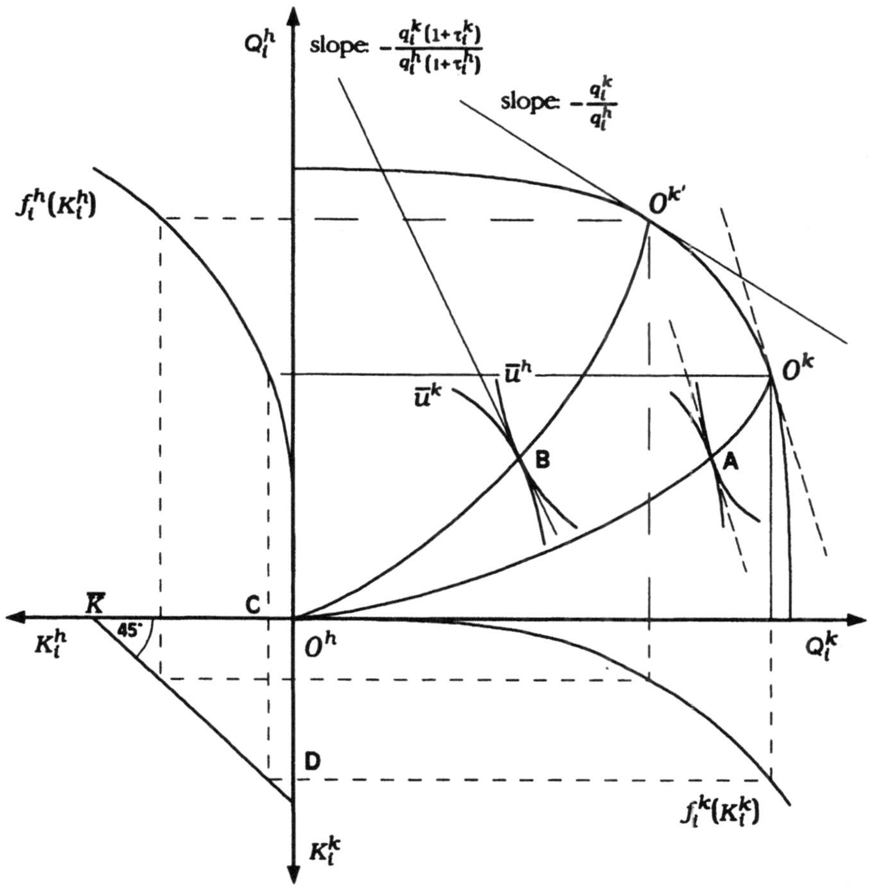

Figure 2. Distortion of international consumption and production decision under the origin principle and the credit method

The simplest way to illustrate the second distortion mentioned above is by assuming that consumption goods C_i^{hh} and C_i^{kh} are perfect substitutes (otherwise we would have to introduce a third dimension into our figure). Equation (1h') then may be simplified to

$$\frac{\partial f_i^h}{\partial K_i^h} = \frac{(1+\tau_i^h)}{(1+\tau_i^k)} \frac{\partial f_i^k}{\partial K_i^k}.$$

The resulting allocation of the given world capital stock $\bar{K} = O^h O^k$ is shown in Figure 3. The domestic and foreign marginal product curves intersect at D, where the allocation of capital is efficient. VAT under the origin principle and the credit method drives a wedge between the marginal productivities of capital. If commodity i is more heavily taxed in the foreign country, the allocation of world capital will be at a point such as G, implying that aggregate production is inefficient. Whereas the home country produces too much of the consumption good, the foreign country produces to little. The total loss in world output due to VAT is represented by the shaded Harberger triangle DEF.

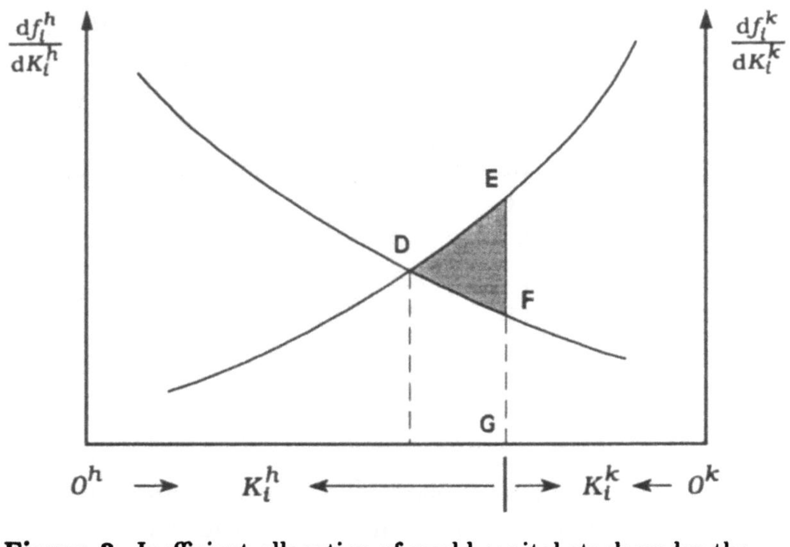

Figure 3. Inefficient allocation of world capital stock under the origin principle

Let us suppose for a moment that capital is internationally immobile. Equations (1h) and (1i) then become[45]

$$\frac{\partial U^h/\partial C_i^{hh}}{\partial U^h/\partial C_i^{kh}} = \frac{(1+\tau_i^h)\partial f_i^k/\partial V_{mi}^{lk}}{(1+\tau_i^k)\partial f_i^h/\partial V_{mi}^{lh}}. \qquad (1i')$$

[45] In this case, $R-1$ first-order-conditions may be dropped, but the same number of constraints has to be added.

International marginal rates of substitution and transformation are still distorted, with the latter now defined by the ratios of marginal products of intermediate inputs. Figures 2 and 3 remain valid with capital input being replaced by intermediate inputs. International distortions vanish only when all countries levy identical tax rates for comparable commodities.

2.4. Origin-based VAT under the Subtraction Method

We now assume that all countries switch from the destination to the origin principle and from the credit to the subtraction method. If only some countries change their international taxation principle or method of calculating tax liabilities, the respective results – if at all feasible – would emerge as a combination of the subsections 2.2. to 2.4.

Under the origin principle and the subtraction method, consumers and producers are faced with tax-inclusive prices. As before, consumers adjust their marginal rates of substitution to relative consumer prices, and equations (3a), (3b'), (3c') remain unchanged. The producer's profit maximization problem now reads as follows:

$$\max p_i^h f_i^h(K_i^h, L_i^h, V_{ji}^{kh} \,|\, j \in N, k \in W) - (1+\tau_i^h)(rK_i^h + w^h L_i^h) - \sum_{k \in W} \sum_{j \in N} p_j^k V_{ji}^{kh},$$

with the first-order conditions

$$p_i^h \frac{\partial f_i^h}{\partial K_i^h} = r(1+\tau_i^h); \quad p_i^h \frac{\partial f_i^h}{\partial L_i^h} = w^h(1+\tau_i^h); \quad p_i^h \frac{\partial f_i^h}{\partial V_{ji}^{kh}} = p_j^k.$$

By appropriately combining these equations with the necessary conditions for the consumer's maximization problem, one obtains equations (1d') and (1e') for domestic resource allocation. Therefore, these first-order conditions do not depend on the international taxation principle applied. International efficiency conditions, however, become:

$$\frac{\partial U^h/\partial C_i^{hh}}{\partial U^h/\partial C_i^{kh}} = \frac{(1+\tau_i^h)\partial f_i^k/\partial K_i^k}{(1+\tau_i^k)\partial f_i^h/\partial K_i^h} \qquad k \in W_h \quad (1h") = (1h')$$

$$\frac{\partial f_i^h/\partial K_i^h}{\partial f_i^h/\partial V_{mi}^{lh}} = \frac{(1+\tau_i^h)\partial f_i^k/\partial K_i^k}{(1+\tau_i^k)\partial f_i^k/\partial V_{mi}^{lk}}. \qquad m \in N;\ k \in W_h;\ l \in W \quad (1i")$$

Regardless of whether the origin principle is combined with the credit or the subtraction method, VAT introduces the same kind of wedge between international marginal rates of substitution and transformation. But there is one additional distortion to be considered under the subtraction method. According to equation (1i") the marginal rates of technical substitution between tradable factors in different countries no longer coincide. The economic reason for this is that primary factors and intermediate inputs are treated asymmetrically under the subtraction method. Whereas the latter do not enter that VAT base, primary inputs do.

Therefore, when the subtraction method is used, losses in aggregate world output occur for two reasons. The first is the inefficient allocation of the world capital stock according to equation (1h'), the second is the inefficient international allocation of tradable factors. This does not necessarily imply that aggregate output losses are larger under the subtraction than under the credit method. From second-best theory it is well-known that when several distortions are present, removing one of them may not improve welfare. It may very well be that one distortion compensates for another.

Let us finally consider the case where capital is immobile internationally and only intermediate factors are traded. In this case the last two equations combine to

$$\frac{\partial U^h/\partial C_i^{hh}}{\partial U^h/\partial C_i^{kh}} = \frac{\partial f_i^k/\partial V_{mi}^{lk}}{\partial f_i^h/\partial V_{mi}^{lh}} \qquad m \in N; k \in W_h; l \in W$$

and international distortions vanish. Production is on the world production frontier and international marginal rates of substitution and transformation coincide, with the latter now being defined by the ratios of marginal productivities of intermediate inputs. Note that this result is independent of whether or not tax rates are differentiated between commodities or countries.

Recently, Sinn (1990), and earlier, Grossman (1980), came up with a similar conclusion. Although Sinn's model incorporates consumption and investment goods, the main economic mechanisms in his and our models are the same because outlays for investment goods and intermediate inputs are treated symmetrically under a consumption-type VAT. An important point to note, however, is that Sinn's and Grossman's results depend heavily on the assumption that primary factors are internationally immobile. In an integrated Europe this is not a sensible assumption. If capital is mobile between countries, an efficient international allocation under the origin principle can only

Table 2. Domestic and international tax distortions

	Interference with first-order conditions								
	domestic allocation					international allocation			
Taxes	(1a)	(1b)	(1c)	(1d)	(1e)	(1f)	(1g)	(1h)	(1i)
Income tax on									
...wages					×				
...capital income									
Production tax				×	×			×	
Tariffs						×	×	×	×
VAT									
...DP				×	×	×			
...OP/credit				×	×			×	
...OP/subtraction				×	×			×	×

be guaranteed if tax rates for comparable commodities are fully harmonized. Table 2 summarizes the distortions generated by the taxes included in our equilibrium model.

3. Trade Neutrality and the Exchange Rate Argument

Trade neutrality is one of the main issues of discussion regarding the effects of taxes on international trade. There has been some concern, especially in the United States, that the destination-based VAT of the EU constitutes an export subsidy and requires imposition of some countervailing duty. Trade theorists, on the other hand, argue that nationally uniform VAT rates are trade-neutral under the destination as well as under the origin principle. A switch from the former to the latter is believed to leave all real variables unchanged if accompanied by a realignment of exchange rates. This has been a standard proposition in international taxation theory since the Tinbergen Report (1953) was published. We now examine these issues in the context of our equilibrium model.

3.1. Trade Neutrality

In order to avoid the confusion surrounding the early debate on trade distortions between Whalley (1979, 1981) and Berglas (1981), we shall start with some precise definitions. In the following, trade neutrality is understood to be a distinctive feature of an equilibrium allocation corresponding to a particular taxation principle. More precisely, an international taxation principle is said to be trade-neutral if all of the first-best marginal conditions concerning foreign trade are fulfilled. In our model this means that equations (1f) to (1i) must hold. We call this *Paretian trade neutrality.* Note that this definition does not include any propositions on domestic marginal conditions. Paretian trade neutrality is compatible with the existence of domestic distortions and, hence, is not equivalent to Pareto-efficiency. As a corollary, Paretian trade neutrality is not desirable on a priori grounds. Whenever domestic distortions prevail, a country or even the world economy as a whole, may gain by appropriately deviating from Paretian trade neutrality. This is one basic message of the theory of second-best. Table 3 summarizes the restrictions on VAT rates necessary to guarantee Paretian trade neutrality under different taxation principles.

Table 3. Tax rates and trade neutrality for VAT taxation principles

	Restrictions on VAT rates		
Capital Intermediates	mobile mobile	immobile mobile	immobile immobile
VAT taxation principle			
OP/subtraction	$\tau_i^h = \tau_i^k \quad i \in N$	none	none
OP/credit	$\tau_i^h = \tau_i^k \quad i \in N$		none
DP	$\frac{1+\tau_j^h}{1+\tau_i^h} = \frac{1+\tau_j^k}{1+\tau_i^k} \quad i, j \in N$		

The following conclusions refer to trade between two countries h and k. For Paretian trade neutrality to be valid globally, the restrictions on tax rates must hold for all countries involved.

The conditions for trade neutrality under the DP are independent of whether or not factors of production are internationally mobile. The ratios of tax factors for different commodities, i.e. $(1+\tau_j)/(1+\tau_i)$, have to coincide in all countries. Sufficient conditions for trade neutrality under the DP are uniformity of VAT rates within, but not necessarily across, countries. In contrast, conditions for trade neutrality under the origin principle depend on the method of calculating tax liabilities and on which factors of production are mobile.

When both capital and intermediate inputs are internationally mobile, the required tax rate restrictions are the same under the credit and under the subtraction method. Tax rates for comparable goods have to be the same in both countries. Uniformity of tax rates within countries is not required. Uniform tax rates within, but not across countries are not compatible with trade neutrality if the origin principle is applied, and capital and intermediates are internationally mobile. The intuition behind this non-neutrality was derived from Figures 2 and 3 in the previous subsection.

If only intermediate inputs are internationally mobile, the necessary conditions for Paretian trade neutrality under the origin principle depend on whether the credit or the subtraction method is applied. If the subtraction method is used, trade neutrality is ensured in any case, quite independently of national tax structures. The economic reason for this is that gross expenditures for internationally traded (as well as domestically produced) intermediate inputs are deducted when calculating the tax base. On the other hand, under the credit method, production and consumption decisions will still be distorted between countries h and k. This is illustrated by Figures 2 and 3, when capital is replaced by the use of intermediate inputs. Low tax countries use too much and high tax countries too little of the internationally mobile factor.

As a final remark, note that the origin principle in combination with the credit method is trade neutral irrespective of national VAT rate structures, whenever all factors of production – primary factors as well as intermediate inputs – are internationally immobile. This conclusion depends heavily on the Armington assumption and is not valid in the traditional Heckscher-Ohlin type of model. The Armington assumption implies complete specialization of production. Without factor mobility there is no link between domestic and foreign production decisions and, hence, no meaningful definition of international marginal rates of transformation or international marginal rates of technical substitution. The neutrality of the origin principle and the credit method under complete factor immobility is thus model-specific and has to be regarded with some caution.

3.2. The Exchange Rate Argument

Let us now relate our remarks about Paretian trade neutrality to the so-called exchange rate argument. In contrast to Paretian trade neutrality, this argument does not refer to the characteristics of one specific equilibrium, but rather to a comparison between two equilibria corresponding to different VAT systems. Our goal is to identify the conditions under which a switch in international taxation principles leaves all real variables of the economy completely unchanged and is accompanied only by an exchange rate realignment. The adjustment of exchange rates is inessential for the argument, however, because changes in absolute producer and factor prices would have exactly the same effect. All that matters is that all real variables (and relative prices) remain unaffected. In order to emphasize the importance of physical quantities remaining unchanged, we will speak of *physical trade neutrality* in the following discussion.

To illustrate the argument, consider two countries, Italy and Germany, each producing one tradable commodity from a single, internationally immobile factor with a constant returns to scale technology. In the reference equilibrium, the destination principle is applied with Italy levying a tax rate of 21 per cent and Germany one of 10 per cent. In national currencies, producer prices of the two commodities are assumed to be 1000 lire and 1 DM, respectively. Given an exchange rate of 1 DM = 1000 lire, the absolute after-tax (or consumer) prices of both commodities will be 1.10 DM in Germany and 1210 lire in Italy. Thus, relative consumer prices will be 1.0 in both countries. The trade accounts, valued at producer prices, will be balanced. Assume now that the origin principle is adopted,[46] but that tax rates remain the same. Now German as well as Italian consumers will shift their demand to the commodity produced in Germany, implying a short run surplus (deficit) in the German (Italian) trade account. As a consequence, the German mark will appreciate (or the Italian lira depreciate) until the trade accounts are balanced, now being valued at consumer prices. This requires an exchange rate of 1 DM = $(1.21/1.1) \times 1000$ lire = 1100 lire. After this adjustment, relative consumer prices, national

[46] In our simple example there is no need to distinguish between the credit and the subtraction method.

tax revenues, and all quantities produced and demanded will be the same as under the destination principle. Relative consumer prices in Germany are now determined by 1.10 DM/[(1210 lire) $\times$ (1 DM/1100 lire)] = 1.0, and analogously for Italy. Instead of an exchange rate realignment, a 10 per cent increase in the German wage rate and producer price, at a fixed nominal exchange rate, would have exactly the same effect.

We shall now slightly generalize the above example to gain greater insight into the problem. Returning to our general equilibrium model, let us make the following assumptions: tax rates are uniform within countries, but may differ between them; intermediate production is neglected;[47] labor supply is constant; primary factors are internationally immobile; and tariffs and other taxes are neglected. With these assumptions, value-added taxation is trade-neutral under the DP as well as under the OP. Furthermore, VAT is equivalent to a lump-sum tax, and there are no domestic distortions. Under these circumstances physical trade neutrality holds when switching from the DP to the OP.

Until this point, exchange rates have not been explicitely considered in our pure trade model, which expresses all monetary values in a common currency unit, namely the ECU. Now let e^{hk} be the exchange rate, i.e. the amount of domestic currency in country h, which is received for one unit of foreign currency from country k (e.g. DM/£, DM/lira etc.). All producer prices q_i^k are now expressed in domestic currency units. For physical trade neutrality to hold, quantities demanded and produced have to be identical under the DP and under the OP. Assuming that national tax revenues are transferred back to domestic households in a lump-sum manner, demand functions of the representative consumer in country h under the DP and the OP are given in the first row of Table 4, where T^h denotes transfer payments. Note that producer and factor prices as well as exchange rates and national tax revenues in general differ under the two international taxation principles. The above-mentioned simplifying assumptions ensure that value-added taxes do not induce substitution effects. Income effects are only generated if a switch from DP to OP changes national tax revenues or will result in a transfer of real income between countries. To illustrate the exchange rate argument in more detail, the equations for tax revenues as well as balance of payments are given in the last two rows of Table 4.

---

[47] Hence, we still do not have to distinguish between the credit and the subtraction method.

Table 4. Demand functions, tax revenues and the balance of payments in country h under the destination and the origin principle

	Destination principle
Demand functions	$C_i^{lh}(q_j^h(1+\tau^h),\ e^{hk}q_j^k(1+\tau^h),\ r^h\bar{K}^h + w^h\bar{L}^h + T^h \mid j \in N, k \in W_h)$
Tax revenues	$\tau^h\left(\sum_{i\in N} q_i^h C_i^{hh} + \sum_{k\in W_h}\sum_{i\in N} e^{hk} q_i^k C_i^{kh}\right)$
Balance of payments	$\sum_{k\in W_h}\sum_{i\in N} q_i^h C_i^{hk} = \sum_{k\in W_h}\sum_{i\in N} e^{hk} q_i^k C_i^{kh}$
	Origin Principle
Demand functions	$C_i^{lh}(q_j^h(1+\tau^h),\ e^{hk}q_j^k(1+\tau^k),\ r^h\bar{K}^h + w^h\bar{L}^h + T^h \mid j \in N, k \in W_h)$
Tax revenues	$\tau^h\left(\sum_{i\in N} q_i^h C_i^{hh} + \sum_{k\in W_h}\sum_{i\in N} q_i^h C_i^{hk}\right)$
Balance of payments	$\sum_{k\in W_h}\sum_{i\in N} q_i^h(1+\tau^h) C_i^{hk} = \sum_{k\in W_h}\sum_{i\in N} (1+\tau^k) e^{hk} q_i^k C_i^{kh}$

Consider now a global switch from the DP to the OP, accompanied by an exchange rate realignment according to

$$e^{hk}\Big|_{OP} = \frac{1+\tau^h}{1+\tau^k}\, e^{hk}\Big|_{DP}. \tag{4}$$

When compared to a high-tax country k, the domestic currency of country h will appreciate by the factor $(1+\tau^h)/(1+\tau^k)$ after the transition to the OP, and depreciate when compared to low-tax trading partners. This adjustment in exchange rates will leave transfer payments to domestic consumers unchanged. Closer inspection of the second and the third rows of Table 4 reveals that after the exchange rate adjustment the trade account will again be balanced and that income transfers between countries do not occur. Furthermore, tax revenues remain the same, implying unchanged transfer payments. Because the switch from DP to OP induces neither substitution nor income effects, relative prices will not change, and quantities demanded and produced are the same in both equilibria. Under the assumptions mentioned above, physical trade neutrality holds when switching from the DP to the OP. Exchange rate adjustments with unchanged factor and producer prices may be substituted by price adjustments in a fixed exchange rate regime. All real variables and relative prices will be unaffected by the change in VAT taxation principles if foreign factor and producer prices in country k adjust by the factor $(1 + \tau^h)/(1 + \tau^k)$.

Let us now try to generalize the lessons from the above considerations. Quite obviously, physical trade neutrality will only hold if the switch from one VAT principle to any other induces neither subsitution nor income effects. The former appear as wedges between some marginal rates of substitution and/or marginal rates of transformation. The latter are associated with changes in relative prices and changes in consumers' income.

Considerable additional insight may be gained by distinguishing between domestic income effects on the one hand, and international income effects on the other. Domestic income effects occur because taxes reduce the consumer's real income, whereas transfers increase it. Hence, there is a positive as well as a negative income effect. If it is assumed that all tax revenues are spent as transfers, negative and positive income effects cancel out and domestic income effects may be neglected. International income effects, however, play an important role. In our context these effects have to be attributed to a change in tax exports or imports. Tax exports arise whenever the tax revenue accrues to the home country whereas the tax burden is partly shifted to foreign residents. Tax exporting is thus equivalent to a transfer from the foreign to the home country. Tax imports work the other way round. Under the DP, tax exports or imports cannot arise, but under the OP they can and generally will – independent of whether or not the OP is administered with the credit or the subtraction method.

The conditions for physical trade neutrality following a switch from one taxation principle to another are a predominant concern in the international trade and taxation literature.[48] In view of our above

---

[48] Georgakopoulos, in particular, has dealt with this question in a whole series

remarks the answer to this question is obvious and requires a two-step procedure. The first step is to investigate whether such a change induces any substitution effects. This will be the case if the sets of first order conditions corresponding to different taxation principles are characterized by *different* tax wedges. Note that it is not the *existence*, but rather the *change* in tax wedges that is important.[49] Hence, a necessary, but not sufficient condition for physical trade neutrality is that tax wedges are exactly the same under the destination and the origin principle. Sufficiency may be established in a second step by proving that no international redistribution due to tax exporting or importing occurs.

Let us now briefly apply this procedure to a comparison of different VAT principles. The general assumption is that VAT rates remain unchanged and only the tax base changes. The conclusions may differ, however, if tax rates as well as the tax base change.

A cursory glance at Table 2 reveals that, although domestic distortions are the same under the DP and the OP, the tax wedges distorting the international allocation are different under these taxation principles. Hence, in the general case, any switch from one taxation principle to another will induce substitution effects and be incompatible with physical trade neutrality. Only if two taxation principles are trade-neutral in a Paretian sense are tax distortions the same and no additional substitution effects generated. Paretian trade neutrality is thus a necessary condition for physical trade neutrality.

From Table 3 one can infer the conditions under which Paretian trade neutrality jointly holds under any two taxation principles. If these conditions are fulfilled one can proceed to investigate whether tax exports or imports are associated with the change in tax bases. Physical trade neutrality then requires that net tax exports, i.e. the difference between tax exports and imports, are zero for all countries involved. Of course, all net tax exports can be neutralized by an international redistribution mechanism, in which case physical trade neutrality may be restored. The determination and computation of tax exports under different VAT reform options will be of central concern in Chapter V. Here, the following remarks should suffice.

---

of articles; see, for example, his articles (1989, 1992) and Georgakopolous and Hitiris (1991, 1992).

[49] To our knowledge, Lockwood (1993, p. 149) is the only one who – in a footnote – emphasizes this point.

Suppose that the EU switches to the CMP but retains the DP when trading with third countries. This is compatible with Shibata's (1967) restricted origin principle. We depict this case here because it provoked some heated discussion in the literature. On closer examination it will become clear[50] that country h's tax exports and imports under this variant of the restricted origin principle are given by[51]

$$\underbrace{\sum_{k\in EU_h}\sum_{i\in N}\tau_i^h q_i^h X_i^{hk}}_{\text{tax exports}} - \underbrace{\sum_{k\in EU_h}\sum_{i\in N}\tau_i^k q_i^k M_i^{kh}}_{\text{tax imports}}. \tag{5}$$

The first term indicates the tax revenue which accrues to country h but is shifted to its EU trading partners. Conversely the second term shows the VAT payments of domestic agents for import purchases from other EU member states, to which the revenue in question accrues. International income effects only vanish if tax exports and tax imports cancel out or net tax exports are neutralized by international transfers between countries. Paretian trade neutrality under the DP as well as under the OP and the credit method requires $\tau_i^h = \tau_i^k$ for $i \in N$. Even if tax rates are uniform within and between EU member states, net tax exports will be positive for EU member countries that have trade surpluses with other member countries.

We may now relate our conclusions to the relevant literature. Berglas (1981, p. 378), for example, states that there will be no transfer of real income between the member countries of a tax union who all adopt the same tax rate, if "each member country's trade with the rest of the world is initially balanced". This assertion requires the additional restriction, not mentioned by Berglas, that capital is internationally immobile. In this case, indeed, commodity trade between country $k \in EU_h$ and all other tax union members taken together is balanced, and net tax exports under the CMP are zero.

To quote one more example, Georgakopoulos and Hitiris (1991, p. 333) conclude that the destination principle and the restricted origin principle "are equivalent (production, consumption and trade remain unaffected) when tax rates are equal in the member countries, and are set in inverse relation to the bilateral trade balance of the initial

[50] Expression (5) will be explicitly derived in Chapter V.

[51] Here, we neglect some complications such as the special VAT treatment of services or non-tradable commodities.

equilibrium".[52] We can reproduce this result by assuming: firstly, a three-country world, where two countries form a tax union and adopt the origin principle and the credit method; and secondly, that all factors of production are internationally immobile. In this case, Paretian trade neutrality is ensured if tax rates are uniform within but not necessarily across countries. Furthermore, net tax exports are zero if

$$\frac{\tau^h}{\tau^k} = \frac{\sum_{i \in N} q_i^k M_i^{kh}}{\sum_{i \in N} q_i^h X_i^{hk}}.$$

With some imagination, these result could be generalized or other equally curious results derived. We do not think that this is a worthwhile task. Suffice to say that Paretian and, particularly, physical trade neutrality hold only under very restrictive and empirically void assumptions.

Under realistic settings, any switch from one international taxation principle to another will provoke substitution as well as (international) income effects. We will now investigate what can be said about the welfare consequences of these effects.

4. Welfare Effects of VAT in Open Economies

In order to evaluate tax effects, income and substitution effects have to be separated. In open economies there are two sorts of both effects; the domestic and the international income effects on the one hand, and the domestic and international substitution effects on the other. As explained in the preceding section, domestic income effects can be neglected if changes in national tax revenues are counterbalanced by identical changes in transfer payments to domestic consumers. In our context, international income effects can only arise in the presence of net tax exports. The domestic substitution effects reflect the distortion of consumer choices due to the tax wedges between consumer and producer prices. International substitution effects only have to be considered in the large-country case. By appropriate manipulation of the tax wedges between domestic and foreign marginal rates of substitution or international marginal rates of transformation, the home economy can exercise some monopoly power on international markets. As a consequence, world market prices or international terms

[52] The precise meaning of this assertion will be become clearer in the following.

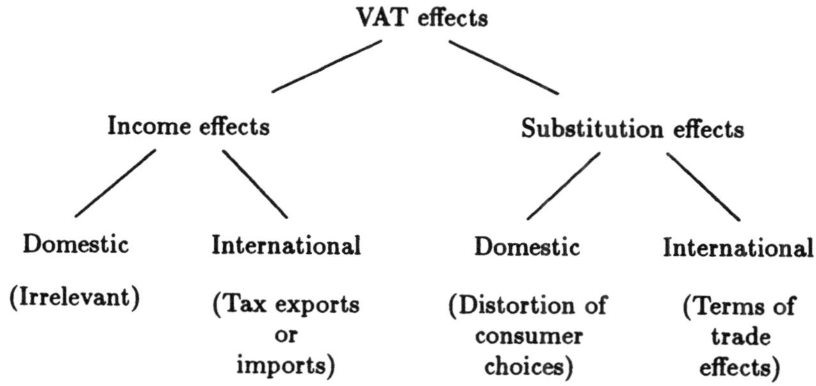

Figure 4. VAT effects in open economies

of trade may change in favor of the home country. Figure 4 summarizes the different VAT effects in open economies.

For a first depiction of the welfare effects of indirect taxes in open economies, consider the following diagrams. These diagrams are strictly partial in nature and all the usual caveats apply.

Figure 5 illustrates a situation in which the home country is importer of a commodity produced in country f. In the left-hand quadrant, S^f is the (inverse) supply curve and D^f the (inverse) demand curve in country f. The Armington assumption implies that these curves do not intersect. Hence, at each price there is some excess supply, corresponding to country f's export supply curve X^{fh}, as shown in the right-hand quadrant. D^h is the home country's (import) demand curve. In the absence of distortions, the free trade equilibrium is determined by point A, with q^f as the equilibrium producer and consumer price. In our single market context, the producer price q^f can be interpreted as the international terms of trade. Country f produces the quantity GJ and consumes GI, whereas exports and imports are given by GA (or JI). Suppose now that the home country introduces a selective commodity tax and applies the destination principle. The indirect tax may be a specific tax per physical unit or an ad-valorem tax as a proportion of the producer price. Graphically, a specific tax is simpler to illustrate. Remember that under the DP, VAT is a tax on consumption, shifting the home country's demand curve from D^h

to $D^{h'}$. This drives the foreign producer price down to $q^{f'}$, with the new production and consumption quantities in countries f and h being given by FK, FH and FB, respectively.

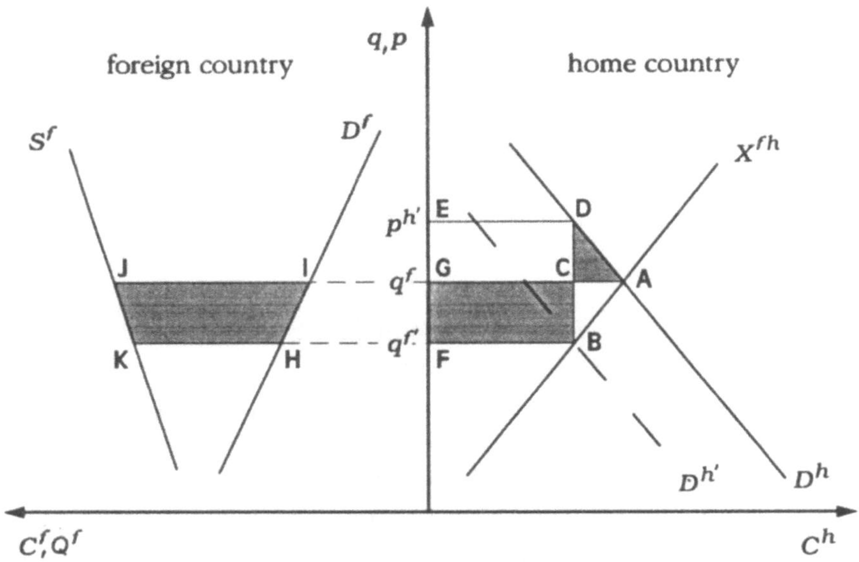

Figure 5. Tax effects under the destination principle; home country importing

Our main interest is on the welfare effects of tax changes. In this section we assume that consumer and producer surpluses are appropriate welfare measures. This is not really problematic in a partial equilibrium context. Net social welfare is computed as the sum of these surpluses together with government tax revenue. In the foreign country, the lower producer price implies a gain in consumer surplus corresponding to area GIHF and a loss in producer surplus of area GJKF. The net loss in country f, the area IJKH, is caused by the deterioration (for country f) of the international terms of trade by $(q^f - q^{f'})$ per unit. From country h's perspective, this constitutes a terms of trade gain. The welfare effects in the home country have to be calculated as follows. After the imposition of the tax, domestic consumers in country h are faced with consumer prices $p^{h'}$, inducing a loss in consumer surplus equal to area EDAG. On the other hand, the government collects tax revenue as represented by the rectangle DEFB. The overall welfare effect is the sum of revenue gains and losses in consumers' surplus. Netting out the overlapping areas, total welfare change is the difference between area CGFB and area DCA. The latter triangle may be regarded as the welfare loss due to domestic substitution effects and the former area as the welfare gain due to the terms of trade effect or the international substitution effect of indirect taxation.

The question then is whether the gains from the international substitution effect are larger or smaller than the losses from the domestic effect. From Figure 5 it becomes clear that welfare losses due to the domestic substitution effect definitely increase with the tax rate, whereas the terms of trade change is dubious, depending on the elasticities of demand and supply. At least for low tax rates the international substitution effect dominates the domestic substitution effect. Technically speaking, welfare losses due to domestic substitution effects are second order effects only (as the product of quantity changes and price changes), whereas terms of trade gains are of first order. Finally note that the terms of trade losses in country f exceed the terms of trade gains in country h by the area ACB (because areas IJKH and AGFB are equal). The total loss in world welfare due to indirect taxation in country h is represented by the Harberger triangle ADB. Even if a single country can gain at the expense of its trading partners, the overall effect of indirect taxes will be a loss in total welfare.

An example in which the home country is the producer and exporter of the commodity is illustrated in Figure 6. The curves drawn in this figure should be self-explanatory, except perhaps for the curve $(D^h + D^f)$, which represents the aggregate demand curve. The free trade equilibrium is represented by points A or M. As above, we assume that country h introduces a specific tax, but contrary to above the origin principle applies. In this case, the tax burdens domestic production, not domestic consumption, and the supply curve shifts to $S^{h'}$. The consumer price rises from q^h to $p^{h'}$, and the producer price falls to $q^{h'}$. Points B or J are the new equilibrium allocations. In the next chapter we will show that the international terms of trade are measured by consumer prices under the OP. Hence, there is a terms of trade gain for the home country and a terms of trade loss for the foreign economy. The latter is represented by the trapezoid CBAD, corresponding to the loss in foreign consumers' surplus. As to the domestic economy, there is a loss in consumer surplus equal to area

FCDI, a loss in producer surplus equal to area MDEL and a gain in tax revenue corresponding to rectangle JCEL. Netting out the overlapping areas, the total change in domestic welfare is given by the difference between trapezoid JFIK and triangle MKL. Whereas the former reflects the international substitution (or terms of trade) effect, the latter is due to the domestic substitution effect. Because areas CBAD and JFIM are identical, indirect taxation in country h induces a deadweight loss in the world economy equal to the Harberger triangle JLM. As a final remark, note that total tax revenue in the home country consists of two components. The first, area FCEH, is the tax revenue generated by taxing domestic consumption. The second, rectangle JFHL, is the revenue from taxing the exports to country f. This revenue accrues to country h under the OP, but burdens the consumers in country f, therefore representing a gain to the domestic economy due to the international income effect or, equivalently, due to tax exports.[53] From the geometry of Figure 6 it is obvious that the international income effect dominates the international substitution effect, which, for its part, dominates the domestic substitution effect, if tax rates are not too high. This will be confirmed by our numerical calculations in Chapter V.

Figure 6 could now be modified to deal with the case when the home country applies the DP instead of the OP. This exercise is left to the reader, but the economic results should be obvious. Under the DP, VAT is a tax on domestic consumption, shifting the domestic demand curve inwards. This lowers the equilibrium producer price and constitutes a terms of trade loss for the home country, because terms of trade are now measured at producer prices. Additionally, there will be a loss in consumer surplus from the domestic substitution effect. Hence, the domestic economy definitely experiences a welfare loss when taxing its exportables under the DP.

Our simple diagrams yield considerable insight into the welfare effects of indirect taxes in open economies, but they are incomplete because of their partial equilibrium nature. Let us therefore take a closer look at the international income effect as well as at domestic and international substitution effects.

As previously mentioned, international income effects are due to tax exports or tax imports. These effects can arise under the OP,

[53] Except for the special case in which the utility functions are quasi-linear, the international income effect will shift domestic and foreign demand curves (in opposite directions). These effects are not captured in our diagram.

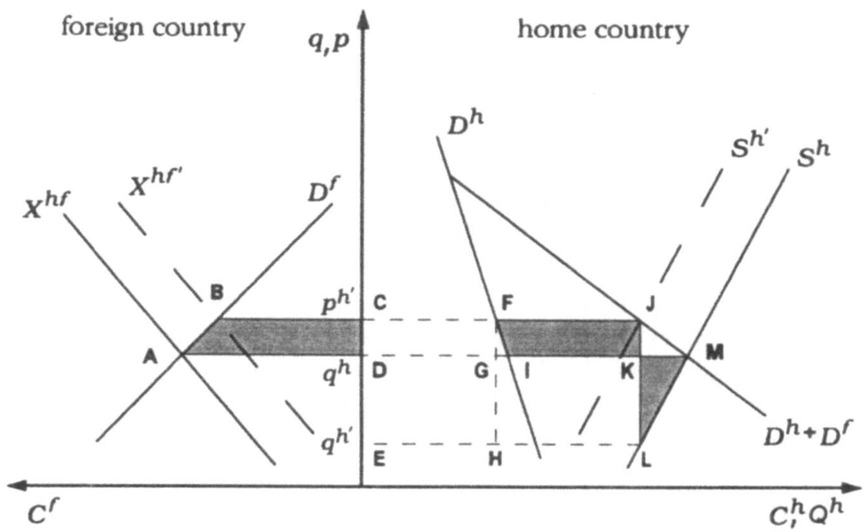

Figure 6. Tax effects under the origin principle; home country exporting

but not under the DP. From a welfare point of view, only net tax exports – the difference between tax exports and tax imports – are relevant. The sign and size of net tax exports depends on two factors: international VAT rate differentials, and trade balances with those countries applying the OP. Net tax exports will be positive for high-tax countries with trade surpluses. Positive net tax exports are equivalent to a transfer from the foreign to the home country. From the discussion of the so-called transfer problem in international trade theory[54] it is known that a transfer from one country to another will generally decrease welfare in the donating country and deteriorate its terms of trade. In the absence of inferior goods, the transferor's demand will be reduced while that of the transferee increases. With heterogeneous goods (due to the Armington assumption) and a home good preference in both countries, overall demand for goods produced in the donating country will fall and rise for goods produced in the transfer-receiving country. The resulting excess demands and supplies will deteriorate the terms of trade for the donating country. Transfer paradoxes, which are dealt with extensively in the literature, cannot arise under these

[54] See, for example, Bhagwati and Srinivasan (1983, Chapter 12).

assumptions. We conclude our discussion on international income effects with two final remarks. Firstly, tax exports for one country are exactly offset by tax imports in another country. In the aggregate, tax exports and tax imports sum up to zero. Secondly, there is reason to assume that welfare gains due to tax exports quantitatively dominate welfare changes from domestic and international substitution effects. The intuition for this was developed in Figure 6. A more technical reason is that international income effects are first order in tax rates.

The domestic substitution effects of indirect taxes and the associated welfare losses are the focus of interest in optimal taxation theory. Essentially, the optimal indirect tax structure depends on the structure of preferences and the availability of other tax instruments, e.g. optimal non-linear income taxes. In our context, only efficiency aspects are relevant within each country (but not between countries). Furthermore, in our simulation model it is assumed that the utility tree of the representative consumer is separable in leisure and consumption bundles and that the latter are composed of a combination of homothetic sub-utility functions. Given these assumptions, we know from the literature[55] that domestic efficiency losses are minimized when the indirect tax structure is uniform. Although optimal indirect taxes are not our concern, they may be important as a reference point for welfare-increasing tax reform programs. Unfortunately matters are somewhat complicated by the fact that not all moves in tax rates from an arbitrary rate structure towards the optimal one are welfare increasing. This at least holds if the reform stops short of the full optimum. This is another basic lesson of second-best theory. However, under fairly general conditions, a step toward uniformity by lowering the highest and raising the lowest indirect tax rates will increase welfare. This was first shown by Hatta (1986) and later generalized by other authors.[56] The intuition is that efficiency losses due to domestic substitution effects will decrease if the spread of tax rates is reduced and vice versa. Quantitatively, these welfare losses depend on compensated elasticities of labor supply and consumption demand and, approximately, on the square of (marginal) tax rates. If tax rates or tax rate changes are small, welfare changes will be small, too.

We are left with the international substitution or terms of trade effects. The idea is that differentiated indirect taxes may serve as a

[55] An early reference is Sandmo (1974); the standard textbook on modern public finance and optimal taxation is still Atkinson and Stiglitz (1980).

[56] See, for example, Gordon (1991), or Fane (1991).

kind of second best substitute for tariffs. Figures 5 and 6 suggest that the home country can influence the terms of trade in its favor by taxing more heavily its importables under the DP and its exportables under the OP. In a more general context the argument goes as follows. Suppose the home country taxes its importables more heavily than its exportables. Under the DP, this will change relative consumer prices in favor of the exportables, thereby increasing demand for them while reducing it for the importables. With constant producer prices, supply would remain unchanged and an excess demand (supply) for exportables (importables) on world commodity markets would result. As a consequence, producer prices will rise for export goods and fall for import goods. Terms of trade, which are defined with respect to producer prices under the DP, will then change in favor of the country in question. This improvement in the terms of trade goes hand in hand with an increase in national welfare. Similarly, a country will lose by taxing its exportables more heavily under the DP.

Under the OP increasing the tax rates on export goods is a welfare increasing strategy. Remember that VAT is a tax on value added, or on production if intermediate inputs are neglected. Furthermore, international terms of trade now coincide with relative consumer prices. A production tax on the exportables will then shift production away from the more heavily taxed goods. At given terms of trade and, hence, given demand, we observe excess demand for the exportables. This changes relative consumer prices in favor of export goods, being equivalent to an improvement in terms of trade to the home country. All these effects have been clearly worked out by Georgakopoulos (1974) in a two-country world with two homogeneous commodities, by Vandendorpe (1972) in an optimal taxation framework, and by a number of other authors in more recent literature.

Note that domestic and international substitution effects may work in opposite directions. Whereas the former requires more uniformity of VAT rates, the latter suggests some rate differentiation. For low tax rates or small tax rate changes, the international will dominate the domestic substitution effect, because the latter is second order in tax rates. Ideally, one would decompose total price and welfare effects of tax changes according to a Slutzky-type equation into domestic and international substitution effects on the one hand and income effects on the other. We have not succeeded in doing this analytically, but a numerical simulation analysis allows separation of the overall substitution effect from net tax export effects. This is accomplished by neutralizing any net tax exports by means of an appropriate international redistribution scheme. What remains are the domestic and international substitution effects. All of our interpretations in Chapter V rely heavily on these basic arguments.

Chapter IV

From Theory to Application: A Computable General Equilibrium Model

We are now equipped with some theoretical insights into the welfare effects of value-added taxes in open economies. We know that international income effects as well as domestic and international substitution effects matter and we have elaborated on the determinants of these effects. Theoretical reasoning alone, however, does not tell us much about the quantitative significance of these effects, which are exactly what we are interested in. Which countries realize welfare gains, and which suffer welfare losses, when the EU switches from one international taxation principle to another? Furthermore we want to know whether or not welfare changes are quantitatively significant, and what counts more for welfare changes, international income effects or efficiency considerations due to substitution effects? In Chapter I we argued that computable general equilibrium (CGE) models were the best way of answering these and related questions. Hence, the aim of the present chapter is to develop and describe our computable general equilibrium model in more detail.

We will start with some general remarks on the CGE methodology in Section 1. Following that we discuss functional forms for utility and production functions and present the complete set of equations characterizing our theoretical model. We then describe the construction of a micro-consistent data set and comment on data sources and manipulations. In the final section, parameter values are determined such that the numerical solution of our theoretical model replicates the observed data base. This is known as "calibration" of the model. Readers who are not interested in technical details may skip this chapter.

1. Operationalizing Walras with CGE models[57]

In the last ten to fifteen years, computable general equilibrium models have become a widespread and increasingly recognized scientific tool. When the *Journal of Economic Literature* reorganized its classification system for publications in March 1991, a special heading "Computable General Equilibrium Models" was introduced, signalling the increasing importance of this kind of model. In the policy arena too, CGE models dealing with tax, trade and other policy issues seem to be gaining in popularity. A recent example is the policy debate on the Uruguay Round of the GATT; the OECD and other research institutions relied heavily on CGE models[58] in order to assess the benefits of trade liberalization.

One of the most important areas of CGE modelling application has always been in the design of tax reforms. Based on work by Harberger (1962, 1966) on the incidence of the corporate income tax, Shoven and Whalley (1972) developed a numerically specified general equilibrium model, which was considerably more disaggregated than the $2 \times 2 \times 2$ models then dominating the literature. The numerical solution of highly non-linear equilibrium models was made possible by a break-through in the computation of equilibrium prices in the 1960s. Herbert Scarf (1967, 1969, 1973) developed a constructive proof of the existence of a general equilibrium, which has since been continually improved and refined. Today the numerical solution of complex economic models no longer poses severe restrictions.

The fundamentals of CGE methodology are summarized in Figure 1. The natural starting point is, of course, to design an appropriate economic model. On the one hand, the model has to be sufficiently rich to capture some institutional features of VAT such as rate differentiation, the credit or subtraction method and so on. On the other hand, simplifications are unavoidable. This implies a considerable degree of

---

[57] For a more complete introduction and an overview of the literature see, for example, Shoven and Whalley (1984, 1992) or Borges (1986). Public sector issues are surveyed in Shoven (1983) and Piggott (1988); Bovenberg (1987) evaluates the significance of CGE methodology for public policy.

[58] See, for example, OECD (1990, 1993) or Nguyen, Perroni and Wigle (1993).

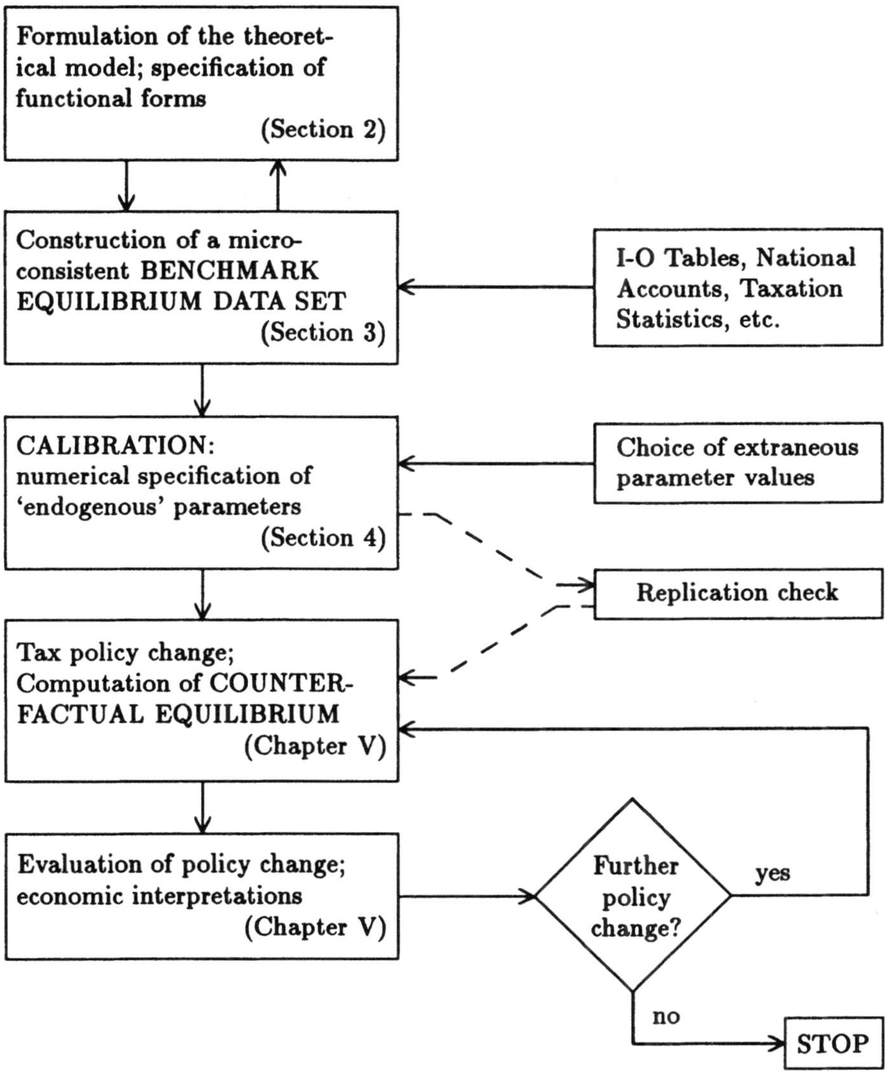

Figure 1. Flow chart for CGE taxation models

subjectivity in model design. For numerical solutions of general equilibrium models, functional forms for utility and production functions have to be specified. These are typically restricted to the convenient forms of Cobb-Douglas or Constant Elasticity of Substitution (CES) functions. In the next section we will describe our choice of functional forms and give a complete list of model equations.

The development of the theoretical model proceeds in close coordination with the construction of a micro-consistent data set. This implies choosing a base year where the usual equilibrium conditions were approximately met. This base year's equilibrium is called the benchmark equilibrium. The data set is constructed from the national accounts, input-output tables and other government statistics. The details are given in Section 3.

The theoretical model could be solved numerically if all the parameters of utility and production functions were known. Without any further restrictions the computed model solution would not, however, match the data base of the benchmark equilibrium. The problem, therefore, is in determining parameter values that exactly reproduce the micro-consistent data set of the base year. This requires the specification of a number of extraneous parameter values, mainly elasticities. In most cases these elasticity values are taken from current econometric literature. The next step involves determining the values of the remaining (or 'endogenous') parameters so as to replicate[59] the observed data in the benchmark equilibrium. This procedure, known as *calibration*, is described in Section 4 of this chapter.

Finally, one can start carrying out policy simulations. Policy conclusions are reached by making comparisons between different equilibria. Hence, starting from the benchmark equilibrium, some policy parameters – such as tax rates or international taxation principles – are changed and a new equilibrium (the counterfactual equilibrium) is computed. At least in principle, all the endogenous variables in the counterfactual equilibrium may be compared with the benchmark equilibrium. Usually one concentrates on various summary statistics such as Hicks' equivalent variation for welfare changes or the Gini-index in distributional studies. This is the numerical counterpart of comparative statics. In Chapter V, we will report our policy simulation experiments and evaluate the results.

---

[59] This is the replication check referred to in Figure 1. It also serves as a convenient device in checking the accuracy of the computer code.

2. The Theoretical Model

In principle, our theoretical model is just a higher dimensional analogue of the standard $2 \times 2 \times 2$ general equilibrium model commonly used in international trade theory. It is, however, much more complicated and deviates in a number of points from the traditional Heckscher-Ohlin framework. Besides including a greater number of commodities and countries, these deviations are:

- the Armington assumption;
- parameters of demand and production that differ from country to country;
- unbalanced trade;
- the existence of taxes and tariffs in the original equilibrium;
- non-tradable commodities;
- intermediates with price-dependent input coefficients;
- international transfers (in the case of the clearing system).

The most notable point is probably the Armington assumption: it states that commodities are distinguished by their place of origin. This is particularily convenient for CGE models, because it allows us to include observable features such as cross-hauling, i.e. the simultaneous export and import of the same commodity category. Contrary to Heckscher-Ohlin models, this implies complete specialization by every country. For example, German cars are distinct from French cars and are only produced in Germany. This and other deviations of our model from the traditional Heckscher-Ohlin world imply that certain theorems about foreign trade, which are known from the literature (e.g., the factor-price equalization theorem), must not necessarily hold. Nevertheless, the basic patterns of explanation of the Heckscher-Ohlin model still remain valid.

The following model description uses the same notation as in Chapters II and III. Each national economy exhibits the same dimensionality and the same structure of production and consumption decisions and government activities. Therefore, we can restrict ourselves to looking at the behavioral assumptions and equilibrium conditions of one typical country. This also enables us to supress the country-specific index h in most parts of the following presentation. All in all, there are R countries with J production sectors each. Consequently, we have a total of $J \times R$ commodities in the model.

This section is organized in the same way as our computer program: given a set of factor prices, producers minimize costs which implicitly determines producer prices (Section 2.1.). On the basis of these producer prices and tax rates or transfer levels, households then calculate their demand quantities (Section 2.2.). Assuming that markets for goods and services always clear, commodity demand is set equal to supply so that factor demand quantities can be derived. Finally, government revenues are calculated (Section 2.3.). This constitutes a system of non-linear equations, which may be solved for the equilibrium values of the endogenous variables (Section 2.5.). Due to Walras' Law, the foreign sector (Section 2.4.) is automatically in balance if all markets clear and all other agents fulfill their budget constraints.

2.1. The Production Sector

Within each country we identify $J - 1$ domestically produced commodities which may be used for domestic consumption, as intermediate inputs in domestic production or as exports. Additionally, we consider a collective consumption good G produced by the public sector. This commodity is not traded, but is consumed (free of charge) by the domestic household sector and is used as an intermediate input (at producer prices) in domestic production. There are two primary production factors, labor and capital. Labor is mobile between production sectors, but not internationally. Capital, however, is mobile between production sectors *and* countries. Moreover, it is assumed to be homogeneous, i.e. firms do not distinguish between source countries and only face one international rental rate for capital. In addition to primary inputs and domestically produced inputs, firms use intermediates from abroad, which – according to the Armington assumption – might be similar, but are not identical to their domestic counterparts.

The firm's decision-making process concerning the use of primary inputs and intermediates is modelled as a hierarchically nested system of constant-returns-to-scale production functions.[60] Cost minimization on a "higher" nest determines the quantity constraints and, hence, demand functions on the "lower" level. All in all, our model features four such nests: composite intermediate commodity use versus value added, labor versus capital, domestic versus foreign intermediates and, finally, intermediates from different foreign countries. The structure of the production side of the model can most easily be represented by

[60] For details of this procedure see Keller (1976), for example.

a "production tree", as shown in Figure 2. In the next sections we will describe the different nests of the tree in more detail.

When computing an equilibrium, we generally start with the production side of the model. At given factor prices, and recalling that with constant-returns-to-scale technologies the zero profit condition holds, cost-covering producer prices can be calculated, which then serve as the basis of household decisions. Consequently, at every level of the price determination process we are interested in a per-unit representation of the use of (composite) factors and intermediates.

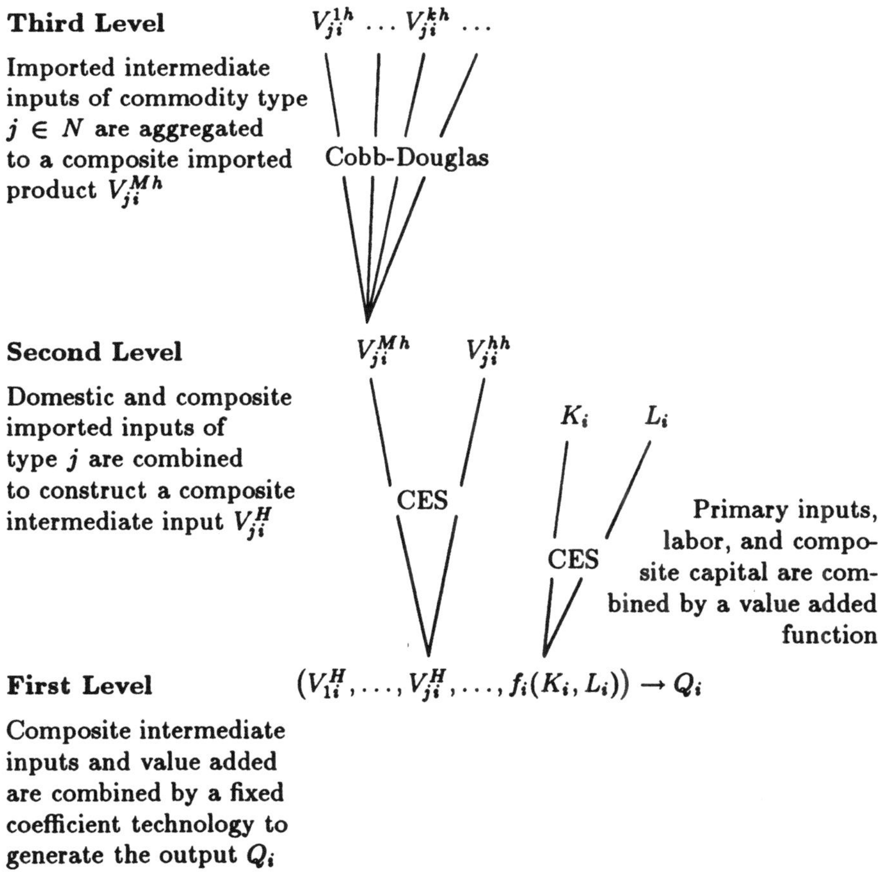

Figure 2. Hierarchical production structure in the i-th sector of country h

2.1.1. Value Added and Composite Intermediate Products

The production function on the first level of the firm's cost minimization problem is a Leontief technology, and does not depend on relative prices.

$$Q_i = \min\left[\frac{1}{a_{0i}} f_i(L_i, K_i); \frac{V_{1i}^H}{a_{1i}}; \ldots; \frac{V_{Ji}^H}{a_{Ji}}\right], \tag{1}$$

where Q_i is total output of commodity i (produced in the home country h by industry or sector i), f_i the value-added function, V_{ji}^H the intermediate use of composite commodity j in the production of commodity i, and a_{ji} the corresponding fixed coefficient, which represents the per-unit demand on this level.

2.1.2. Primary Input Demand

Let us first turn to the right branch of the production tree in Figure 2. After having decided how much overall value added will be employed, firm i now determines its need of primary factors labor, L_i, and capital, K_i. We employ the following CES function to describe the functional relationship between the two production factors:

$$f_i(L_i, K_i) = \phi_i\left[\delta_i L_i^{\varrho_i} + (1 - \delta_i) K_i^{\varrho_i}\right]^{\frac{1}{\varrho_i}}, \tag{2}$$

where ϕ_i is a scale parameter, δ_i a share parameter and σ_i the elasticity of substitution between composite capital and labor. To simplify the notation, we have set $\varrho_i = {}^{(\sigma_i - 1)}/_{\sigma_i}$.

The cost function is

$$Cost_i(L_i, K_i) = wL_i + rK_i, \tag{3}$$

where w is the domestic wage rate, and r a rental rate on the world capital market (remember that capital is homogeneous, i.e. there is no difference between capital from different source countries).[61]

[61] If world capital is heterogeneous (i.e. there is a world market for capital from every possible source country), a further nest would have to be added to the production tree. After having determined their overall capital demand, firms would then choose their optimal capital use from different countries according to the respective national rental rates. The exact modelling of this variant can be found in Fehr, Rosenberg, Wiegard (1991).

Minimizing the cost funtion (3) subject to $f_i = a_{0i}\bar{Q}_i$ gives us factor demands for labor and composite capital at a given output level $\bar{Q}_i$:

$$L_i = \frac{a_{0i}}{\phi_i}\bar{Q}_i \left\{ \delta_i + (1-\delta_i)\left[\frac{\delta_i r}{(1-\delta_i)w}\right]^{1-\sigma_i} \right\}^{-\frac{1}{\varrho_i}} \tag{4}$$

and

$$K_i = \frac{a_{0i}}{\phi_i}\bar{Q}_i \left\{ (1-\delta_i) + \delta_i \left[\frac{(1-\delta_i)w}{\delta_i r}\right]^{1-\sigma_i} \right\}^{-\frac{1}{\varrho_i}} . \tag{5}$$

The per unit factor requirements we are interested in are derived by dividing (4) and (5) by the given output quantity $\bar{Q}_i$. This yields

$$l_i = \frac{L_i}{\bar{Q}_i} \tag{6}$$

and

$$k_i = \frac{K_i}{\bar{Q}_i}. \tag{7}$$

2.1.3. Demand for Domestic and Imported Composite Inputs

Let us now turn to the left branch of the production tree. On the first level the representative firm i has decided on the use of the composite intermediate input V_{ji}^H. Each of these $J-1$ (traded) composites is some aggregate of domestic and imported inputs, with the substitution possibilities between them being captured by a CES technology. Note that imported intermediates V_{ji}^{Mh} themselves are composites. The production function for the composite input commodity can be written as

$$V_{ji}^H = \xi_{ji}\left[\lambda_{ji}(V_{ji}^M)^{\theta_{ji}} + (1-\lambda_{ji})(V_{ji})^{\theta_{ji}}\right]^{\frac{1}{\theta_{ji}}} , \tag{8}$$

with the scale parameter ξ_{ji}, the share parameter λ_{ji}, and the elasticity of substitution between imported and domestic intermediates ω_{ji}. For simplification we have set $\theta_{ji} = {}^{(\omega_{ji}-1)}/_{\omega_{ji}}$ and have omitted the country index h in V_{ji}^{Mh} and V_{ji}^{hh}. We can now formulate a cost function regarding the composite input use of commodity j:

$$Cost_{ji}^H(V_{ji}, V_{ji}^M) = q_j V_{ji} + q_{ji}^M V_{ji}^M , \tag{9}$$

where q_j is the producer price of the domestically produced intermediate commodity j and q_{ji}^M is a price index which can be calculated from the foreign country's producer prices in the following way:

$$q_{ji}^M = \sum_{k \in W_h} \frac{V_{ji}^{k\cdot}}{V_{ji}^M} q_j^k (1 + t_j^{\cdot k}). \tag{10}$$

Note that the tariff rate $t_j^{\cdot k}$ (applied by country h on commodity j from country k) enters the price index formula. In our case, tariffs are zero except for trade between ROW and EU, i.e.

$$t_j^{hk} \begin{cases} = 0 & \text{if } h, k \in EU \; ; \\ \neq 0 & \text{otherwise.} \end{cases}$$

Minimizing (9) subject to (8) and writing intermediate demands in per-unit form yields

$$v_{ji}^M = \frac{V_{ji}^M}{V_{ji}^H} = \frac{1}{\xi_{ji}} \left\{ \lambda_{ji} + (1 - \lambda_{ji}) \left[\frac{\lambda_{ji} \, q_j}{(1 - \lambda_{ji}) q_{ji}^M} \right]^{1-\omega_{ji}} \right\}^{-\frac{1}{\theta_{ji}}} \tag{11}$$

as the composite imported input coefficient and

$$v_{ji} = \frac{V_{ji}}{V_{ji}^H} = \frac{1}{\xi_{ji}} \left\{ (1 - \lambda_{ji}) + \lambda_{ji} \left[\frac{(1 - \lambda_{ji}) q_{ji}^M}{\lambda_{ji} \, q_j} \right]^{1-\omega_{ji}} \right\}^{-\frac{1}{\theta_{ji}}} \tag{12}$$

as the domestic input coefficient.

Furthermore, we can now calculate input-specific producer prices using the following formula:

$$q_{ji} = v_{ji} q_j + v_{ji}^M q_{ji}^M . \tag{13}$$

2.1.4. Demand for Imported Inputs

At the last stage of the hierarchical cost minimization problem the representative firm i decides in which country to purchase its imported intermediates. We model the substitution possibilities between comparable intermediates of different origin as a Cobb-Douglas function:

$$V_{ji}^{M} = \zeta_{ji} \prod_{k \in W_h} (V_{ji}^{k\cdot})^{\kappa_{ji}^{k}} \qquad \text{with} \qquad \sum_{k \in W_h} \kappa_{ji}^{k} = 1, \tag{14}$$

where ζ_{ji} is the scale parameter and κ_{ji}^{k} the share parameter. The cost function for the composite imported input j used in the production of commodity i is

$$Cost_{ji}^{M}(V_{ji}^{k\cdot} \mid k \in W_h) = \sum_{k \in W_h} V_{ji}^{k\cdot} q_j^k (1 + t_j^{\cdot k}) \tag{15}$$

with intermediate use of commodity j from country k, $V_{ji}^{k\cdot}$, and the corresponding producer price q_j^k. We can now calculate the intermediate demand coefficients of all imported inputs by minimizing (15) subject to (14). Writing the result in per-unit form yields:

$$v_{ji}^{k\cdot} = \frac{V_{ji}^{k\cdot}}{V_{ji}^{M}} = \frac{1}{\zeta_{ji}} \prod_{m \in W_h} \left[\frac{q_j^k (1 + t_j^{\cdot k}) \kappa_{ji}^{m}}{q_j^m (1 + t_j^{\cdot m}) \kappa_{ji}^{k}} \right]^{-\kappa_{ji}^{m}} . \tag{16}$$

2.1.5. Calculating Producer Prices Under the Tax Credit Method

We are now able to compute producer prices for all $J \times R$ commodities. This is possible because in our model the zero profit condition holds, enabling us to write every producer price as a function of factor prices and all (including its own) producer prices. As was already shown in Chapter II, applying the destination principle with the tax credit method for calculation of VAT liabilities yields the following zero-profit condition[62]

$$q_i \bar{Q}_i = \sum_{k \in W} \sum_{j \in N} q_j^k (1 + t_j^{\cdot k}) V_{ji}^{k\cdot} + wL_i + rK_i + \frac{\tau_{qi}}{1 + \tau_{qi}} q_i \bar{Q}_i . \tag{17}$$

---

[62] Note that we have to distinguish between producer prices and manufacturing prices, where the first exceed the latter by production taxes net of subsidies paid per unit. The tax base of production taxes is output valued at *manufacturing* prices. In order to avoid a separate symbol we compute tax liability as a percentage of output, valued at *producer* prices.

Dividing (17) by the output quantity $\bar{Q}_i$ and, for notational simplification, setting gross factor costs $b_i = wl_i + rk_i$, gives us the cost-covering producer price

$$q_i = (b_i + \sum_{j \in N} a_{ji} q_{ji})(1 + \tau_{qi}). \tag{18}$$

According to (13) in combination with (10), composite input prices q_{ji} are non-linear functions of all producer prices $q_i^k (k \in W, i \in N)$. Hence, (18) is a non-linear equation. On the whole, we have a system of $J \times R$ non-linear producer price equations which has to be solved by an appropriate solution algorithm.

Figure 3 summarizes the procedure of calculating producer prices (as described above) and shows how it may be imbedded in any numerical non-linear equation solution algorithm. For each variable computed within the process we give the relevant equations, which can be found in the preceeding sections. Note that in Figure 3 we assume that the tax credit method is used, which enables us to neglect consumption taxes within the price determination procedure.

The starting points are exogenously given country-specific factor prices for labor and a uniform rental rate for capital. The determination of factor prices itself will be explained at a later stage. With given factor prices, we can calculate the composite capital and labor demand coefficients for every industry. These in turn determine the gross factor costs for a certain configuration of factor prices.

The next step is the evaluation of composite input prices q_{ji} in equation (18). For all equations from (16) on, producer prices have to be known. Hence, we have to assume some "best guesses" for producer prices q_j^k in order to calculate input demand coefficients. Aggregation of the appropriate coefficients, valued at the assumed producer prices including tariffs, gives us the price indices of the composite imported inputs. These price indices enable us to compute the coefficients of imported intermediate inputs. Adding the value of composite imported inputs and domestic inputs yields the price index for each of the $J \times J \times R$ intermediate inputs. Since the (fixed) coefficients of the composite inputs as well as the production tax rates are given exogenously, and gross factor costs have already been calculated, the $J \times R$ producer prices $\hat{q}_i^h$ can now be computed.

We then have to check whether our "first guess" is sufficiently accurate to fulfill the zero profit condition. We specify some criterion ϵ and compare the computed producer prices $\hat{q}_i^h$ with their starting values q_i^h.

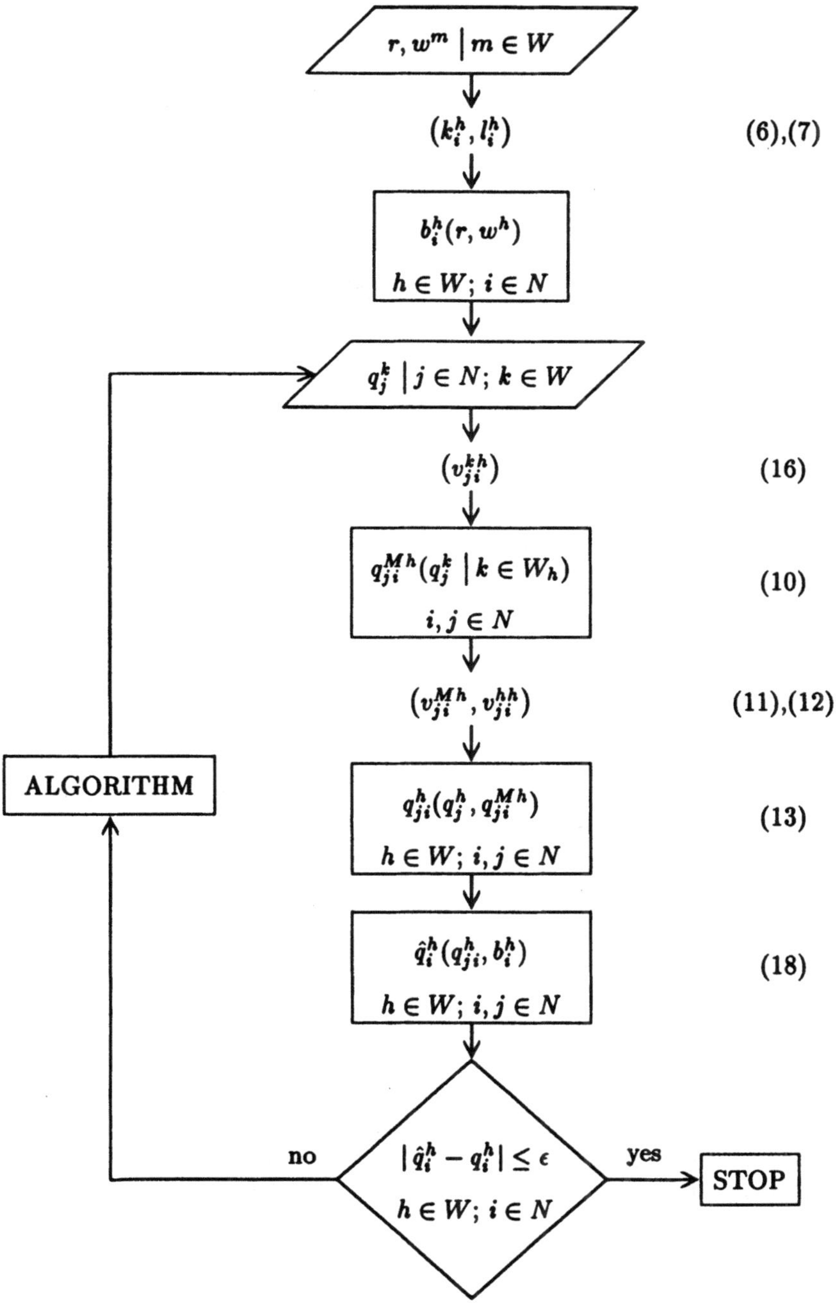

Figure 3. Flow chart for the calculation of producer prices (credit method)

If the difference between the two is sufficiently small (i.e. within the bounds of the criterion), a solution has been found. If the criterion is not fulfilled, we re-iterate with the computed producer prices until the criterion is fulfilled. Even if convergence is not guaranteed, our hand-made procedure produces a solution after only a few iterations.

Once a set of producer prices is found, we can turn to the computation of demand quantities. The representative household's determination of final demands will be described in the next section. For calculating intermediate demand quantities we need the matrix of intermediate input coefficients. These can easily be calculated according to

$$av_{ji}^{k\cdot} = a_{ji} \cdot v_{ji}^{M} \cdot v_{ji}^{k\cdot} ,$$

or, for domestic intermediate inputs,

$$av_{ji} = a_{ji} \cdot v_{ji}$$

where av_{ji}^{kh} $(h,k \in W;\ i,j \in N)$ is the price-dependent coefficient of input j from country k in the production of commodity i in country h.

Note that the above method of calculating producer prices will only work if the credit method is used. Under the subtraction method, production decisions depend on consumer prices. Therefore, instead of producer prices, consumer prices have to be determined by an iteration process analogous to the one described above.

2.2. The Household Sector

We assume only one representative household in each country. In CGE studies it has become standard to model the decision-making process of the household sector as a multi-stage utility maximization problem regarding leisure and various aggregates of consumption. The underlying idea is that a representative agent makes his choices step by step. Therefore, decisions on a higher level determine the budget set for choices on the next, lower, level. In our model, we distinguish four such utility nests regarding the choice between leisure and aggregate consumption, different consumption goods, imported and domestic commodities and, finally, imported consumption goods from different source countries. Note that collective consumption goods are provided free of charge and enter the utility function in an additively separable manner (and consequently can be omitted).

Fourth Level

Aggregation of direct consumption of commodity $i \in N$, imported from country $k \in W_h$, to a composite imported commodity (C_i^{Mh})

Third Level

Aggregation of comparable imported and domestic consumption goods to a composite consumption commodity (C_i^H)

Second Level

Aggregation of the different consumption categories in the home country to an aggregate composite consumption commodity

First Level

CES utility function over aggregate consumption and leisure

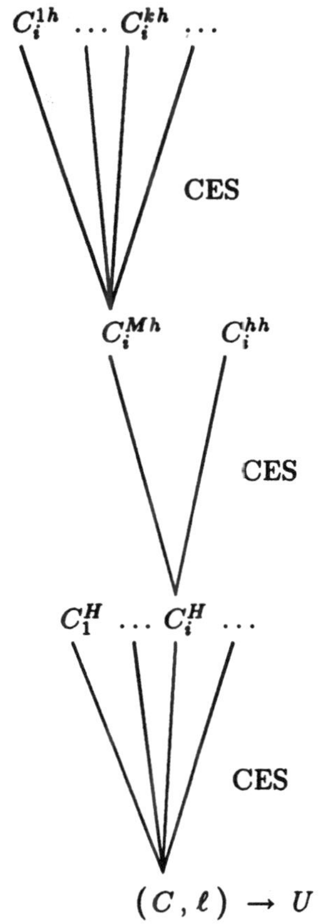

Figure 4. Nested utility functions

Figure 4 shows the structure of the decision-making process of the representative household as a utility tree. The different utility nests will be described in detail in the following sections.

2.2.1. Calculating Price Indices

As a first step, we have to compute all consumer prices and consumer price indices. The latter is necessary because the calculation of demand quantities starts at the first level of the utility tree, and requires price indices that are derived on lower levels. For given producer prices and utility function parameters we work our way up from fourth level to first level price indices. Because we attempt to keep our representation as close as possible to the actual computation procedure, we present the calculation of price indices in this first section, and not – as rigorous economic modelling would probably require – as constraints on the maximization problems at every stage of the decision making process.

In the following, p_i^h (with index h omitted whenever possible) denotes the consumer price for commodity i produced *and* consumed in country h. It is related to the respective producer price by

$$p_i^h = (1 + \tau_i^h)q_i^h \ ,$$

where τ_i^h is the VAT rate applied to commodity i by country h. Note that producer prices are defined only if the credit method is used. We define p_i^{kh} as the consumer price of the i-th commodity which is produced in country k but consumed in country h. If the destination principle of international commodity taxation is applied, similar demand categories are taxed at the same rate, regardless of whether they are produced abroad or domestically. Hence, domestic consumer prices for commodities produced in country k are given by

$$p_i^{kh} = (1 + \tau_i^h)(1 + t_i^{hk})q_i^k \ , \tag{19a}$$

where the tariff t_i^{hk} is equal to zero whenever $h, k \in EU$.

In our simulation runs we sometimes apply the origin principle[63] where commodities are taxed according to their place of production. Equation (19a) then changes to

$$p_i^{kh} = (1 + \tau_i^k)(1 + t_i^{hk})q_i^k, \tag{19b}$$

provided that the credit method is retained. Because the utility function on the lowest level is a CES function, we can calculate the price

[63] The origin principle is generally applied to direct imports of market services, i.e. expenditures of domestic residents on services abroad.

index at this level (p_i^M) from the consumer prices for commodities i from country k as follows[64]

$$p_i^M = \left[\sum_{k \in W_h} \beta_i^k \left(p_i^{k\cdot} \right)^{1-\nu_i^M} \right]^{\frac{1}{1-\nu_i^M}} \qquad \text{with} \quad \sum_{k \in W_h} \beta_i^k = 1. \quad (20)$$

At the next level we use a CES function again. The price index at this level is calculated by using p_i^M and the consumer price of domestically produced goods p_i:

$$p_i^H = \left[\beta_i^H (p_i)^{1-\nu_i} + (1 - \beta_i^H)(p_i^M)^{1-\nu_i} \right]^{\frac{1}{1-\nu_i}}. \quad (21)$$

Finally, we can calculate the price index p of the composite consumption good C by using the lower level price indices p_i^H:

$$p = \left[\sum_{i \in N} \beta_i \left(p_i^H \right)^{1-\nu_c} \right]^{\frac{1}{1-\nu_c}} \qquad \text{with} \quad \sum_{i \in N} \beta_i = 1. \quad (22)$$

Here again we have omitted the country index h. The underlying utility functions and their parameters are explained in the next sections.

2.2.2. Demand for Leisure and Consumption

On the first level the representative consumer decides on aggregate consumption C and leisure ℓ. His preferences are represented by the following CES utility function:

$$U(C, \ell) = \left[(1 - \beta)^{\frac{1}{\nu}} C^{\mu} + \beta^{\frac{1}{\nu}} \ell^{\mu} \right]^{\frac{1}{\mu}}, \quad (23)$$

with the substitution elasticity ν, the budget share parameter β and the definition $\mu = {}^{(\nu - 1)}/_{\nu}$.

The consumer's budget is constrained by his maximal achievable income, including government transfers, less income tax payments:

$$pC + w\ell = wE + r\bar{K} - T_Y + Tr, \quad (24)$$

[64] Price indices are derived by rearranging the indirect utility function to fulfill the budget constraint. For details see Keller (1976).

where w and r are the factor prices of labor and capital, E the total time endowment, $\bar{K}$ capital ownership (at home and abroad), T_Y income tax payments, and Tr transfer payments received. Applying the residence principle to international capital transactions, income tax payments are determined by

$$T_Y = \tau_y[w(E - \ell) + r\bar{K} - All] \, ,$$

where All is an income tax allowance for the representative domestic consumer.

After substituting T_Y and performing some rearrangements the consumer's budget constraint may be written:

$$pC + w(1 - \tau_y)\ell = (1 - \tau_y)\left[wE + r\bar{K}\right] + \tau_y All + Tr =: Y \, . \quad (25)$$

Here Y is defined as net maximal income. The composite consumption bundle C is valued by the price index p, which is derived as described above. For the valuation of labor or leisure we have to apply the net wage rate $w_n = (1 - \tau_y)w$.

Maximization of (23) subject to (25) yields the demand functions for composite consumption and leisure

$$C = \frac{(1 - \beta)Y}{p^{\nu}\Omega} \quad (26)$$

and

$$\ell = \frac{\beta Y}{w_n^{\nu}\Omega} \quad (27)$$

with

$$\Omega = (1 - \beta)p^{1-\nu} + \beta w_n^{1-\nu}. \quad (28)$$

Labor supply L is then given by

$$L = E - \ell.$$

2.2.3. Demand for Different Consumption Commodities

On the second level of the utility tree the consumer decides on the demand for different consumption categories C_i^H, for example cars or food. His preferences are represented by the following CES utility function

$$C(C_1^H, \ldots, C_J^H) = \left[\sum_{i \in N} \beta_i^{\frac{1}{\nu_c}} (C_i^H)^{\mu_c}\right]^{\frac{1}{\mu_c}} , \quad (29)$$

where β_i is the share parameter, and ν_c represents the elasticity of substitution between demand categories. We have set $\mu_c = {}^{(\nu_c - 1)}/_{\nu_c}$ for notational simplification. Now the consumer's budget is constrained by disposable income Y^H, defined by the difference between maximal income Y and optimal "leisure" income, determined at the next higher stage:

$$Y^H = Y - w\ell = \sum_{i \in N} p_i^H C_i^H. \tag{30}$$

Maximizing (29) subject to (30) yields the demand for different commodity categories

$$C_i^H = \frac{\beta_i Y^H}{(p_i^H)^{\nu_c} \Omega_c} \tag{31}$$

with

$$\Omega_c = \sum_{i \in N} \beta_i (p_i^H)^{1-\nu_c}. \tag{32}$$

Again, p_i^H represents a price index which is derived as described above.

2.2.4. Demand for Domestic and Imported Commodities

On the third level, the representative agent decides whether to buy a commodity at home or abroad, for example, whether to purchase an imported or a domestic car. According to the Armington assumption, commodities are distinguished by their place of origin and are consequently treated as different, though closely substitutable, commodities. This enables us to model the choice of comparable commodities from domestic or foreign origin as a CES-utility function for home products C_i and composite imports C_i^M:

$$C_i^H(C_i^M, C_i) = \left[(\beta_i^H)^{\frac{1}{\nu_i}} (C_i)^{\mu_i} + (1 - \beta_i^H)^{\frac{1}{\nu_i}} (C_i^M)^{\mu_i} \right]^{\frac{1}{\mu_i}}, \tag{33}$$

with the share parameter β_i^H and the elasticity of substitution ν_i between domestic and composite imported commodity. Again we set $\mu_i = {}^{(\nu_i - 1)}/_{\nu_i}$.

Given the choices made at the previous stages of the decision making process, the representative agent is now confined by his disposable income which has not yet been "planned" for other commodity categories. Hence, his budget constraint is

$$Y_i^H = Y^H - \sum_{j \in N_i} p_j^H C_j^H = p_i C_i + p_i^M C_i^M. \tag{34}$$

Maximizing the utility function (33) subject to the budget constraint (34), yields the demand for the composite imported commodity

$$C_i^M = \frac{(1-\beta_i^H) Y_i^H}{(p_i^M)^{\nu_i} \Omega_i} \tag{35}$$

and the demand for the comparable good of domestic origin

$$C_i = \frac{\beta_i^H Y_i^H}{(p_i)^{\nu_i} \Omega_i}, \tag{36}$$

with

$$\Omega_i = \beta_i^H (p_i)^{1-\nu_i} + (1-\beta_i^H)(p_i^M)^{1-\nu_i}. \tag{37}$$

2.2.5. Demand for Different Imported Commodities

At the last level, the representative consumer decides where to buy his direct consumption imports; for example, a German final consumer decides whether to buy an imported car from Italy or from France. Again using CES utility functions, we have

$$C_i^M(C_i^{1\cdot}, \ldots, C_i^{R\cdot}) = \Big[\sum_{k \in W_h} (\beta_i^k)^{\frac{1}{\nu_i^M}} (C_i^{k\cdot})^{\mu_i^M} \Big]^{\frac{1}{\mu_i^M}}, \tag{38}$$

where $C_i^{k\cdot}$ is the final demand for commodity i from country k, β_i^k the corresponding share parameter, ν_i^M is the elasticity of substitution between commodity categories i from different source countries, and R the number of countries in the model. We have set $\mu_i^M = {(\nu_i^M - 1)}/{\nu_i^M}$.

The household faces as a budget constraint that part of disposable income that has not yet been allocated to other demand categories or to domestic commodities C_i comparable to commodity $C_i^{k\cdot}$ with $k \in W_h$:

$$Y_i^M = Y_i^H - p_i C_i = \sum_{k \in W_h} p_i^{k\cdot} C_i^{k\cdot}. \tag{39}$$

Maximizing (38) subject to (39) gives us the following CES-demand functions for imported commodities i:

$$C_i^{k\cdot} = \frac{\beta_i^k Y_i^M}{(p_i^{k\cdot})^{\nu_i^M} \Omega_i^M} \tag{40}$$

with

$$\Omega_i^M = \sum_{k \in W_h} \beta_i^k (p_i^{k\cdot})^{1-\nu_i^M}. \tag{41}$$

2.3. The Public Sector

2.3.1. Public Revenues

In our model the government levies various taxes and tariffs in order to finance its expenditures. Let us first turn to tax revenues.

Value-added taxes play a decisive role in our simulations. In Chapter II we have already shown how the government revenue equation changes under different VAT liability calculation methods. Therefore, it may suffice to present our benchmark case, the destination principle with VAT administration according to the credit (invoice) method. Remember that there are no border tax adjustments for direct service imports. Hence, total VAT revenue T_C is calculated as follows:[65]

$$T_C = \sum_{k \in W} \sum_{i \in N_s} \tau_i q_i^k C_i^{k\cdot} + \sum_{k \in W} \tau_s q_s C_s^{\cdot k}. \tag{42}$$

Note that the revenue from taxing the consumption of services accrues to the home country, whereas the tax burden is partly shifted to foreign consumers. Hence, there is some tax exporting associated with the taxation of services. With respect to the production of public goods, we assume zero rating in all countries; the public sector is thereby permitted to claim a credit for taxes paid on purchases of intermediate goods. Actually, the government sector is tax-exempt and not zero rated (Pohmer, 1981, p. 94), which makes quite a difference.

Income taxes T_y are the other major source of revenue. We assume a constant marginal tax rate and an allowance which diminishes the

[65] For trade between the EU and ROW, tariff payments have to be included in the tax base for physical goods.

tax base. In accordance with common practice, we apply the residence principle. The linear income tax function already given above is

$$T_Y = \tau_y \left[wL + r\bar{K} - All \right]. \tag{43}$$

Furthermore, the government levies production taxes T_Q, which, in our model, also include certain excises such as the gasoline tax. The tax base is the (gross) value of domestic production of commodity i:

$$T_Q = \sum_{i \in N} T_{Q_i} = \sum_{i \in N} \frac{\tau_{qi}}{1 + \tau_{qi}} q_i Q_i. \tag{44}$$

Note that production taxes may also be negative. In such cases they can be interpreted as subsidies and represent a public expenditure.

Finally, EU member countries levy a common tariff on all (intermediate and direct) imports from ROW, while ROW applies a tariff on all its imports from the EU. In accordance with the Treaty of Rome, trade within the EU is not subject to tariffs. Consequently, tariff revenue for EU member countries $h \in EU$ is

$$\begin{aligned} TAR &= \sum_{i \in N} TAR_i^Q + TAR^H \\ &= \sum_{j \in N} \left[t_j^{\cdot ROW} q_j^{ROW} \left(\sum_{i \in N} V_{ji}^{ROW \cdot} + C_j^{ROW \cdot} \right) \right], \end{aligned} \tag{45}$$

whereas tariff revenue for ROW is

$$TAR^{ROW} = \sum_{k \in EU} \sum_{j \in N} \left[t_j^{ROWk} q_j^k \left(\sum_{i \in N} V_{ji}^{kROW} + C_j^{kROW} \right) \right]. \tag{46}$$

2.3.2. Public Expenditure

There are two expenditure categories in the government sector. The first are lump-sum transfer payments Tr to the representative consumer. The second are outlays on the provision of a collective commodity (or non-market services) that – as already mentioned above – is offered free of charge to the domestic household sector (public services such as police and health care) and sold at producer prices to domestic firms. The public commodity is not traded and is produced in the same way as any other good, combining primary factors and intermediates, bought at market prices. Furthermore, we assume that the total supply of the public good is fixed. Net public expenditure for the collective commodity in country h is $q_g^h G^h$.

2.4. The Foreign Sector

2.4.1. Balance of Payments

Our model includes several transborder activities: international trade in goods and services, international capital income flows and, when the clearing system is in operation, international transfer payments between governments. All these transactions are captured in the balance of payments (BP), which may be decomposed – in our context – into three parts. Note that in our static context the balance of payments is reduced to the current account.

First, the trade balance captures all international transactions in (physical) goods. In our model the trade balance of country h is

$$TB = \sum_{k \in W_h} \sum_{j \in N_*} q_j \Big(\sum_{i \in N} V_{ji}^{\cdot k} + C_j^{\cdot k} \Big) - \sum_{k \in W_h} \sum_{j \in N_*} q_j^k \Big(\sum_{i \in N} V_{ji}^{k \cdot} + C_j^{k \cdot} \Big) . \quad (47)$$

Whenever the destination principle applies, all international transactions leave the country tax-free and therefore have to be valued at producer prices. Under the origin principle, however, consumer prices would be the appropriate price concept.

The second relevant sub-account in our model is the service account. This account not only captures international transactions in services, but also flows of capital income between countries. Imports of services by domestic consumers are generally taxed according to the origin principle and are therefore valued at consumer (tax-inclusive) prices. Imports of services for intermediate production are valued at producer or consumer prices, depending on whether the destination or the origin principle is applied. Under the former, we can write the service balance SB for country h as

$$SB = \sum_{k \in W_h} \sum_{j \in N} (q_s V_{sj}^{\cdot k} - q_s^k V_{sj}^{k \cdot}) + \sum_{k \in W_h} \Big[q_s(1+\tau_s) C_s^{\cdot k} - q_s^k (1+\tau_s^k) C_s^{k \cdot} \Big] + \sum_{k \in W_h} \sum_{i \in N} r \big(\bar{K} - \sum_{i \in N} K_i \big) . \quad (48)$$

If transfers between countries (such as clearing payments) exist, these transactions additionally enter the balance of payments as unilateral transfers TRB.

For every country the sum of these three accounts has to equal zero:

$$BP = TB + SB + TRB = 0. \tag{49}$$

The current account is balanced unilaterally. Bilateral accounts, however, do not have to be in balance.

2.4.2. Terms of Trade

In an open economy, a change in VAT will generally change the international terms of trade (ToT). Terms of trade effects are associated with international substitution as well as with international income effects. This section focusses on the measurement of ToT.

The basic measure we use is the net-barter ToT. This is the most common ToT definition in the empirical literature and is often used in simulation studies such as that by Whalley (1985).[66] The net-barter ToT are generally defined as

$$ToT_N = \frac{p_x}{p_m} \cdot 100 ,$$

where p_x and p_m represent price index numbers for exports and imports. Using a Laspeyres price index with the base year's export and import quantities as weights, the indices for country h are:[67]

$$p_m = \frac{\sum_{k \in W_h} \sum_{i \in N} (q_i^k)_1 \, (M_i^{kh})_0}{\sum_{k \in W_h} \sum_{i \in N} (q_i^k)_0 \, (M_i^{kh})_0} \tag{50}$$

and

$$p_x = \frac{\sum_{k \in W_h} \sum_{i \in N} (q_i^h)_1 \, (X_i^{hk})_0}{\sum_{k \in W_h} \sum_{i \in N} (q_i^h)_0 \, (X_i^{hk})_0} , \tag{51}$$

where M_i^{kh} is country h's total imports of commodity i from country k and X_i^{hk} country h's total exports of commodity i to country k. The additional index 0 indicates quantities and prices in the benchmark

[66] The theoretical literature relies mostly on the so-called "gross barter terms of trade", a quantity index. In large-scale empirical models, however, this definition seems less practicable. See Allen and Ely (1953, pp. 207-209) or Kemp (1968) for a discussion.

[67] Whalley (1985, p. 130) uses domestic production quantities as weights, obviously in order to correct for distortions by tariffs already in place in the base year.

equilibrium, and index 1 stands for the counterfactual equilibrium. In the former, all prices $(q_i^k)_0$ are all equal to one and we can simply add up quantities. This is due to the special normalization assumptions for the benchmark data set, which will be described in the next section.

In our context, the question arises of whether producer or, rather, consumer prices should be used when calculating these price indices. Since the ToT are basically designed to capture the value of exports and imports vis-à-vis trading partners, it seems appropriate to use world market prices. In simulations in which the destination principle is applied in the benchmark as well as in the counterfactual equilibrium, producer prices would be the correct evaluation. This is because of the border tax adjustment procedure, which ensures that all goods leave a country without any VAT. If, however, the origin principle is applied in the counterfactual equilibrium, exports and imports will have to be valued at consumer prices because domestic goods are traded at a VAT-inclusive price on the world market. In this case, price indices are calculated as follows:[68]

$$p_m = \frac{\sum_{k \in W_h} \sum_{i \in N} (p_i^k)_1 \, (M_i^{kh})_0}{\sum_{k \in W_h} \sum_{i \in N} (q_i^k)_0 \, (M_i^{kh})_0} \tag{52}$$

and

$$p_x = \frac{\sum_{k \in W_h} \sum_{i \in N} (p_i^h)_1 \, (X_i^{hk})_0}{\sum_{k \in W_h} \sum_{i \in N} (q_i^h)_0 \, (X_i^{hk})_0} . \tag{53}$$

Furthermore the ToT then also include tax exporting effects, which always occur when the origin principle is applied.

2.5. Equilibrium Conditions of the Model

As a final step, we have to specify equilibrium conditions in markets for commodities[69] and factors:

$$\text{Commodity market } i: \qquad Q_i = \sum_{k \in W} \Big(\sum_{j \in N} av_{ij}^{:k} Q_j^k + C_i^{:k} \Big) \tag{54}$$

[68] If only a partial shift to the origin principle takes place (e.g., only for direct consumption trade), only these relevant quantities are valued at consumer prices.

[69] The commodity market clearing condition also holds for the public commodity G.

Factor markets:
$$\sum_{k\in W}\bar{K}^k = \sum_{k\in W}\sum_{i\in N} K_i^k \tag{55}$$

$$L = \sum_{i\in N} L_i. \tag{56}$$

Additionally, the government budget has to be balanced:

$$q_g G + Tr = T_C + T_Q + T_Y + TAR. \tag{57}$$

According to Walras' Law, the current account is automatically balanced if all private agents fulfill their budget constraints.

The special structure of our model, however, enables us to reduce the dimensionality of the problem drastically. Since we assume constant returns to scale and, consequently, zero profits, commodity prices are a function of factor prices. Hence, any vector of factor prices that clears the markets for capital and labor automatically ensures that commodity markets are cleared as well. The problem of finding an equilibrium for the economy can then be confined to finding a set of factor prices and government parameters (tax rates or transfer payment levels) that balance factor markets and the government budget in each country.

The factor demands in each country are derived as follows. Rearranging (54) and writing it in matrix notation we have

$$\mathbf{Q} = (\mathbf{I} - \mathbf{AV})^{-1}\mathbf{C}\,,$$

where $\mathbf{Q}$ is a column vector of the output quantities Q_i^h ($i \in N$; $h \in W$), $\mathbf{I}$ the identity matrix and $\mathbf{AV}$ the matrix of the (variable) input coefficients. Finally, $\mathbf{C}$ is a column vector with elements $\sum_{k\in W} C_i^{hk}$ ($i \in N; h \in W$). The factor demand quantities in each industry (of every country) are then calculated as follows:

$$L_i = l_i Q_i \quad \text{and} \quad K_i = k_i Q_i,$$

where unit factor demands and output supplies depend only on factor prices. Inserting factor demands L_i, K_i into the equilibrium conditions (55) and (56), we can solve for the equilibrium factor prices. Because only relative prices matter, we can normalize the price system by choosing one numeraire commodity.

Figure 5 presents a flow chart of the entire model, summarizing the derivation of market clearing conditions for any set of factor prices

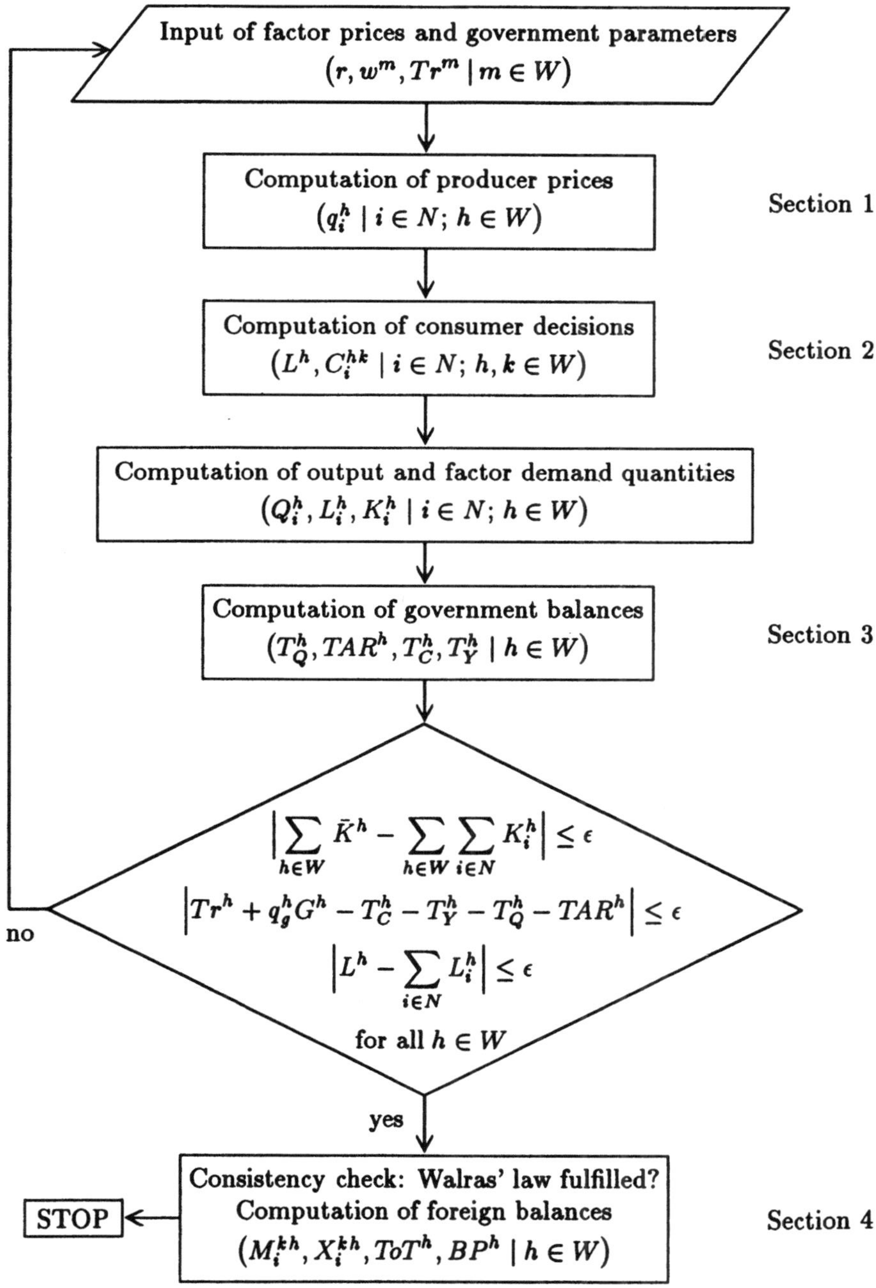

Figure 5. Flow chart for the solution of our CGE model

and government parameters, as described in detail above. The final system of non-linear equations was solved by using a "state of the art" algorithm available in any FORTRAN library.

3. A Micro-consistent Data Set for the EU

The essence of CGE economics is the combination of general equilibrium theory with a consistent data set from the national accounts in order to derive policy insights. In this section, we describe the manipulations that were undertaken in order to arrive at a data set that meets all requirements of micro-consistency. This usually is the most time-consuming part of every CGE study, and a detailed listing of each and every step in constructing a micro-consistent data set is not very interesting.[70] We therefore confine ourselves to the more important adjustments. We start by presenting the consistency requirements for a Walrasian benchmark data set and comment on the sources of our raw data. Next, we explain the manipulations necessary to reconcile the different data sources. We conclude with some final remarks on our data set.

3.1. Consistency Requirements and Data Sources

One of the basic assumptions of most CGE models is that the economy is characterized by Walrasian equilibrium. In our context the base year's data set has to comply with the following equilibrium conditions:[71]

- Demand equal supply for all goods and factors. The market equilibrium conditions were given above as

supply		demand	
		domestic	foreign
Q_i	$=$	$C_i + \sum_{j\in N} V_{ij}$	$+\sum_{k\in W_h}\left(C_i^{\cdot k} + \sum_{j\in N} V_{ij}^{\cdot k}\right)$
$\sum_{k\in W} \bar{K}^k$	$=$	$\sum_{i\in N} K_i$	$+\sum_{k\in W_h}\sum_{i\in N} K_i^k$
L	$=$	$\sum_{i\in N} L_i$	

[70] St-Hilaire and Whalley (1983, 1987) give a more complete description of what is involved in constructing micro-consistent data sets.

[71] In the following we assume that the credit method is used. Under the subtraction method some conditions would look different.

- Zero profits in all industries in (long-run) equilibrium

$$q_i Q_i = wL_i + rK_i + \sum_{j \in N} \sum_{k \in W} q_j^k V_{ji}^{k\cdot} + T_{Q_i} + TAR_i^Q.$$

- All agents satisfy their budget constraints. For the representative consumer this means

$$r\bar{K} + wL + Tr - T_Y = \sum_{k \in W} \sum_{i \in N} q_i^k C_i^{k\cdot} + T_C^H + TAR^H,$$

  whereas the government budget constraint is[72]

$$T_C + T_Y + T_Q + TAR^H + TAR^Q = Tr + q_g G.$$

- The current account is balanced

$$TB + SB + TRB = 0.$$

To construct a micro-consistent data set we need data on interindustry transactions, value added, final demand, bilateral trade and capital income flows and, finally, government revenues and outlays. Unfortunately, these data are often mutually inconsistent. Hence, various adjustments are necessary in order to guarantee consistency. In the following we present the major data sources for our data set and describe some of the more important causes of mutual inconsistency.

The interindustry transaction table in intermediate products and the final demand table are mainly derived from data provided by Langer (1987). This author estimated interregional transactions within the EU for 1981 based on national input-output tables (for 1975) and on EU trade statistics for 1977, 1979, and 1981. With one minor exception we use the same disaggregation of commodities and countries as Langer did. Because Langer's data on aggregate trade flows within the EU are not compatible with those given in official statistics, we borrowed the structure of bilateral trade flows from his work but

[72] National VAT revenue (T_C) and VAT payments by domestic consumers (T_C^H) will differ because the direct consumption of services is taxed according to the origin principle.

took aggregate values from EUROSTAT (1982). For ROW we calculated input-output coefficients as well as final demand coefficients from national account and input-output data provided by the United Nations (1985) and by MITI (1989).

Langer's work does not contain any data on value added so we relied on data from EUROSTAT (1986) and MITI (1989). In order to compute tariff payments we used tariff rates published in Whalley (1985, pp. 162 f., p. 286). We used conversion factors given in EUROSTAT (1983, p. 66) to convert data in national currencies into our general accounting unit, the ECU.

With respect to government revenues, information on tax rates or revenues was taken from the German Ministry of Finance (1981) or OECD (1988). VAT rates for ROW were chosen more or less arbitrarily. Average income tax rates were calculated using revenue statistics from the OECD (1989), and marginal income tax rates were derived from McKee et al. (1986). Details of our adjustment procedure are given in the next section.

Obviously, a number of problems arise when combining data from so many different sources. Here only the more important problems are mentioned.

- *Different classification concepts.* The sectoral classifaction in input-output statistics may not always match commodity classification in trade statistics. Moreover, the definition of the government sector in the US-Japan input-output tables differs considerably from that in the EUROSTAT tables.
- *Different price concepts.* International trade statistics are sometimes based on cif, and sometimes on fob prices. Industry output values may be measured on a net-of-retail, wholesale margin, or net-of-transportation cost basis as in input-output data or on a gross basis as in consumer expenditure data.
- *Different nationality concepts.* National accounting data are generally estimated on a national basis, i.e. income is assigned to the residence of the owners of factors of production, while input-output data are determined on a domestic basis, allocating income to the region in which it is earned.
- *Different observation years.* We combine data from different observation years. This makes inflating/deflating – with all its well-known problems – necessary.

Even within the EU, where most measurement concepts are harmonized by the Statistical Office of the European Communities (EU-

ROSTAT), considerable differences prevail between bilateral trade and factor income flows reported by the exporting countries and those reported by the importing countries.[73]

These data inconsistencies make a number of adjustments necessary, which may be arguable in their detail, but are unavoidable when constructing a micro-consistent data base. These will be explained in the following section.

3.2. Data Adjustments

3.2.1. Updating the Intermediate Transaction and Final Demand Tables

The starting point of our calculations is an estimated interregional input-output table for the EU contained in Langer (1987). His country disaggregation features the following EU countries:[74] France (F), the Netherlands (NL), Germany (D), Italy (I), Denmark (DK) and the aggregations Belgium-Luxembourg (B-L) and UK-Ireland (UK-IRL). For these countries Langer aggregated the 44 production sectors of the national input-output tables for 1975 as given in EUROSTAT (1986) to 13 sectors. He then used the bilateral intra-EU trade statistics and some rather crude adjustment procedures to estimate his interregional transaction table. In some aspects the purpose of our study is different, requiring modifications to his data set.

First, we disaggregated Langer's service sector into market services and non-market services (public good's sector). This is because non-market services are treated differently from other commodities (not traded and zero-rated under VAT) in our model. The commodity or industry disaggregation is then: agriculture and forestry; energy, water, and mining; chemicals; metal products; electric products; machinery; office equipment and computers; cars; other motor vehicles; food and drink; textiles and leather; market services; non-market services. Our disaggregation of the service sector requires the disaggregation of the sectors' inputs and outputs. Since data on non-market service inputs to the other production sectors were not available for all EU

[73] Compare Boomsma et al. (1991) for a comment on this phenomenon which is sometimes referred to as the *mirror puzzle*.

[74] Greece, which was a member of the EU in 1981, is excluded because of data difficulties.

countries, we applied the structure of the German input-output tables as published by the Statistical Office (1986) to all other countries. For the column-wise disaggregation of the service sector we borrowed from the national input-output tables supplied by EUROSTAT. On the final demand side we introduced the additional demand category "collective consumption", taking the data from EUROSTAT (1986).

Secondly, Langer's study provides only the bilateral tables of EU imports from ROW. We still needed to add ROW's bilateral import tables and the input-output table for ROW's internal transactions. The latter was computed by consolidating the four tables on US-Japanese input-output transactions provided by MITI (1989) to one table with 14 production sectors. The calculation of ROW import tables was performed in two steps. First, we consolidated an initial import matrix for ROW with our sectoral aggregation from the US-Japan trade tables with other countries. The total sectoral exports from every EU country to ROW could be found in EUROSTAT (1986). In the second step we therefore derived the bilateral import tables of ROW with respect to every EU country by scaling up the row sums of the initial import matrix to the respective EU countries' sectoral exports to ROW.

Thirdly, although Langer consolidated the intraregional transaction tables (intermediate and final demand), these tables still contained the 1975 values. We therefore had to scale them up to our base year, retaining the structure of the 1975 data. The numbers for 1981 were obtained by inflating the 1980 tables of intermediate and final uses with the corresponding national price indices. The procedure for ROW was different, because no such table exists. First we calculated the GDP of ROW by simply subtracting the GDP of the EU countries from world gross product as provided in United Nations (1985). The next step was to calculate a weighted average of the coefficients of the relation between GDP and intraregional transactions in the EU countries, the US, and Japan. Multiplying this average coefficient with the the GDP of ROW yielded the benchmark value we were looking for. The original Japan-US table was then scaled up to this value.

Fourth, when comparing the bilateral trade flows from Langer's data base with bilateral trade statistics from EUROSTAT, we found considerable differences in volume and direction of flow data. Because trade flows between countries play a decisive role in our study, we relied on the official data for bilateral trade in merchandise and services. Intra-community data on commodity trade were taken from

Table 1. Bilateral trade flows (total and intermediate products; no services) – in mill. ECU, 1981[a]

Exports to → / Imports from ↓	F	B-L	NL	D	I	UK-IRL	DK	ROW	$\sum$ exports
F	-	7551	4029	13483	10325	6481	609	47213	89691
	-	*6127*	*3055*	*9986*	*8231*	*5660*	*532*	*37434*	*71025*
B-L	9559	-	7367	10033	2540	4292	661	14451	48903
	7345	-	*5528*	*7532*	*2049*	*3791*	*584*	*12196*	*39025*
NL	6438	8817	-	18114	3453	5105	1031	16300	59258
	5301	*7423*	-	*14013*	*2945*	*4582*	*896*	*13503*	*48663*
D	20656	11514	13469	-	12457	10444	2989	83131	154660
	16986	*10190*	*11261*	-	*10331*	*9473*	*2661*	*65969*	*126871*
I	9268	1871	2084	10574	-	3941	373	37896	66007
	6743	*1447*	*1515*	*7440*	-	*3317*	*311*	*30054*	*50827*
UK-IRL	6824	4513	7274	10006	3142	-	1925	55994	89178
	4429	*3113*	*5081*	*6604*	*2106*	-	*1503*	*44545*	*67381*
DK	709	250	500	2431	656	2048	-	7756	14350
	481	*172*	*348*	*1585*	*422*	*1423*	-	*6134*	*10565*
ROW	52245	22932	23611	71134	44173	48378	8954	-	271426
	46224	*20545*	*21035*	*61371*	*41413*	*41257*	*7517*	-	*239362*
$\sum$ imports	105699	57248	58334	135775	76746	80689	16541	262441	-
	87509	*49017*	*47823*	*108531*	*67497*	*69503*	*14004*	*209835*	-

[a] EUROSTAT (1982, p. 105) for intra-EU trade; EUROSTAT (1987) for EU-ROW trade

EUROSTAT (1982, p. 105), while unpublished data for flows of services and capital income were directly provided by EUROSTAT. Data on commodity trade and capital income flows between the EU and ROW were taken from EUROSTAT (1987). In order to ensure a unilateral external sector balance we had to perform some adjustments on international flows of capital income, which will be described below. One last adjustment had to be made with respect to direct consumption imports. Because original data were not available, we derived our estimates by scaling up Langer's bilateral import matrices to the aggregate trade figures of EUROSTAT. In input-output accounting, wholesale trade imports that are sold by domestic retailers to final consumers are recorded as final consumption imports whereas the corresponding trade margin is reported as service imports. These figures largely exceed the purchases of domestic consumers from foreign retailers through distance selling, which is our understanding of direct consumption imports. Due to the lack of better information, we therefore halved the figures obtained between intermediate imports of the respective industries and cross-border purchases by final consumers. Since direct consumption imports are of decisive importance for our results, we perform some sensitivity analysis with respect to these data in the next chapter. Table 1 summarizes total bilateral trade flows and trade in intermediate products (in slanted numbers). The difference between these numbers is equivalent to direct consumption imports or exports.

3.2.2. Value Added by Industry

Value added data by industry are composed of four major parts: labor income, capital income, production taxes minus subsidies, and tariff payments. As mentioned above, Langer (1987) provides no information on these data. To compute tariff payments by industry we took the post-Tokyo Round tariff rates from Whalley (1985, p. 162) for the EU and ROW. Tariff payments were then obtained by multiplying tariff rates with the respective intermediate imports. Production taxes minus subsidies as well as returns to labor and capital are generally reported in EUROSTAT input-output tables. For some countries, however, only net value added at market prices was provided for our base year, 1981. In these cases we isolated labor from capital income by splitting the total values according to some older input-output tables.[75] Additionally, national input-output tables do not necessarily

[75] For France we used input-output tables from 1965, for Italy those from 1970,

include any figures on the net operating surplus in the non-market service sector. In these cases we used data from EUROSTAT (1987) to get information on capital income in this sector.

Value added data for ROW were obtained by consolidating MITI's input-output tables to our 14 production sectors. We then scaled this table up to the GDP of ROW, which was computed from data provided by the United Nations (1985, p. 5). In Table 2 we compare the GDP figures as resulting from our data base with those from EUROSTAT statistics.

Table 2. Comparison of GDP figures (mill. ECU, 1981)

Country	Data base	EUROSTAT[a]
F	521.2	514.3
B-L	86.7	88.5
NL	141.9	126.3
D	609.2	614.2
I	368.7	370.5
UK-IRL	474.1	474.7
DK	51.6	52.3
ROW	7307.2	

[a] EUROSTAT (1983, p. 39)

Finally, we employed the RAS (row-and-column adjustment) algorithm[76] to ensure the consistency requirements of input-output tables.

3.2.3. Government Revenues and Expenditures

On the revenue side of the government budget, our model features tariffs, taxes on production, value-added taxes, and income taxes.[77] Government expenditures include outlays on public goods (non-market services) and on transfer payments to households.

The origin of our data on production taxes less subsidies, as well as on tariff payments by industries was described in the last section. Tariff payments on trade in direct consumption between the EU and

and for Belgium those from 1975.

[76] See Bacharach (1970) for details.

[77] Taxes on the use of capital services in production are neglected but could easily be incorporated.

Table 3. Tax rates in the benchmark equilibrium

Countries →		F		B-L		NL	
Industries ↓	EU tariffs	VAT	Prod. taxes	VAT	Prod. taxes	VAT	Prod. taxes
1 Agriculture, forestry	2.0	7.0	1.5	6.0	−3.3	4.0	1.0
2 Energy, water, mining	2.0	17.6	3.0	16.0	5.3	18.0	3.5
3 Chemicals	7.0	17.6	6.6	16.0	−1.3	18.0	−0.2
4 Metal products	5.0	17.6	15.0	16.0	−0.7	18.0	−0.3
5 Electrical products	5.0	17.6	10.1	16.0	−0.8	18.0	−0.5
6 Machinery	6.0	17.6	10.3	16.0	−0.6	18.0	−0.6
7 Office equipment and computers	8.0	17.3	12.9	16.0	−0.8	18.0	−0.8
8 Cars	6.0	33.3	11.7	25.0	−0.8	18.0	0.0
9 Other motor vehicles	6.0	17.6	2.8	16.0	−2.4	18.0	−3.7
10 Food and drink	4.0	7.0	14.9	6.0	5.5	4.0	−0.8
11 Textiles and leather	9.0	17.6	10.3	16.0	−1.0	18.0	−1.1
12 Other goods	4.0	17.6	9.8	16.0	−0.8	18.0	−0.3
13 Market services	-	8.6	10.7	7.14	−1.3	7.3	0.2
14 Non−market (public) services	-	0.0	-	0.0	-	0.0	-
Income tax rates marginal/average		24.4	6.4	40.5	15.8	32.0	11.8

Sources: VAT rates for EU countries were taken from Ministry of Finan (1981); tax rates on market services are average values; VAT rat for ROW are arbitrary. Production tax rates were computed fro values given by EUROSTAT (1986); negative values indicate sub dies.

Marginal income tax rates were computed as a weighted avera for single earners and married couples with two children from T ble 4 in McKee et al. (1986, p. 67). Average income tax rates we computed from data given in OECD (1989).

D		I		UK-IRL		DK		ROW		
VAT	Prod. taxes	VAT	Prod. taxes	VAT	Prod. taxes	VAT	Prod. taxes	Tariffs	VAT	Prod. taxes
6.5	−1.2	3.5	−3.0	0.0	−3.5	22.0	−0.2	5.0	10.0	1.8
13.0	7.0	15.0	11.3	15.0	7.3	22.0	11.3	2.0	10.0	8.2
13.0	0.8	15.0	0.1	15.0	0.5	22.0	−0.9	5.0	10.0	1.8
13.0	0.7	15.0	−0.3	15.0	1.4	22.0	−0.2	4.0	10.0	2.3
13.0	0.8	15.0	−0.2	15.0	1.2	22.0	−0.1	3.0	10.0	1.6
13.0	1.5	15.0	−2.5	15.0	0.7	22.0	−0.5	5.0	10.0	1.4
13.0	0.1	15.0	−0.1	15.0	0.8	22.0	1.0	4.0	10.0	1.6
13.0	0.8	20.0	−0.1	15.0	7.1	22.0	0.0	2.0	10.0	3.7
13.0	−1.4	15.0	−3.1	15.0	−0.4	22.0	8.3	2.0	10.0	1.0
6.5	9.4	3.5	3.7	0.0	19.3	22.0	6.5	20.0	10.0	7.6
13.0	0.2	15.0	−0.4	15.0	0.3	22.0	−1.2	12.0	10.0	1.0
13.0	0.3	15.0	−0.4	15.0	1.2	22.0	−0.4	3.0	10.0	1.5
7.3	1.2	3.4	−0.6	5.8	4.3	15.4	−1.1	-	10.0	7.7
0.0	-	0.0	-	0.0	-	0.0	-	-	0.0	-
24.5	12.5	27.0	11.6	30.0	14.5	53.4	29	33.9		22.6

ROW are calculated similarly by multiplying tariff rates and direct consumption imports from ROW or the EU.

VAT rates were taken from the German Ministry of Finance (1981) supplemented by additional information from the OECD (1988). For simplicity we assumed a uniform VAT rate of 10 per cent in ROW, which is somewhat close to the average consumption tax rates in the US and Japan. As for market services, we calculated a weighted average tax rate, the weights depending on the share of zero-rated (or tax-exempt) industries in the service sector. Our model includes a linear income tax featuring a constant marginal tax rate and an allowance. Marginal income tax rates τ_y were calculated as a weighted average of the figures for singles and married couples with two children, reported in McKee et al. (1986, p. 67). Taking total income tax revenues from OECD revenue statistics (1989), the allowances were determined endogenously as $A\ell\ell = wL + rK - Ty/\tau_y$. For ROW we have chosen a somewhat different procedure. Here we simply assumed the marginal tax rate to be 1.5 times the average rate. Table 3 summarizes the assumed tariff and tax rates in the benchmark equilibrium. Table 4 presents some key figures on tax revenues in our data base and in OECD statistics.

Table 4. Key revenue figures: tax revenues in % of GDP

	Total revenue		VAT revenue	
Country	Data base	OECD[a]	Data base	OECD[a]
F	29.2	24.0	9.6	8.8
B-L	24.6	30.0	9.2	8.0
NL	19.8	27.0	8.4	7.1
D	23.1	24.0	7.3	6.3
I	17.8	19.0	6.2	4.7
UK-IRL	26.6	30.0	6.1	4.6
DK	44.4	44.0	14.0	10.3
ROW	36.5	-	7.6	-

[a] OECD (1989, p. 84)
[b] OECD (1989, p. 96)

Turning to the expenditure side of the government budget, outlays on public good supply were obtained from the input-output tables. Transfer payments from the government to the household sector were then determined so that the government budget balanced.

3.3. Some Final Remarks

Even if our data set performs quite well with respect to key aggregates such as GDP or tax revenues, there are a number of deficiencies which should not be left unmentioned.

The most obvious shortcoming is the neglect of investment as a demand category. As a consequence, private consumption expenditures and VAT revenues are exaggerated in our benchmark data set. Furthermore, our data on direct consumption imports were "guesstimated" due to the lack of reliable data. This is particularly unfortunate because some of our numerical results presented in Chapter V depend heavily on these trade flows. We perform some sensitivity analysis to get a feeling for how our quantitative results vary with these data. As a final point, one might argue that a data base for 1981 is not really appropriate for investigating tax reform proposals in the 1990s.

We are aware of these restrictions, which mean that the empirical base of our simulation model is rather weak. Consequently, the computed numbers should not be taken too seriously. The broad policy lessons which emerge from our exercises are more important. Our simulations will show which data are crucial for the welfare effects of indirect taxes in open economies. We feel quite confident that we, and hopefully the reader, too, can assess even without any further general equilibrium computations how welfare results will change if better and more recent data were available. In our concluding chapter we will return to these remarks.

4. Model Calibration

We now have a theoretical model for the analysis of taxation problems, and an empirical data base. For given values of parameters and exogenous variables the theoretical model can be solved numerically. If the equilibrium allocation is unique, this numerical solution should exactly reproduce the benchmark data set. With some reservation, one could then claim that the theoretical model "explains" the observed reality. In order to match the benchmark equilibrium's data set, the theoretical model is calibrated to the base year's observation. The observed data set is used for the determination of parameter values which are consistent with that observation. The benchmark data set alone, however, is usually not sufficient to uniquely determine all parameter values of the model. This under-identification problem is solved by extraneously specifying a sufficient number of parameters. The common practice is to adopt as many price, income or other elasticities from the econometric literature as necessary to uniquely determine the remaining parameters with the benchmark data and model equations.

Calibration procedures have caused some degree of discomfort, especially among econometricians. We will not elaborate on the details here, but refer the reader to the articles by Mansur and Whalley, Lau, and Jorgenson in Scarf and Shoven (1984). In the following, we will first describe our choice of exogenous parameters values and then turn to the endogenous determination of parameter values.

4.1. Specification of Exogenous Parameter Values

The calibration of the free parameters requires the a priori specification of a sufficient number of parameters. On the production side of the economy, we extraneously specify the substitution elasticities between capital and labor (σ_i) and between imported and domestic intermediates for every industry and every import commodity (ω_{ji}). For the former we took the sector-specific values provided by Whalley (1985, p. 100) and applied them to every country. In order to compute sector- and country-specific elasticities of substitution between the imported and the domestic product, we used the procedure described by Harrison, Rutherford and Wooton (1991, p. 100).

Starting with their sectoral elasticities η_i we first computed a (imported weighted) country specific elasticity

$$\rho = \sum_{i \in N} a_i \eta_i,$$

where a_i is the share of sector i's imports in the total imports of country h. The sector specific elasticities of substitution in country h are then derived by

$$\omega_{ij} = \eta_i \frac{\psi}{\rho},$$

where ψ is the (extraneously specified) aggregate import elasticity in country h. Therefore, we did not distinguish between different import elasticities within a specific sector.

On the household side we fixed the uncompensated elasticity of labor supply with respect to the wage rate (e), the price elasticities of import demand (ε_i), and the substitution elasticities between composite demand categories (ν_c) as well as between imports of commodity i from different source countries (ν_i^M). As in Ballard, Fullerton et al. (1985, p. 135), the uncompensated labor supply elasticity was assumed to be 0.15 in every country. In addition, we assumed that the representative consumer in the benchmark equilibrium supplies 40 hours out of a possible 70 hour week. The ratio of labor time to total time endowment is therefore given by $E/L = 1.75$. We restrain from questioning the 70-hour assumption; a discussion of the economics of sleeping and related activities is beyond the scope of our book.[78] Price elasticities of imports can be transformed into substitution elasticities ν_i between domestic and comparable foreign commodities (see equation 66 below). Starting with the import price elasticities as given in Stern, Francis and Schumacher (1976, p. 20), we computed substitution elasticities ranging between 1.2 and 1.7. For simplicity we have chosen a "central case" value of 1.5. The other two substitution elasticities were chosen more or less arbitrarily.

The general idea is that in an Armington demand system the elasticity of substitution increases with the decision level as described in our Figure 2 above. The price sensitivity when choosing between cars and food is probably less than the price sensitivity when choosing between imported and domestic cars. Therefore, we employed the elasticity of substitution $\nu_c = 1.1$ for the first level and $\nu_i^M = 2.0$ on the lowest level. Table 5 summarizes our choice of exogenous parameter values. We will refer to it as our "central case" parameter set.

4.2. Calibration

Having extraneously specified the above parameter values we can now use our benchmark data base to solve for the remaining parameter values. This requires one additional assumption. All data are given in value terms, i.e. they are products of prices and quantities. General equilibrium theory, on the other hand, requires the separation of prices and quantities. The by now common procedure is to adopt appropriate unit conventions on quantities, allowing one to translate data in value terms into information on physical quantities. The most convenient assumption is to choose physical factor quantities such as to earn 1 ECU net of all taxes and subsidies in the benchmark equilibrium. Similarly, quantities of commodities are implicitely defined by assuming prices of goods net of indirect taxes and tariffs to be 1 ECU in

[78] The reader is referred to the interchange between Bergstrom (1976) and Hoffman (1977).

Table 5. Exogenous parameter values ("central case")

Production sector:

Country-specific elasticity of substitution between imported and domestic intermediates[a] (ψ^h)

F	1.05	D	1.70	DK	0.88
B-L	1.24	I	1.16	ROW	1.41
N	0.68	UK-IRL	0.53		

Sector	Sector-specific elasticities of substitution between imported and domestic intermediates[b] (η_i)	Elasticity of substitution between capital and labor[c] (σ_i)
Agriculture	2.0	0.6
Energy, water	2.0	0.8
Chemicals	2.0	0.8
Metal products	0.5	0.8
Electric prod.	1.3	0.75
Machinery	0.5	0.6
Office equipment	2.0	0.9
Cars	5.0	0.8
Other motor veh.	0.5	0.8
Food and drink	1.5	0.8
Textiles, leather	2.0	0.9
Other man. goods	2.0	0.9
Market services	2.0	0.95
Non-market serv.	2.0	0.95

Household sector:

Uncompensated elasticity of labor supply (e)[d]	0.15	Ratio of total time endowment/working time[d]	1.75

Elasticities of substitution between ...

imports from different source countries (ν_i^M)	home goods and composite imported goods (ν_i)	different consumption categories (ν_c)
2.0	1.5	1.1

[a] Harrison, Rutherford, Wooton (1991, p. 100)
[b] Harrison, Rutherford, Wooton (1991, p. 101)
[c] Whalley (1985, p. 100)
[d] Ballard, Fullerton, Shoven, Whalley (1985, p. 135)

the base year. Hence, the vector of factor and producer prices in the benchmark equilibrium consists only of 1's. After these preliminary remarks we can now turn to the calibration of the free parameters.

4.2.1. Calibration in the Production Sector

Let us first consider the primary input side of the production tree in Figure 2. With the substitution elasticities σ_i being given, the remaining parameters to be determined by calibration are the share parameters δ_i and the scale parameters ϕ_i. The former are obtained by simply rearranging the marginal condition of each producer's cost minimization problem to yield

$$\delta_i = \frac{wL_i^{\frac{1}{\sigma_i}}}{wL_i^{\frac{1}{\sigma_i}} + rK_i^{\frac{1}{\sigma_i}}}. \tag{58}$$

The latter then follows from rearranging the CES value added function (2)

$$\phi_i = \frac{f_i}{[\delta_i L_i^{\varrho_i} + (1-\delta_i)K_i^{\varrho_i}]^{\frac{1}{\varrho_i}}}, \tag{59}$$

with
$$f_i = wL_i + rK_i + T_{Q_i} + TAR_i^Q.$$

The next step is to calibrate the share parameters κ_{ji}^k and the scale parameters ζ_{ji} entering the demand functions for imported inputs. Here no exogenous specification of parameters is necessary because we have assumed a Cobb-Douglas function on the lowest level of the production tree. The share parameters are then given by

$$\kappa_{ji}^k = \frac{q_j^k(1+t_j^{\cdot k})V_{ji}^{k\cdot}}{V_{ji}^M} \tag{60}$$

with
$$V_{ji}^M = \sum_{k\in W_h} q_j^k(1+t_j^{\cdot k})V_{ji}^{k\cdot}.$$

Rearranging the intermediate demand function (14) gives us the scale parameters

$$\zeta_{ji} = \frac{V_{ji}^M}{\prod_{k\in W_h}(V_{ji}^{k\cdot})^{\kappa_{ji}^k}}. \tag{61}$$

Turning to the parameters for domestic and composite intermediate inputs in the demand functions, the free parameters to be determined are the λ_{ji}'s and the ξ_{ji}'s. Having specified a CES technology for this part of the production tree and with the substitution elasticities ω_{ji}, the share parameters λ_{ji} are derived by

$$\lambda_{ji} = \frac{q_{ji}^M (V_{ji}^M)^{\frac{1}{\omega_{ji}}}}{q_{ji}(V_{ji})^{\frac{1}{\omega_{ji}}} + q_{ji}^M (V_{ji}^M)^{\frac{1}{\omega_{ji}}}}. \tag{62}$$

The scale parameter ξ_{ji} can now readily be computed as

$$\xi_{ji} = \frac{V_{ji}^H}{\left[\lambda_{ji}(V_{ji}^M)^{\theta_{ji}} + (1-\lambda_{ji})(V_{ji})^{\theta_{ji}}\right]^{\frac{1}{\theta_{ji}}}} \tag{63}$$

with

$$V_{ji}^H = q_j V_{ji} + q_j^M V_{ji}^M .$$

What remains are the fixed coefficients on the first level of the production tree. These are obtained by the equations

$$a_{ji} = \frac{\sum_{k \in W} V_{ji}^{k\cdot}}{Q_i} \quad \text{and} \quad a_{0i} = \frac{f_i}{Q_i}. \tag{64}$$

4.2.2. Calibration in the Household Sector

Once again we start with the lowest level of the utility tree (Figure 4). The exogenous parameters are the substitution elasticities ν_i^M. Solving equation (40) for β_i^k and combining it with (39) and (41) yields

$$\beta_i^k = \frac{(p_i^{k\cdot})^{\nu_i^M} C_i^{k\cdot}}{\sum_{k \in W_h} (p_i^{k\cdot})^{\nu_i^M} C_i^{k\cdot}}, \tag{65}$$

where $C_i^{k\cdot}$ comes directly from the data set and consumer prices can easily be calculated for given tax and tariff rates, provided our unit convention $q_i^k = 1$ ECU holds.

Proceeding to the demand functions for composite imports and domestic commodities, the CES function on the third level of the utility tree involves the composite input commodity C_i^M. Its value is not contained in the data set, but, given the β_i^k on the fourth level, can be computed according to equation (38).

The price index p_i^M of the composite imported commodity is calculated from consumer prices on the fourth level as described above in equation (20). A key parameter of the CES function is the elasticity of substitution between imported and domestic commodities, ν_i. If this value is known, the share parameters β_i^h can be derived. The literature, however, provides hardly any estimates of such elasticities of substitution. We therefore have to rely on the price elasticity of import demand

$$\varepsilon_i \equiv \frac{\partial C_i^M}{\partial p_i^M} \frac{p_i^M}{C_i^M},$$

for which information is available in empirical trade literature. Performing some manipulations involving equations (34) and (38) we can derive the following formula for ν_i [79]

$$\nu_i = \frac{\varepsilon_i \cdot Y_i^H + p_i^M C_i^M}{p_i^M C_i^M - Y_i^H}, \tag{66}$$

where p_i^M and C_i^M are calculated according to (20) and (38) and Y_i^h is given by (34). Given the elasticity of substitution ν_i, we obtain

$$\beta_i^H = \frac{(p_i)^{\nu_i} C_i}{(p_i)^{\nu_i} C_i + (p_i^M)^{\nu_i} C_i^M}. \tag{67}$$

On the second level of the utility tree, parameters β_i have to be calibrated. This again involves several values which are not directly contained in our data base, but can be computed given the parameters on the next lower level. Hence, we first evaluate composite commodities C_i^H according to (33), price indices p_i^H according to (21), and disposable income of this stage according to (30). Because the elasticity of substitution between different consumption categories is specified exogenously, the share parameter of the CES function is given by

$$\beta_i = \frac{(p_i^H)^{\nu_c} C_i^H}{\sum_{i \in N} (p_i^H)^{\nu_c} C_i^H}. \tag{68}$$

As a final step, utility parameters on the first level of the decision process have to be calibrated. We first show how to compute the substitution elasticity ν between composite consumption and leisure from

[79] For simplicity we have specified ν_i exogenously in Table 5.

the extraneously specified uncompensated elasticity of labor supply (e) and the assumed ratio of total time endowment to working time (E/L).

Firstly, translate the uncompensated labor supply elasticity e into the corresponding elasticity of leisure demand $\hat{e}$. This is done by combining the definitions

$$e \equiv \frac{\partial L}{\partial w_n} \frac{w_n}{L} \quad \text{and} \quad \hat{e} \equiv \frac{\partial \ell}{\partial w_n} \frac{w_n}{\ell}, \quad \text{where} \quad w_n = w(1 - \tau_y).$$

Expanding $\hat{e}$, we get

$$\begin{aligned} \hat{e} &= \frac{\partial (E - L)}{\partial w_n} \frac{w_n}{(E - L)} \\ &= -\frac{\partial L}{\partial w_n} \frac{w_n}{E - L}, \qquad \text{since} \quad \partial E / \partial w_n = 0. \end{aligned}$$

We have assumed E/L has a value of 1.75. After some manipulation we obtain

$$\hat{e} = -e \quad \frac{1}{1.75 - 1}.$$

We can now determine the elasticity parameter ν. This is done by evaluating $\partial \ell / \partial w_n$ from (27)

$$\frac{\partial \ell}{\partial w_n} = \frac{\beta E}{w_n^{\nu} \Omega} - \frac{(1 - \nu)\beta^2 Y}{(w_n^{\nu} \Omega)^2} - \frac{\nu \beta w_n^{-\nu - 1} Y}{\Omega},$$

where Ω is given by (28).
Substituting into the definition of $\hat{e}$, one obtains

$$\hat{e} = \frac{w_n E}{Y} - \frac{(1 - \nu)\beta w_n^{1-\nu}}{\Omega} - \nu.$$

Defining the share of leisure 'expenditure' to full disposable income by

$$s_{\ell} \equiv \frac{w_n \ell}{Y} = \frac{\beta w_n^{1-\nu}}{\Omega}$$

and defining

$$s_e \equiv \frac{w_n E}{Y}$$

as the ratio of time endowment value and full disposable income, we can finally solve for the elasticity of substitution:

$$\nu = \frac{s_e - s_{\ell} - \hat{e}}{1 - s_{\ell}}. \tag{69}$$

The share parameter β is then given by

$$\beta = \frac{(w_n)^{\nu}\ell}{p^{\nu}C + (w_n)^{\nu}\ell}. \tag{70}$$

This completes the calibration of utility parameters.

By performing sensitivity analysis around our central case parameter specification we will gain some insights into the importance of key parameters for our welfare results.

We shall close this chapter with a final remark on the shortcomings of calibration procedures. To the econometrician, parameter determination by calibration is unacceptable for at least three reasons. There is no statistical test of the model specification, there is a serious under-identification problem, and there is a lack of "flexibility" in the assumed functional forms of utility and production functions. The econometric approach to CGE, described for example by Jorgenson (1984), seems to be superior to calibration, but is a very difficult and time-consuming undertaking. In the meantime, some policy advice is required, and calibration is a convenient procedure for a quick answer. As Lawrence Lau (1984, p. 136) says: "It is useful shortcut for a modeler in a hurry".

Chapter V

Simulation Results and Economic Interpretations

This chapter contains our simulation results and explains them in economic terms. Starting with the data set for 1981, we used the fully specified CGE model from Chapter IV to compute a number of hypothetical ("counterfactual") equilibria corresponding to different VAT reform options. Using summary statistics, the results are then compared with the original pre-change ("benchmark") equilibrium. We then try to explain the numerical results in economic terms.

A short section on methodological issues preceeds the presentation and interpretation of our simulation results. One section is devoted to each of the following VAT reform options: the transitional system, the origin principle with the credit method, and the origin principle with the subtraction method. In these sections, results are based on our "central case" parameter specifications. Some sensitivity analysis is performed in the final section of this chapter.

1. Some Methodological Issues

1.1. Reliability of CGE Results

Our model is much more detailed and complicated than those used in most other studies on VAT reform issues. The advantage of this is that we can accurately model some relevant institutional features of actual VAT systems or reform proposals – without, of course, being able to capture all the intricacies of VAT as it works in practice. An unavoidable consequence, however, of a more "realistic" modelling is that CGE models increasingly become impenetrable "black boxes" to outside observers. Even if all the model equations, the parameter specifications, and data sources are honestly reported (as we did in Chapter IV), it usually is neither possible nor rewarding for other researchers to verify the accuracy of the numerical results. Besides possibly expressing one's admiration for the presumed competence and technical skills of the respective authors, all the general reader can do is to deliver summary grunts of belief or disbelief – depending on whether or not the simulation results accord with the reader's own intuition. Obviously, this is not a solid foundation for good economics.

In fact, this is a more general problem, concerning computational studies not only in the CGE field, but likewise in optimal tax calculations or econometric work. There are plenty of examples in the economics literature that suggest a sound scepticism when faced with the alternative of whether or not to accept the results from computational studies. Here, we only refer to "The Journal of Money, Credit and Banking Project" conducted by Dewald, Thursby and Anderson (1986). These authors requested the data, the algorithms, and all other ingredients necessary to replicate a number of empirical articles published in that journal. All in all, their results were rather devastating. Some authors had lost or discarded the original data so that replication was impossible on a priori grounds. Where replication was possible, the findings of Dewald et al. suggest "that inadvertent errors in published empirical articles are a commonplace rather than a rare occurance" (p. 587 f.). Though correcting the errors did not affect most *qualitative* conclusions, there seem to be enough reasons to distrust the precise numbers.

There are no easy ways out of this dilemma. In our view the best way to gain some confidence in the validity of the numerical results of CGE models is to check them against our economic knowledge and intuition.[80] These models have a very clear theoretical underpinning. Therefore, with some effort, it should be possible in each case to grasp and explain computational results in an intuitive manner. Economic intuition, of course, is best developed for simple model structures. However, with suitable assumptions, complex general equilibrium problems can usually be reduced to special cases where results are either unambiguously known from the literature or can be intuitively understood. A few simulation runs will reveal whether the expected results are generated by the computer. This is a convenient way for the model-builders themselves to become familiar with the economic mechanisms inherent in their models.

In our context, for example, we drastically simplified our theoretical model by assuming – together or in isolation – fixed intermediate input coefficients, international immobility of capital, trade in all goods, constant labor supply, no tax distortions in the benchmark equilibrium, and so on. The introduction of a uniform VAT under the destination principle should then leave all real variables unaffected if tax revenue is returned to consumers in a lump-sum manner. The introduction of a not too large tariff should clearly improve this country's terms of trade and its welfare. Furthermore, a change from the destination to the origin principle while retaining the credit method should guarantee physical trade neutrality if uniform tax rates prevail, and Paretian trade neutrality should hold if tax structures $(1+\tau_j)/(1+\tau_i)$ coincide in the countries concerned. If net tax exports were neutralized by installing an international redistribution mechanism, even physical trade neutrality could be restored in the latter case. Our numerical model reproduced all the results we expected. This equipped us with a high degree of confidence that our policy simulations in more sophisticated environments would produce the correct results as well. By presenting detailed economic explanations we will also try to convince the sceptical reader that our numerical results are indeed reliable.

---

[80] We assume that the replication check has successfully been passed. This is a very first and purely formal test as to the accuracy of the computer code and the consistency of the equilibrium model.

1.2. Measuring Welfare Changes from Tax Reforms

In conducting policy experiments with our CGE model, the general procedure is as follows. Starting with our 1981 data set, which is interpreted as the result of an equilibrium allocation (benchmark equilibrium), we consider a VAT policy change and compute the alternative equilibrium associated with a specific VAT reform proposal (counterfactual equilibrium). Evaluation of different reform proposals then proceeds on the basis of comparisons between the counterfactual and the benchmark equilibrium. Even if, at least in principle, all adjustments in prices and quantities following a tax change could be reproduced, this would be a boring and hardly illuminating activity. After all, our model features 105 consumption goods in each country and our interregional input-output table is of dimension 112 × 112. It is therefore necessary to use some summary statistics when comparing different equilibria.

Our main focus is on the comparison of welfare levels in different states of the economy. In the literature there has been an extensive debate about the accuracy of different welfare measures.[81] Here we use the Hicksian equivalent variation (HEV), which is now widely accepted as a monetary welfare measure. The equivalent variation is defined as the amount of money that must be given to or taken from a consumer in order to make him as well off as he would have been after a change in prices. A positive HEV indicates a welfare improvement, a negative one a welfare loss. More formally, the HEV is defined as

$$HEV = E(p_0, w_0, V(p_1, w_1, Y_1)) - E(p_0, w_0, V(p_0, w_0, Y_0)).$$

Here, lower indices 0 and 1 indicate variables in the benchmark and counterfactual equilibrium, respectively, $E(\cdot)$ is the expenditure function and $V(\cdot)$ the indirect utility function,[82] depending on the price vector of consumption goods p, the wage rate w and net maximal income Y. If direct utility functions are homogeneous, the equivalent variation can be written as

$$HEV = \frac{U_1 - U_0}{U_0} Y_0.$$

[81] Textbook expositions may be found in McKenzie (1983), Boadway and Bruce (1984), Johansson (1987) and Ahlheim and Rose (1989).

[82] More precisely, $E(p, w, V(p, w))$ is the indirect compensation function and $E(p, w, U)$ the expenditure function, where $V(p, w, Y) = \max U(C, \ell)$.

This can easily be shown for the specific functional forms as chosen in Chapter IV. Inserting the composite consumption demand and the leisure demand functions (IV-26), (IV-27) together with (IV-28) into the direct utility function (IV-23), one obtains the indirect utility function

$$V(p,w,Y) = \left[(1-\beta)p^{1-\nu} + \beta w^{1-\nu}\right]^{\frac{1}{\nu-1}} Y$$

and the expenditure function

$$E(p,w,U) = \underbrace{\left[(1-\beta)p^{1-\nu} + \beta w^{1-\nu}\right]^{\frac{1}{1-\nu}}}_{=\Omega} U.$$

We therefore have

$$\begin{aligned} HEV &= \Omega_0^{\frac{1}{1-\nu}}(U_1 - U_0) \\ &= \frac{U_1 - U_0}{U_0} Y_0, \end{aligned}$$

where the second equality follows from the indirect utility function.

The equivalent variation is a reliable welfare indicator when applied to single-consumer economies, and the results presented in the next sections clearly show which countries experience welfare losses or gains as a consequence of a VAT reform program. Additionally, it is interesting to know whether the EU as a whole would gain or lose. In the former case, the gainers from the change could compensate the losers, either hypothetically or in reality, out of a EU-wide redistribution funds. In CGE models and applied welfare economics it is common practice to measure aggregate welfare by simply summing the HEVs across all countries. The problem with this procedure is that the aggregate equivalent variation may not correctly indicate whether a welfare improvement in terms of the Pareto criterion has taken place, i.e. whether the gainers were able to compensate the losers. This apparent paradox has been noted by Boadway (1974) and is more fully discussed by Ebert (1985). As is often the case, theoretical paradoxes are of little empirical relevance. In our context this paradox did not occur. We checked this by running the following simulation experiments. Starting from the counterfactual equilibrium we redistributed income between the gainers and losers of a VAT reform such that all but one EU member state realized their welfare levels from the benchmark equilibrium. The remaining country realized either a welfare gain or loss after redistribution, depending on whether the aggregate equivalent variation was positive or negative. Hence, at least in our context, a positive value of aggregate HEV is a solid indicator for a Pareto improvement.

Evaluating policy reform proposals by comparing welfare levels in different states of the economy is commonplace for the applied welfare economist. This is in marked contrast to discussions in the policy arena, where welfare changes hardly play a role and the equivalent variation is a completely unknown measurement concept. From the exchequer's point of view, only changes in VAT revenue are important, whereas they are less important to the welfare economist. In the following sections, we concentrate on explaining the computed welfare changes, but for the sake of completeness we also present and comment on VAT revenue changes.

We conclude these preliminary remarks with a warning. The tables presented on the following pages contain a large number of seemingly precise numbers. In view of some legitimate reservations against our choice of functional forms, parameter values, and some aspects of our data base, the precise numerical results should not be overemphasized. More important are the broad policy lessons that emerge from the interpretation, and, above all, the valuable insights one gains into the forces underlying the results.

2. The Transitional System

In this section we present our simulation results for the welfare and revenue effects of the transitional VAT system which has been effective since January 1, 1993. The institutional details have been laid out in Chapter II. There, we modelled different variants of the transitional system. In our opinion, what we referred to as the switching option is the most likely variant to occur. Under the switching option, consumers in EU countries will make use of the most favorable tax option. Consumers in high-tax countries will settle their direct consumption purchases according to the origin principle, whereas consumers in low-tax countries will stick to the destination principle. The welfare results are presented in the next subsection. This is contrasted with the so-called mixed system, where all trade in direct consumption is taxed according to the origin principle. This variant assumes that the special provisions with regard to distance selling, car sales and so forth are not enforceable at all. There is, of course, a third possibility. If all special provisions could be made effective, the transitional system will not deviate (by much) from the allocation under the destination principle.

2.1. The Switching Option[83]

Table 1 contains the quantitative effects when switching from the destination principle, as it was in effect until 1993, to the present transitional system, where the switching option is effective. The first column represents the HEV values for each country in millions of ECU, the second shows monetary welfare changes as a percentage rate of national VAT revenues in the benchmark equilibrium. Columns (3) and (4) represent VAT revenue changes in per cent. Here, the third column gives general equilibrium (g.e.) revenue changes, whereas the fourth contains so-called first round (f.r.) changes. (These will be explained shortly.) Note that for ROW we only present absolute HEV values and do not go into further details. This is for two reasons. The first is that numbers for ROW are very small and more or less meaningless. Secondly, data for ROW are rather artifical and unreliable; the modelling of ROW merely serves as some kind of consistent closing-rule.

The welfare effects as measured by the HEV will be explained in more detail below. Here we will briefly comment on VAT revenue changes. Even if they are only of limited (or no) interest from an efficiency point of view, they are the primary concern of national exchequers.

National VAT revenues under the DP on the one hand, and under the transitional system on the other, are given by equations (II-4) and (II-8), where prices and quantities are evaluated in the benchmark and the counterfactual equilibrium, respectively. The numbers in the third column were then computed by expressing the revenue difference in percentage form. In contrast, first round revenue changes in the fourth column were calculated by evaluating VAT revenue under the transitional system with the benchmark equilibrium's prices and

[83] This subsection heavily relies on Fehr, Rosenberg and Wiegard (1993). Whereas the numerical results differ due to revised estimates of cross-border direct consumption sales, the economic explanations remain the same.

Table 1. Welfare and revenue effects of the transitional system

	HEV		VAT revenue in %	
	in mill. ECU	in % of VAT	g.e.	f.r.
Country	(1)	(2)	(3)	(4)
F	−1141	−2.23	−2.65	−2.57
B-L	145	1.81	1.66	1.08
NL	−610	−5.24	−7.10	−6.54
D	810	1.85	2.40	1.60
I	259	1.13	1.66	1.04
UK-IRL	554	1.91	2.30	1.48
DK	−149	−2.06	−3.14	−2.64
EU	−132			
ROW	5			
$\sum$	−127			

quantities. The first round tax revenue difference is then given by[84]

$$\underbrace{\sum_{k\in EU_h^H}\sum_{i\in N_*}\tau_i q_i C_i^{\cdot k}}_{\text{VAT revenue gain}} - \underbrace{\sum_{k\in EU_h^L}\sum_{i\in N_*}\tau_i q_i^k C_i^{k\cdot}}_{\text{VAT revenue loss}}\,. \tag{1a}$$

Remember that under the transitional system country h's direct consumption deliveries to high-tax EU member states as well as its direct consumption purchases from low-tax trading partners within the EU are taxed according to the origin principle. The first constitutes a VAT revenue gain, the second a revenue loss due to foregone import VAT accruing to country h under the destination principle. It should be clear that low-tax countries within the EU are the revenue gainers from the transitional system and high-tax member states are the losers. In 1981, the latter were France, the Netherlands and Denmark. This is confirmed by the numbers given in column (4) of Table 1. Whether or not one considers first round revenue calculations (column 4) as reasonable approximations for general equilibrium VAT revenue changes (column 3) is a matter of personal opinion. In any case, first round

[84] Strictly speaking, EU_h^H and EU_h^L should include the commodity index i, because a country may be a high tax country for one commodity and a low tax country for another commodity. In our simulations we have taken this into account.

revenue calculations, neglecting any price or quantity reactions, give reasonable lower bounds to "true" revenue changes. A comparison of column (2) with columns (3) or (4) shows that HEV and VAT revenue changes do not differ too much and in all cases have the same sign. This might suggest some causality, which, however, would be grossly misleading. Changes in national VAT revenues and HEV values have the same causality as stork's nests and birthrates.

HEV values have to be explained not by national revenue changes but with recourse to net tax export effects on the one hand, and substitution effects on the other. This is done in Table 2. The first column reproduces the percentage form of the HEV values from Table 1. The next two columns represent net tax exports, calculated in a general equilibrium framework in column (2) and as first round effects in column (3). Column (4) contains aggregate, i.e. domestic and international substitution effects. The next column gives the total terms of trade effects (in per cent) associated with the switch to the transitional system, whereas the final column contains the terms of trade changes which are solely attributable to the international substitution effect.

Table 2. Decomposing welfare effects of the transitional system[a]

Country	HEV (1)	Net tax exports g.e. (2)	f.r. (3)	Subst. effect (4)	Terms of trade (in %) Total (5)	Int'l (6)
F	−2.23	−2.03	−1.95	−0.17	−0.80	−0.04
B-L	1.81	1.91	1.95	−0.06	0.36	−0.01
NL	−5.24	−5.19	−5.05	−0.19	−1.08	−0.05
D	1.85	2.02	1.90	0.08	0.54	0.02
I	1.13	1.23	1.19	0.04	0.41	0.01
UK-IRL	1.91	1.56	1.52	0.39	0.56	0.06
DK	−2.06	−1.71	−1.56	−0.30	−0.78	−0.11

[a] The values in columns (1)-(4) are in per cent of the benchmark equilibrium's VAT revenues.

First of all, note that, on average, around ninety per cent of total welfare changes are due to net tax exports. This is surprisingly high even if one expects net tax export effects to dominate substitution effects. Secondly, as far as HEV values and net tax exports are concerned, we now indeed have a causal relationship. Because VAT revenue and net tax export changes do not greatly differ, welfare changes and revenue changes roughly coincide as well.

Net tax exports for country h are given by the difference

$$\sum_{k\in EU_h^H}\sum_{i\in N_*}\tau_i q_i C_i^{\cdot k} - \sum_{k\in EU_h^L}\sum_{i\in N_*}\tau_i^k q_i^k C_i^{k\cdot}. \tag{2a}$$

When computing general equilibrium effects in column (2), both terms have to be evaluated in the counterfactual equilibrium. First order effects in column (3) are obtained if prices and quantities are taken from the benchmark equilibrium.

Note that when comparing first round VAT revenue changes – column (4) in Table 1 – with first round net tax exports – column (3) in Table 2 –, the latter exceeds the former, with the difference given by

$$\sum_{k\in EU_h^L}\sum_{i\in N_*}(\tau_i^h - \tau_i^k)q_i^k C_i^{kh} > 0.$$

A second point to note is that, in the case of net tax exports, first round effects are much better approximations for general equilibrium values. This is because first round and general equilibrium net tax exports only differ in so far as they have to be evaluated in different equilibria, but direct consumption exports and imports valued at producer prices do not change too much between the benchmark and the counterfactual equilibrium. On the other hand, first round VAT revenue changes as given by expression (1a) are only part of general equilibrium revenue changes, as determined by equations (II-4) and (II-8). As a final remark, remember that whereas net tax exports are quite considerable for a single country, they cancel out for the EU as a whole. EU-wide welfare gains of 132 million ECU are solely due to domestic and international substitution effects. These effects are extremely small not only in the aggregate but also for single countries. Although we have not been able to isolate, either analytically or numerically, domestic from international substitution effects, there is good reason to believe that international substitution effects dominate domestic ones for the VAT reform under consideration. Let us focus on Denmark as a high-tax and on Germany as a low-tax country to explain the signs of these substitution effects.

Within the EU, Denmark applies the highest standard VAT rate. In 1981 it levied a uniform rate of 22 per cent (which was raised to 25 per cent in late 1992). Under the present transitional system, rational consumers in Denmark should try to settle all direct consumption purchases from other EU countries according to the origin principle. As a consequence, both domestic and international substitution effects contribute to a further reduction in economic welfare, in excess of welfare reducing net tax imports. The domestic substitution effect is negative because VAT rates on final consumption will be differentiated and the international substitution effect is negative because Denmark's importables carry a lower tax load than its exportables.

Germany, on the other hand, was – and still is – a low tax country with respect to the *standard* rate. Therefore, all other EU countries will apply the origin principle when importing German commodities to which the standard rate applies. The corresponding shift in demand towards German exports will change the terms of trade and economic welfare in its favor. There are, however, two countervailing effects, both depending on the fact that Germany's *reduced* rate is higher than in other EU countries. As a consequence, Germany will import the commodities concerned according to the origin principle. This will not only contribute to a deterioration in its terms of trade but will also induce a welfare-decreasing domestic substitution effect. The latter occurs because some imported products now bear a lower tax load than before, which increases the variance of tax rates. Since the reduced rate applies to only a few commodities, these countervailing effects are comparatively small. This may explain why the overall welfare effects due to the aggregate substitution effect are positive but rather modest for Germany. Note that net tax export effects on the one hand and the aggregate substitution effect on the other sum up to yield the HEV values in the first column of Table 2.

The fact that Germany and Denmark are at the lower and upper end of the tax rate range admittedly facilitates interpretation. But with some effort and intuition, the welfare effects for all other countries could be explained by analoguous reasoning.

We now come to the numbers given in the last two columns. Terms of trade effects are associated with net tax exports and with international substitution effects. The latter effects may be isolated by neutralizing any net tax exports by implementing a hypothetical EU-wide redistributional mechanism. It is important to note that the signs and orders of magnitude of the numbers in columns (4) and (6) coincide. This reassures us that the international substitution effects indeed dominate the domestic ones. The terms of trade effects due to net tax exports are obtained by taking the difference between columns (5) and (6). One realizes that not only the signs of net tax exports and total welfare changes coincide, but terms of trade effects due to net tax exports do also have the same sign. The explanation follows the same lines as our discussion of the transfer problem above. Due to international income effects, the transferor's demand will be reduced while that of the transferee will be increased. With a universal preference for domestic goods, the terms of trade will deteriorate (improve) for the country suffering a welfare loss (gain).

2.2. The Mixed System

In this subsection we assume that *all* trade in direct consumption is taxed according to the origin principle. In view of the transitional system's special provisions with respect to distance selling, this is not a very realistic assumption. Nevertheless, a closer look at the mixed system may be of interest. It not only sharpens the eyes for the quantitative significance of different taxation principles applying to cross-border direct consumption purchases, but also forms a convenient link between this and the following section, in which all trade in direct consumption goods as well as in intermediate products is taxed according to the origin principle.

Table 3. Welfare and revenue effects of the mixed system

	HEV		VAT revenue in %	
	in mill. ECU	in % of VAT	g.e.	f.r.
Country	(1)	(2)	(3)	(4)
F	−494	−0.96	−1.31	−0.92
B-L	258	3.22	3.75	3.50
NL	−247	−2.13	−2.76	−2.42
D	−653	−1.49	−0.68	−1.41
I	119	0.52	1.50	0.89
UK-IRL	783	2.71	3.72	2.62
DK	111	1.53	1.98	3.23
EU	−123			
ROW	−17			
$\sum$	−140			

Table 4. Decomposing welfare effects of the mixed system[a]

	HEV	Net tax exports		Subst.	Terms of trade (in %)	
		g.e.	f.r.	effect	Total	Int'l
Country	(1)	(2)	(3)	(4)	(5)	(6)
F	−0.96	−0.33	0.17	−0.60	−0.04	−0.15
B-L	3.22	3.66	4.08	−0.28	0.75	−0.03
NL	−2.13	−1.77	−1.53	−0.36	−0.49	−0.06
D	−1.49	−2.01	−2.69	0.28	−0.72	0.11
I	0.52	0.56	0.28	0.04	0.27	0.03
UK-IRL	2.71	2.17	1.89	0.65	0.76	0.13
DK	1.53	2.96	4.55	−1.47	1.74	−0.40

[a] The values in columns (1)-(4) are in per cent of the benchmark equilibrium's VAT revenues.

Tables 3 and 4 have the same structure as the preceeding tables. As is evident from a comparison of these tables, high-tax countries Denmark, the Netherlands, and France gain in welfare and VAT revenue when comparing the mixed system to the switching option, whereas the low-tax countries Germany and Italy lose in both respects. This can be explained by considering first round VAT revenue changes and net tax exports under the mixed system and comparing them with the benchmark equilibrium. The former are given by

$$\sum_{k \in EU_h} \sum_{i \in N_s} \tau_i (q_i C_i^{\cdot k} - q_i^k C_i^{k \cdot}), \tag{1b}$$

whereas the latter correspond to

$$\sum_{k \in EU_h} \sum_{i \in N_s} (\tau_i q_i C_i^{\cdot k} - \tau_i^k q_i^k C_i^{k \cdot}). \tag{2b}$$

The signs and magnitudes of revenue changes are determined by intra-community trade balances in direct consumption deliveries as well as by the structure of VAT rate differentiation within a country. Those countries with a positive overall trade balance with respect to direct consumption deliveries will realize a revenue gain. This effect is reinforced if VAT rates are highest for those commodities of which the country in question is a large net exporter. Net tax exports on the other hand depend on trade balances and tax rate differentials between countries. Here, high-tax countries with a positive trade balance in direct consumption trade will gain.

The difference in first round effects between the mixed system and the switching option is obtained by combining equations (1a) and (1b) as well as (2a) and (2b). With respect to net tax exports this difference is given by

$$\sum_{k \in EU_h^L} \sum_{i \in N_\cdot} \tau_i q_i C_i^{\cdot k} - \sum_{k \in EU_h^H} \sum_{i \in N_\cdot} \tau_i^k q_i^k C_i^{k \cdot}.$$

For the high-tax country Denmark, the last expression disappears and the first term indicates the additional tax exports under the mixed system when compared to the switching option. For the low-tax country Germany the reasoning goes the other way round. At least with respect to the standard rate, the set EU_h^L is empty and the second term constitutes the additional tax imports. This explains the remarkable gains and losses in net tax exports for high-tax and low-tax countries respectively, when the mixed system is compared with the switching option.

Under the mixed system, first round effects seem to be a less satisfactory approximation for general equilibrium effects. For France, even the signs of the respective net tax exports differ because aggregate substitution effects are now stronger. If all deliveries to final consumers in other member states are taxed according to the origin principle, demand reactions will be stronger and substitution effects will increase. Even if the signs of aggregate substitution effects are the same under both the mixed system and the switching option of the transitional system, the absolute values are two or three times higher under the mixed system. Once again, the bulk of the aggregate substitution effect is due to the international component. Consider Denmark as an extreme example. Its international terms of trade now deteriorate for two reasons. The first, as above, is that direct consumption imports from other member states will carry those countries lower tax rates. Secondly, Denmark's direct consumption exports now bear its high VAT rate, whereas under the switching option its direct consumption exports were taxed according to the destination principle. In subsection 3.2. we will return to the explanation of these substitution effects.

Another result worth mentioning is that for Germany and Denmark the signs of the total terms of trade effects differ between the fifth columns in Tables 2 and 4. This is an immediate consequence of the fact that, for these countries, net tax exports have changed signs, too.

3. The Origin Principle and the Credit Method

As matters currently stand, the transitional system will only be in place until the end of 1996. The definitive VAT system for the EU shall become effective on New Year's Day 1997. As a "medium term objective" the EU Commission and the ECOFIN Council still support their ambitious plan that "taxation will be reserved to the country of origin" (Scrivener, 1990, p. 357). Even though it is not completely clear, "taxation in the country of origin" is understood as a situation without any border tax adjustments, where not only physical border controls but, in addition, any fiscal frontiers have been abolished within the EU. Trade with other countries will be taxed according to the destination principle. In this section we will analyze the welfare effects of this change in taxation principle under the assumption that the credit method in calculating tax liabilities is retained. In the first subsection we consider the abolition of fiscal frontiers without any supplementary measures. This reform alternative is called the common market principle (CMP). In the second subsection the common market principle is supplemented by an international redistribution mechanism in order to prevent major revenue reallocations between EU member states. We will refer to the common market principle in combination with such an international transfer system as the "clearing system".

3.1. The Common Market Principle

Even though the common market principle is not being seriously considered for implementation in the EU after 1997 – it was not even mentioned in any of the EU Commission's draft proposals – it is of interest for its own sake. The basic difference between the CMP and the mixed system, as discussed in subsection 2.2., is that not only direct consumption imports, but also trade in intermediate products, are taxed according to the origin principle, i.e. bear the exporting country's taxes. With the credit method in use, foreign VAT on imported intermediates may be deducted from gross tax liabilities. This ensures that all sales from domestic production to domestic consumers are taxed according to national VAT rates. Only direct consumer purchases from abroad bear the full tax burden of the country of production or origin. As a consequence, aggregate substitution effects should be exactly the same under the mixed system as under the common market principle. Only national VAT revenues and net tax exports or imports differ under the two tax systems. In other words: the efficiency properties of the mixed system and the common market principle are identical, but their redistributional effects differ. In Tables 5 and 6 we report welfare and revenue effects of a switch from the destination to the common market principle, and decompose welfare changes into their constituent parts.

Table 5. Welfare and revenue effects of the common market principle

	HEV		VAT revenue in %	
	in mill. ECU	in % of VAT	g.e.	f.r.
Country	(1)	(2)	(3)	(4)
F	503	0.98	0.65	0.98
B-L	213	2.66	2.87	2.75
NL	1094	9.40	10.66	9.84
D	−568	−1.29	−0.72	−1.11
I	−670	−2.93	−3.10	−3.11
UK-IRL	−891	−3.08	−3.50	−3.47
DK	317	4.38	5.19	5.98
EU	−2			
ROW	−4			
$\sum$	−6			

Table 6. Decomposing welfare effects of the common market principle[a]

	HEV	Net tax exports		Subst.	Terms of trade (in %)	
		g.e.	f.r.	effect	Total	Int'l
Country	(1)	(2)	(3)	(4)	(5)	(6)
F	0.98	1.59	2.07	−0.60	1.00	−0.15
B-L	2.66	3.13	3.33	−0.28	1.36	−0.03
NL	9.40	10.10	10.73	−0.36	1.30	−0.06
D	−1.29	−1.78	−2.39	0.28	−1.05	0.11
I	−2.93	−3.34	−3.69	0.04	−0.35	0.03
UK-IRL	−3.08	−3.84	−4.19	0.65	−0.99	0.13
DK	4.38	5.73	7.30	−1.47	3.67	−0.40

[a] The values in columns (1)-(4) are in per cent of the benchmark equilibrium's VAT revenues.

As is clear from the fourth columns of Tables 4 and 6, aggregate substitution effects are identical. Furthermore, the terms of trade changes in the sixth columns of both tables coincide exactly. Hence, only VAT revenues and net tax exports have to be explained. At least with respect to first round effects, this is a simple exercise. When switching from the destination to the common market principle, VAT revenue changes and net tax exports are obtained by simply adding the expression

$$\sum_{k \in EU_k} \sum_{i \in N} \sum_{j \in N} (\tau_i q_i V_{ij}^{\cdot k} - \tau_i^k q_i^k V_{ij}^{k \cdot}) \tag{4}$$

to equations (1b) and (2b).

When compared with the mixed system, this term reflects the additional gain or loss in VAT revenue, which results from taxing intra-community trade in intermediates as well as direct consumption deliveries according to the origin principle. Note that these revenue changes simultaneously constitute net tax exports or imports. This means that both first round revenue changes and net tax exports effects under the common market principle are greater or smaller by an equal amount than under the mixed system. For France, for example, the difference between first round tax revenues and net tax exports under both taxation systems is 1.90 percentage points, whereas for Denmark the corresponding difference is 2.75 percentage points. Even if HEV values include general equilibrium repercussions, the above numbers correspond approximately to the welfare changes between the mixed system and the common market principle.

The sign and magnitude of the term in (4) depend on international tax rate differentials and the intra-community balance of trade in intermediate products. The Netherlands realizes the largest gain in net tax exports and in economic welfare because it has some of the highest standard VAT rates in the EU and, in 1981, managed to have a large surplus in its intra-community trade in intermediate products. For Germany, on the other hand, tax rate and trade balance effects are countervailing. Germany's enormous intra-community trade surplus in intermediates contributes to additional tax exports, but its imports in intermediate products bear the higher tax rates of the countries of origin. Because VAT on these imports is fully deductible in Germany, this amounts to additional tax imports. Whereas both effects work in opposite directions, the former slightly outweighs the latter. We can explain first round net tax exports for all other countries by similar reasoning.

When proceeding from first round to general equilibrium effects, price and quantity changes have to be considered. Once again the numbers do not change dramatically. It seems to be a matter of opinion whether or not first round calculations are judged to be reasonable approximations to their general equilibrium counterparts. We will offer our view on this question in the concluding chapter.

3.2. The Clearing System

The 1987 Proposal of the EU Commission

The common market principle would result in considerable revenue shifts between member states, making its implementation politically infeasible. This is precisely why the EU Commission proposed a supplementary clearing mechanism in order to ensure that ... "output tax collected on export sales to one Member State is reimbursed to other Member States in which input tax is deducted and in which final consumption takes place." (COM (87) 323 final/2). As already mentioned in Section 4 of Chapter II, there are some serious technical problems associated with the workability of the clearing mechanism. According to the Commission's original idea, all taxable firms would record all their export sales to and purchases from other member states, the first constituting liabilities, the second claims vis-à-vis some central clearing institution. As an immediate consequence, the clearing institution would run a surplus corresponding to the sum of intra-community direct consumption imports. This surplus has to be redistributed to the member states according to a formula which has not yet been decided upon. In the following calculations we assume that direct consumption imports are observable. A natural consequence is that each country can claim its portion from the clearing surplus. Following our notation in the second chapter, we therefore set

$$S^h = \sum_{k \in EU_h} \sum_{i \in N_\bullet} \tau_i^k q_i^k C_i^k.$$

The net position of a country against the clearing institution is then given by

$$\overbrace{\sum_{k \in EU_h} \Big(\sum_{i \in N} \sum_{j \in N} \tau_i^k q_i^k V_{ij}^{k\cdot} + \sum_{i \in N_\bullet} \tau_i^k q_i^k C_i^{k\cdot} \Big)}^{\text{claims}} - \underbrace{\sum_{k \in EU_h} \Big(\sum_{i \in N} \sum_{j \in N} \tau_i q_i V_{ij}^{\cdot k} + \sum_{i \in N_\bullet} \tau_i q_i C_i^{\cdot k} \Big)}_{\text{liabilities}}.$$

Note that this is a somewhat ideal clearing mechanism in that claims include direct consumption imports, which in practice cannot easily be monitored.

The net claims and liabilities against the clearing account, resulting from our calculations, are reported in the first column of Table 7. These numbers coincide exactly with the net tax exports or imports occuring under the common market principle. Net tax exports under the latter result in tax liabilities under the clearing system. Note, however, that the net position against the clearing account is given in absolute numbers in Table 7, whereas the corresponding figures in column (2) of Table 6 are presented in percentage form.

Table 7. Net positions against the clearing institution (mill. ECU)

Country	Claims (+) Liabilities (−) (1)	First round Model (2)	First round Commission (3)	COM (87) 323 final/2 (4)[a]
F	−847	−1061	2003	2421
B-L	−260	−267	53	−747
NL	−1234	−1249	−600	−1509
D	832	1049	−2013	−3534
I	790	842	233	147
UK-IRL	1149	1214	−139	1897
DK	−429	−528	463	690
$\sum$	0	0	0	646

[a] The Commission's calculations also included the member states Greece, Portugal, and Spain. The number in the last line corresponds to the aggregate claims of these countries.

In an annex to the working document concerning the introduction of a VAT clearing mechanism, the EU Commission estimated the revenue flows resulting from the operation of this mechanism. These figures are reported in the last column of Table 7 and as they are vastly different to our own calculations they require some explanation. The first point the CGE modeler notices is that the Commission performed only first round calculations and neglected price and quantity reactions. Unfortunately, this is not the crucial point. If we confine our calculations to first round effects as well, the differences remain as large as before; compare columns 2 and 4. General equilibrium computations are important but cannot explain the deviations from the Commission's calculation.

In essence, there are two reasons for the divergence of results. The first and most important point is that the Commission based its calculations on the assumption of a standard VAT rate of 16.5 per cent and a reduced rate of 6.5 per cent for *all* members of the EU. International differences in taxes were fully neglected. For better comparability we adopted these assumptions and recalculated revenue flows to and from the clearing institution. The results are reported in the third column. The effects of assuming EU-wide uniform VAT rates are tremendous, as a comparison between the second and the third columns of Table 7 illustrates. As one would expect, the position of the high tax countries France, Belgium/Luxembourg, the Netherlands, and Denmark improves, whereas the three low-tax countries (Germany, Italy, United Kingdom/Ireland) suffer considerable losses.

Table 8. Welfare and revenue effects of an ideal clearing system

	HEV		VAT revenue in %		Terms of
	mill. ECU	in % of VAT	g.e.	f.r.	trade
Country	(1)	(2)	(3)	(4)	(5)
F	−307	−0.60	−0.97	−1.09	−0.15
B-L	−22	−0.28	−0.43	−0.58	−0.03
NL	−42	−0.36	−0.76	−0.89	−0.06
D	121	0.28	1.52	1.28	0.11
I	9	0.04	0.83	0.58	0.03
UK-IRL	187	0.65	1.16	0.73	0.13
DK	−106	−1.47	−1.82	−1.32	−0.40
EU	−160				
ROW	−4				
$\sum$	−164				

The remaining discrepancies are due to the fact that the Commission based their calculations on foreign trade data from 1986 whereas our data set refers to 1981. During these five years the balance of intracommunity trade has reversed for several EU countries. The United

Kingdom, for example, became a net importer during this time. The opposite holds for Belgium/Luxembourg. This explains why these countries' net positions vis-à-vis the clearing institution are reversed when comparing our calculations with those of the Commission.

Table 8 contains the relevant welfare and revenue effects of the clearing system. The HEV values in the second column exactly coincide with the substitution effects under the common market principle or the mixed system. Net tax exports are absent due to the clearing mechanism. The first column shows that absolute HEV values are rather modest. They would be even smaller if traveller's allowances under the destination principle had been taken into account. Before offering some remarks on these substitution effects, we will briefly comment on VAT revenue changes. The purpose of the clearing mechanism is to ensure that VAT revenue accrues to the country where consumption takes place, as is the case under the destination principle. Even if the basic idea is the same, the revenue distribution itself deviates between the destination principle and the clearing system as columns (3) and (4) show. Considering first round effects only, the revenue difference is given by

$$\sum_{k \in EU_h} \sum_{i \in N_t} (\tau_i^k - \tau_i^h) q_i^k C_i^{kh}.$$

The reason for this difference is that after abolishing border tax adjustments the clearing mechanism ensures that whereas direct consumption imports by domestic consumers bear the foreign country's tax burden, the corresponding VAT revenue accrues to the country where the consumption takes place. Therefore, the clearing system can be thought of as the destination principle supplemented by an additional tax or subsidy on direct consumption imports according to the tax rate differentials $(\tau_i^k - \tau_i^h)$. The above equation indicates that low-tax countries will gain and high-tax countries will lose revenue.

With this information, the HEV values, which are solely due to substitution effects, can now be easily explained. Due to international tax rate differentials, final consumers in the low-tax countries Germany, Italy, and the UK/Ireland will face higher tax burdens for their purchases from other EU countries after the switch from the destination principle to the clearing system. Following our remarks in the preceding chapter, this changes the terms of trade in favor of these countries and increases national welfare. High-tax countries, on the other hand, have higher tax burdens on their importables under the destination principle than under the clearing system. Accordingly, the terms of trade will deteriorate and national welfare decreases. Hence, one would expect relative terms of trade changes and welfare losses to be highest for Denmark. Relative terms of trade changes associated with international substitution effects are reported in column 5 of Table 8, and these numbers clearly confirm our conclusions.

The welfare consequences of domestic substitution effects are somewhat less clear. The spread of tax rates, after abolishing border tax adjustments, will increase in all EU member countries. Our conjecture is that these effects work in a welfare-decreasing direction, increasing welfare losses in high-tax and weakening welfare gains in low-tax countries. We have argued that international substitution effects will dominate domestic ones in absolute values, and our numerical results seem to confirm this view.

For an assessment of the clearing system one has to recall that our model reflects its ideal form. In practice, direct consumption imports cannot be monitored for taxation purposes if fiscal frontiers are absent. Cross-frontier sales to tax-exempt firms constitute another reason why total claims and liabilities against the central clearing account will not exactly match. An even more serious objection to the workability of the clearing system may be an enforcement assymmetry built into the redistribution mechanism (Lee, Pearson and Smith, 1989, p. 23). National revenue authorities will have an incentive to correctly report all claims against the clearing institution but underreport liabilities. Furthermore, incentives to control dubious and fraudulent claims for input VAT will be diminished for national exchequers if these claims can be passed on to the clearing institution. Again, the consequence will be that net tax exports are unavoidable under the clearing system.

The Proposal of the German Country of Origin Commission

The bilateral clearing proposal made by Germany's *Country of Origin Commission* may be considered a reaction to these severe objections. The decentralized calculation of the clearing payments allows to monitor the actual payments, at least to some degree. In comparison to the ideal clearing system above, the bilateral clearing proposal would be more feasible. When analyzing its welfare properties, it should be clear that the aggregate substitution effects will be the same as under the ideal clearing system (column 2 of Table 8). The redistributional consequences, on the other hand, could be quite different, depending on the volume of distance sales. If distance sales exceed the deviation limit mentioned above, net tax exports occur. For member state h, these are given by the difference

$$S^{kh} - S^{hk} = 0.45 \sum_{k \in EU_h} \sum_{i \in N_*} (\tau_i q_i C_i^{\cdot k} - \tau_i^k q_i^k C_i^{k\cdot})$$
$$+ 0.05 \sum_{k \in EU_h} \sum_{i \in N} \sum_{j \in N} (\tau_i q_i V_{ij}^{\cdot k} - \tau_i^k q_i^k V_{ij}^{k\cdot}),$$

where the correction payments are determined by equation (II-18b).

The sign and magnitude of this expression depend on tax rate differentials between countries h and k, on their bilateral trade balance in distance sales, and, to a very limited degree, on the bilateral trade balance in intermediate products. In general, high-tax countries with a positive balance in direct consumption trade will realize positive international income effects. Table 9 reports the welfare and revenue effects of this proposal when applied to our data set.

Table 9. Welfare and revenue effects of a bilateral clearing system as proposed by the German Country of Origin Commission

	HEV		VAT revenue (%)		Net tax exports	
	mill. ECU	% of VAT	g.e.	f.r.	g.e.	f.r.
Country	(1)	(2)	(3)	(4)	(5)	(6)
F	−443	−0.86	−1.22	−1.11	−0.24	0.02
B-L	108	1.34	1.52	1.30	1.69	1.88
NL	−205	−1.76	−2.37	−2.19	−1.42	−1.31
D	−232	−0.53	0.53	0.06	−0.92	−1.23
I	99	0.43	1.37	0.90	0.45	0.33
UK-IRL	542	1.87	2.68	1.88	1.29	1.16
DK	−18	−0.25	−0.27	0.59	1.20	1.91

As was the case under the mixed system, first round effects do not seem to be a reasonable approximation for general equilibrium effects. The total welfare effects in column 2 are obtained by simply adding the general equilibrium net tax exports (column 5, Table 9) to the aggregte substitution effects resulting from an ideal clearing system (column 2, Table 8).

Due to a lack of better information, our data base presumably exaggerates the volume of distance sales to final consumer. If correction payments were not required under a bilateral clearing system, its feasibility would be much more favorable than the Commission's global clearing system. On the other hand, some of the above mentioned objections remain valid, and our judgement is that prospects of introducing any clearing system in 1997 look gloomy.

4. The Origin Principle and the Subtraction Method

In this section we will assume that the EU and all its trading partners not only switch from the destination to the origin principle, but also from the credit to the subtraction method. We have already mentioned, in a previous chapter, that we do not consider this reform option as an overwhelmingly realistic alternative. On the other hand, the Neumark Committee (1963) favored this harmonization concept and in more recent times, again, a switch to the subtraction method has been suggested. In the following subsections we present welfare and revenue effects under the origin principle and the subtraction method. After that we introduce and calculate effective consumption tax rates from nominal value-added tax rates. This device is helpful, if not necessary, in explaining our welfare results along similar lines as in the preceding sections. These explanations can be found in the final subsection.

4.1. Welfare and Revenue Effects

Table 10 contains the welfare and revenue effects when switching from the destination principle and the credit method to a global origin principle with application of the subtraction method.

First note that welfare as well as revenue gains and losses are quite remarkable under the tax reform option being considered. Once again we will start with some remarks as to the VAT revenue effects. Comparing columns (3) and (4) in Table 10 it becomes obvious that first round calculations give a sufficiently good approximation for general equilibrium VAT revenue changes. Therefore, our explanations can be concentrated on first round effects. According to equations (II-4) and (II-24), the value-added tax base is domestic consumption under the destination principle (if services are neglected) and domestic value added under the origin principle combined with the subtraction method (if investment expenditures are neglected). In our model, the difference between these two tax bases is accounted for by a country's

Table 10. Welfare and revenue effects of the origin principle and the subtraction method

	HEV		VAT revenue in %		base
	mill. ECU	in % of VAT	g.e.	f.r.	effect
Country	(1)	(2)	(3)	(4)	(5)
F	−1255	−2.45	−14.19	−13.78	−15.19
B-L	−798	−9.94	−8.72	−9.23	−7.31
NL	467	4.01	10.74	10.49	7.43
D	1793	4.08	16.36	13.58	6.45
I	−806	−3.53	4.65	2.24	−2.12
UK-IRL	−294	−1.02	20.65	18.67	0.10
DK	−88	−1.22	−6.77	−2.19	−3.89
EU	−981				
ROW	386				
$\sum$	−595				

trade balance. If exports exceed imports, the tax base increases under the origin principle. The last column in the above table contains these changes in tax bases in percentage form. If tax rates were uniform or the shares of low-taxed goods in final consumption were the same as in value added, then only these base effects would be relevant for VAT revenue differences between the two taxation principles. Except for Germany, Italy, and the UK/Ireland tax base effects explain most of the revenue changes. For these three, however, tax base changes are much lower than total revenue changes. This is because in these countries reduced tax rates refer to much higher shares in final consumption than in value added. Hence total VAT revenue changes are higher than pure tax base changes would indicate.

Turning to the welfare effects, several points seem to be noteworthy. Firstly, the EU as a whole, as well as most member countries, will realize considerable welfare losses. We consider this as an economic argument against a possible switch to the subtraction method. Secondly, columns (2) and (3) of Table 10 clearly illustrate our assertion that there is no causal relationship between welfare and revenue effects. Thirdly, our economic explanations of welfare effects as developed in Chapter III and as applied to the VAT reform proposals discussed in the preceding sections are no longer applicable without major qualifications. VAT under the origin principle refers to value added in production when the subtraction method is applied, whereas the notion and quantification of net tax exports as well as of domestic substitution effects requires knowledge of the consumer's tax burden. Remember that tax exports have been defined as the difference between national VAT revenue and tax burdens to domestic consumers. In order to determine the latter, we transformed statutory tax rates on value added into equivalent *effective* tax rates on consumption. Here, equivalence means that under both tax regimes exactly the same equilibrium should be reproduced in a general equilibrium context. This basic idea is due to Kay and Warren (1980) and Hemming and Kay (1981). These authors, however, proceed the other way round, calculating effective tax rates on value added from a given set of observable consumption tax rates; moreover, their calculations are based on a closed economy. Furthermore, there is a close relationship between our concept of effective consumption tax rates and the concept of effective rates of protection, which is extensively used in international trade literature. Tower (1984, Chapter IV) comes very close to our approach. In the following section we will illustrate the concept of effective consumption tax rates in more detail and compute them for our model economy.

4.2. Equivalence of Statutory Tax Rates on Value Added and Effective Tax Rates on Consumption

Under the origin principle in combination with the subtraction method, producer prices, in contrast to consumer prices, are not clearly defined. Profits and production decisions depend on tax-inclusive market prices, as is clear from considering the zero-profit condition for a firm i in country h:

$$p_i^h Q_i^h - (w^h L_i^h + r K_i^h)(1 + \tau_i^h) - \sum_{k \in W} \sum_{j \in N} p_j^k V_{ji}^{kh} = 0. \tag{5a}$$

For the sake of simplicity, tariffs and production taxes have been neglected.

Our question now is whether or not there exist effective tax rates on consumption, called $\tilde{\tau}_i^h$ in the following, which generate exactly the same equilibrium as statutory tax rates τ_i^h on value added do. Clearly a necessary condition is that (relative) consumer prices are exactly the same under both tax regimes. Effective consumption tax rates implicitly define a set of fictive producer prices $\tilde{q}_i^h$ by using the relationship $\tilde{q}_i^h(1+\tilde{\tau}_i^h) = p_i^h$ for all $i \in N$ and $h \in W$. Hence, for a given vector of consumer prices, the existence of effective consumption tax rates is equivalent to the existence of a vector of fictive producer prices $\tilde{q}_i^h$, guaranteeing that production decisions are exactly the same under a system of statutory tax rates on value added as under a system of effective tax rates on consumption.

If fictive producer prices are relevant for production decisions, the zero-profit condition must read

$$\tilde{q}_i^h Q_i^h - (w^h L_i^h + r K_i^h) - \sum_{k \in W} \sum_{j \in N} \tilde{q}_j^k V_{ji}^{kh} = 0. \tag{5b}$$

Converting to a per unit form and defining

$$b_i^h := w^h \frac{L_i^h}{Q_i^h} + r \frac{K_i^h}{Q_i^h} \quad \text{and} \quad a_{ji}^{kh} := \frac{V_{ji}^{kh}}{Q_i^h}$$

as (fixed) value added and intermediate input per unit of output, the last two equations become

$$p_i^h - b_i^h(1+\tau_i^h) - \sum_{k \in W} \sum_{j \in N} p_j^k a_{ji}^{kh} = 0 \tag{6a}$$

and

$$\tilde{q}_i^h - b_i^h - \sum_{k \in W} \sum_{j \in N} \tilde{q}_j^k a_{ji}^{kh} = 0. \tag{6b}$$

We can now ask whether a vector of fictive producer prices $(\tilde{q}_i^h \mid i \in N, h \in W)$ exists that is compatible with the same per unit input coefficients that result under the origin principle and the subtraction method. For this to be true, the following equation must hold

$$\tau_i^h b_i^h = (p_i^h - \tilde{q}_i^h) - \sum_{k \in W} \sum_{j \in N} (p_j^k - \tilde{q}_j^k) a_{ji}^{kh} \qquad i \in N, h \in W.$$

In vector notation we can write

$$\mathbf{B}\tau = (\mathbf{I} - \mathbf{A}^T)(\mathbf{p} - \tilde{\mathbf{q}}),$$

where $\tau, \mathbf{p}, \tilde{\mathbf{q}}$ are column vectors, $\mathbf{I}$ the identity matrix, $\mathbf{A}$ the matrix of input-output coefficients, with $\mathbf{A}^T$ as its transpose, and $\mathbf{B}$ a matrix with b_i^h as diagonal elements and zeros elsewhere. The dimension of all vectors corresponds to the number of commodities (14) in each country times the number of countries (8).[85] Solving the last equation for the unknown vector of fictive producer prices, one obtains

$$\tilde{\mathbf{q}} = \mathbf{p} - \left(\mathbf{I} - \mathbf{A}^T\right)^{-1}\mathbf{B}\tau, \tag{7}$$

provided that the Leontief-inverse $(\mathbf{I}-\mathbf{A}^T)^{-1}$ exists. It is now straightforward to calculate effective consumption tax rates as

$$\tilde{\tau}_i^h = \frac{p_i^h}{\tilde{q}_i^h} - 1 \qquad i \in N, h \in W. \tag{8}$$

If the existence of $\tilde{\mathbf{q}}$ according to equation (7) is guaranteed, the two equilibria under effective consumption tax rates and under statutory tax rates on value added are indeed identical. The consumption bundles demanded and supplied by households coincide because consumer and factor prices are the same. On the production side, per unit input coefficients are identical under both tax regimes and equality of total quantities produced and factors demanded follows when considering market clearing conditions.

Let us now try to characterize the effective consumption tax system in more detail. The first thing to observe is that effective consumption tax rates are only compatible with the tax credit method, because otherwise equation (5b) could not hold. Under the credit method, the individual tax liability of firm i in country h is determined by

$$\tilde{T}_i^h = \tilde{\tau}_i^h \tilde{q}_i^h Q_i^h - \sum_{k\in W} \sum_{j\in N} \tilde{\tau}_j^k \tilde{q}_j^k V_{ji}^{kh}. \tag{9}$$

Equation (5b) is then obtained by inserting the last equation into the zero-profit condition

$$p_i^h Q_i^h - (w^h L_i^h + rK_i^h) - \sum_{k\in W} \sum_{j\in N} p_j^k V_{ji}^{kh} - \tilde{T}_i^h = 0. \tag{10}$$

Collecting terms and using $p_i^h = \tilde{q}_i(1 + \tilde{\tau}_i^h)$ yields (5b).

---

[85] Actually the relevant dimension is only 111. This is due to the fact that Denmark does not produce the eighth commodity (cars) according to our data set. The corresponding effective consumption tax rate is not well-defined for Denmark. This explains why we do not report this tax rate in Table 11 below.

Equation (10) illustrates a second point. Intermediate inputs are traded at gross (or tax-inclusive) prices p_j^k for all $k \in W$. This means that fiscal frontiers must be absent not only within the EU but also with respect to the rest of the world. Hence, effective consumption tax rates require the application of a global origin principle together with the tax credit method.

One might wonder how firms could make exactly the same input decisions under the origin principle, when applying the subtraction method and statutory tax rates on the one hand, and the credit method with effective consumption tax rates on the other. Our explanation uses the concept of "value added prices", which was first applied to international taxation problems by Grossman (1980). Remember that value added coefficients b_i^h as well as intermediate input coefficients a_{ji}^{kh} per unit of output are the same under both tax systems. The open question then is whether or not the shares of primary factors, labor and capital, in value added are also identical. Consider a marginal increase in labor input under both tax systems. Under the subtraction method and statutory tax rates, the marginal costs are $w^h(1 + \tau_i^h)$, whereas marginal revenues net of additional outlays for intermediate inputs are given by $(p_i^h - \sum_{k \in W} \sum_{j \in N} p_j^k a_{ji}^{kh})\ {}^{\partial Q_i^h}/_{\partial L_i^h}$.

Profit maximization requires equality of marginal costs and marginal revenues or, equivalently,

$$\left(\frac{p_i^h}{1+\tau_i^h} - \sum_{k \in W} \sum_{j \in N} \frac{p_j^k}{1+\tau_i^h} a_{ji}^{kh}\right) \frac{\partial Q_i^h}{\partial L_i^h} = w^h. \tag{11a}$$

Note that the marginal product of labor has to be evaluated in the equilibrium corresponding to the origin principle and the subtraction method.

The bracketed term on the left-hand side may be considered as the above-mentioned value added price. It is an obvious generalization of Grossman's (1980) value added price for a "stage of processing" VAT under the origin principle (his equation (3)).

Under the tax credit method with effective consumption tax rates, analogous considerations result in

$$\left(\tilde{q}_i^h - \sum_{k \in W} \sum_{j \in N} \tilde{q}_j^k a_{ji}^{kh}\right) \frac{\partial Q_i^h}{\partial L_i^h} = w^h. \tag{11b}$$

If the use of capital is increased, similar equations can be derived.

It now becomes apparent from equations (6a) and (6b) that value added prices are exactly the same in equations (11a) and (11b). Because the wage rate is identical as well, marginal products of labor and capital and, hence, factor demands coincide under the two tax systems considered.

So far we have assumed fixed input coefficients and neglected tariffs and production taxes. Considering these aspects complicates the analysis,[86] but does not change the general intuition. Therefore the technical details are not included here. Suffice to say that we have accounted for variable coefficients, tariffs, and production taxes when computing effective consumption tax rates.

Table 11. Effective consumption tax rates for the base year 1981

Countries	F	B-L	NL	D	I	UK-IRL	DK	ROW
1 Agriculture, forestry	8.5	7.6	6.1	7.9	4.7	4.4	17.9	9.9
2 Energy, water, mining	13.7	12.0	14.9	11.5	11.5	12.8	15.5	10.0
3 Chemicals	13.2	12.8	14.6	11.8	11.7	12.2	16.8	10.1
4 Metal products	15.4	13.3	14.6	11.9	12.8	12.9	17.3	10.0
5 Electrical products	14.6	13.2	14.2	12.2	12.9	13.0	17.5	10.1
6 Machinery	14.6	13.0	13.9	12.2	12.8	12.6	18.1	10.1
7 Office equipment and computers	14.1	13.5	14.5	12.2	12.8	12.9	17.0	10.1
8 Cars	23.1	14.9	14.8	12.3	15.4	13.0	-	10.3
9 Other motor vehicles	13.9	13.5	13.6	12.1	12.7	13.0	15.3	10.0
10 Food and drink	8.5	8.1	6.9	8.2	6.0	5.9	17.5	9.8
11 Textiles and leather	13.4	12.9	12.9	11.6	12.9	12.4	15.3	10.1
12 Other goods	13.8	12.7	14.5	11.6	12.7	12.8	17.5	10.0
13 Market services	9.4	8.3	8.3	8.2	5.0	7.5	14.3	9.9
14 Non-market (public) services	3.5	2.7	3.6	4.4	2.1	4.6	5.0	2.7

[86] In general, the effective consumption tax rates which indicate the tax burden now differ slightly from those which generate the artificial equilibrium.

Table 11 presents these effective consumption tax rates. Note that these rates are positive for publicly provided non-market services although the corresponding statutory VAT rates are zero throughout. Let us emphasize again that effective consumption tax rates when levied under a global origin principle using the credit method (without any clearing mechanism) generate exactly the same equilibrium as statutory VAT rates under a global origin principle combined with the subtraction method.

4.3. Effective Consumption Tax Rates in General Equilibrium: An Example

Before explaining the welfare effects of a switch from the destination principle to the origin principle and the subtraction method, we will briefly illustrate the computation of effective consumption tax rates in a simple two-country-two-commodity-two-factor-model. We return to our example presented in Figure 2 of Chapter II, which will be extended to a complete general equilibrium model. For simplicity's sake we assume fixed production coefficients with respect to value added and intermediate inputs. Labor supply is assumed to be fixed, and utility and value added production functions are of the Cobb-Douglas variety. These functional forms were chosen in order to enable the reader to cross-check the results by hand. All the necessary information is given in Table 12.

As a reference point, the first column in Table 12 contains functional forms, equilibrium conditions, and equilibrium prices under the destination principle. We believe this column to be self-explanatory. Note that production functions, per unit factor demands and equilibrium conditions are the same for all three columns considered. The parameter values and the data which are necessary to compute the equilibrium quantities are given in the last part of Table 12. The input-output table we used in Chapter II follows from multiplying the input coefficients in Table 12 with the corresponding quantities. Parameters and data remain constant in the following comparative static experiments.

Table 12. Illustration of the equivalence of statutory VAT rates and effective consumption tax rates

	Benchmark equilibrium	Counterfactual equilibrium: Origin principle	
	Destination principle	Subtraction method; statutory VAT rates	Credit method; effective consumption tax rates
Households			
Consumption demand	$C_i^{hh} = \frac{\alpha_i^{hh} Y_v^h}{q_i^h (1+\tau_i^h)}$; $C_i^{kh} = \frac{\alpha_i^{kh} Y_v^h}{q_i^k (1+\tau_i^h)}$	$C_i^{hh} = \frac{\alpha_i^{hh} Y_v^h}{p_i^h}$; $C_i^{kh} = \frac{\alpha_i^{kh} Y_v^h}{p_i^k}$	$C_i^{hh} = \frac{\alpha_i^{hh} Y_v^h}{\tilde{q}_i^h (1+\tilde{\tau}_i^h)}$; $C_i^{kh} = \frac{\alpha_i^{kh} Y_v^h}{\tilde{q}_i^k (1+\tilde{\tau}_i^k)}$
		$Y_v^h := w^h \overline{L}^h + r\overline{K}^h + Tr^h$	
Firms			
Production functions		$Q_i^h = \min \left\{ \frac{1}{a_{oi}^h} f_i^h (L_i^h, K_i^h), \frac{V_{ji}^{kh}}{a_{ji}^{kh}} \right\}$	
		$f_i^h = \theta_i^h (L_i^h)^{\beta_i^h} (K_i^h)^{1-\beta_i^h}$	
Zero profit condition	$q_i^h Q_i^h - VA_i^h - \sum_k \sum_j q_j^k V_{ji}^{kh} = 0$	$p_i^h Q_i^h - VA_i (1+\tau_i^h) - \sum_k \sum_j p_j^k V_{ji}^{kh} = 0$	$\tilde{q}_i^h Q_i^h - VA_i^h - \sum_k \sum_j \tilde{q}_j^k V_{ji}^{kh} = 0$
		$VA_i^h = w^h L_i^h + r K_i^h$	
Per unit factor demands		$\frac{K_i^h}{Q_i^h} = \frac{1}{\theta_i^h} \left[\frac{(1+\beta_i^h) w^h}{\beta_i^h r} \right]^{\beta_i^h} a_{oi}^h$	
		$\frac{L_i^h}{Q_i^h} = \frac{1}{\theta_i^h} \left[\frac{\beta_i^h r}{(1-\beta_i^h) w^h} \right]^{1-\beta_i^h} a_{oi}^h$	

Market equilibrium			
Factor markets		$\overline{L}^h = \sum_i L_i^h$ $\sum_h \overline{K}^h = \sum_i \sum_k K_i^h$	
Commodity markets		$Q_i^h = \sum_k C_i^{hk} + \sum_j \sum_k a_{ji}^{kh} Q_i^h$	
Balance of payments			
	$\sum_i q_i^h \left(C_i^{hk} + \sum_j V_{ij}^{hk}\right)$ $+r\left(\overline{K}^h - \sum_i K_i^h\right)$ $= \sum_i q_i^k \left(C_i^{kh} + \sum_j V_{ij}^{kh}\right)$	$\sum_i p_i^h \left(C_i^{hk} + \sum_j V_{ij}^{hk}\right) + r\left(\overline{K}^h - \sum_i K_i^h\right) = \sum_i p_i^k \left(C_i^{kh} + \sum_j V_{ij}^{kh}\right)$	
Government			
(Budget constraint)	$T_r^h = \sum_i \tau_i^h (C_i^{hh} + C_i^{kh})$	$T_r^h = \sum_i \tau_i^h VA_i^h$	$T_r^h = \sum_i \sum_k \tilde{\tau}_i^h \tilde{q}_i^h C_i^{hk} +$ $\sum_i \sum_j (\tilde{\tau}_i^h \tilde{q}_i^h V_{ij}^{hk} - \tilde{\tau}_i^k \tilde{q}_i^k V_{ij}^{kh})$
fulfilled by Walras' Law			
Equilibrium prices			
Normalization:			
$w^D = 1.0$	$r = 1.0,\ w^F = 1.0$ $p_1^D = 1.05 \quad p_2^D = 1.10$ $p_1^D = 1.05 \quad p_2^D = 1.10$ $q_1^D = q_2^D = q_1^F = q_2^F = 1.0$	$r = 1.0,\ w^F = 0.994$ $p_1^D = 1.076 \quad p_2^D = 1.100$ $p_1^F = 1.104 \quad p_2^F = 1.145$	$r = 1.0,\ w^F = 0.994$ $p_1^D = 1.076 \quad p_2^D = 1.100$ $p_1^F = 1.104 \quad p_2^F = 1.145$ $\tilde{q}_1^D = 0.999 \quad \tilde{q}_2^D = 0.999$ $\tilde{q}_1^F = 0.996 \quad \tilde{q}_2^F = 0.998$

Table 12. continued

Parameters and data	D		F	
Households				
	$\overline{L}^D = 100$	$\overline{K}^D = 60$	$\overline{L}^F = 80$	$\overline{K}^F = 80$
	$\alpha_1^{DD} = 0.490$	$\alpha_2^{DD} = 0.385$	$\alpha_1^{FF} = 0.060$	$\alpha_2^{FF} = 0.196$
	$\alpha_1^{FD} = 0.061$	$\alpha_2^{FD} = 0.064$	$\alpha_1^{DF} = 0.418$	$\alpha_2^{DF} = 0.326$
Production				
	$a_{11}^{DD} = 0.118$	$a_{12}^{DD} = 0.235$	$a_{11}^{DF} = 0.050$	$a_{12}^{DF} = 0.063$
	$a_{21}^{DD} = 0.176$	$a_{22}^{DD} = 0.118$	$a_{21}^{DF} = 0.100$	$a_{22}^{DF} = 0.063$
	$a_{11}^{FD} = 0.059$	$a_{12}^{FD} = 0.118$	$a_{11}^{FF} = 0.200$	$a_{12}^{FF} = 0.313$
	$a_{21}^{FD} = 0.118$	$a_{22}^{FD} = 0.118$	$a_{21}^{FF} = 0.150$	$a_{22}^{FF} = 0.188$
	$a_{01}^{D} = 0.529$	$a_{02}^{D} = 0.412$	$a_{01}^{F} = 0.500$	$a_{02}^{F} = 0.375$
	$\theta_1^D = 1.890$	$\theta_2^D = 1.980$	$\theta_1^F = 1.960$	$\theta_2^F = 1.890$
	$\beta_1^D = 0.667$	$\beta_2^D = 0.571$	$\beta_1^F = 0.600$	$\beta_2^F = 0.333$
Government				
Statutory VAT rates				
	$\tau_1^D = 0.05$	$\tau_2^D = 0.10$	$\tau_1^F = 0.10$	$\tau_2^F = 0.20$
Effective consumption tax rates				
	$\tilde{\tau}_1^D = 0.077$	$\tilde{\tau}_2^D = 0.101$	$\tilde{\tau}_1^F = 0.108$	$\tilde{\tau}_2^F = 0.147$

First we switch from the destination principle to the origin principle and the subtraction method, leaving statutory VAT rates unchanged. In the second column of Table 12, the relevant equations as well as the prices characterizing this counterfactual equilibrium are presented. Taking the consumer prices of this equilibrium as given, we can compute effective consumption tax rates according to equations (7) and (8). In our numerical example, equation (7) becomes[87]

[87] The numbers in the following equations are rounded.

$$\begin{bmatrix} \tilde{q}_1^D \\ \tilde{q}_2^D \\ \tilde{q}_1^F \\ \tilde{q}_2^F \end{bmatrix} = \begin{bmatrix} 1.076 \\ 1.100 \\ 1.104 \\ 1.145 \end{bmatrix} - \begin{bmatrix} (1-0.118) & -0.176 & -0.059 & -0.118 \\ -0.235 & (1-0.118) & -0.118 & -0.118 \\ -0.050 & -0.100 & (1-0.200) & -0.150 \\ -0.063 & -0.063 & -0.313 & (1-0.188) \end{bmatrix}$$

$$\times \begin{bmatrix} 0.529 & & & 0 \\ & 0.412 & & \\ & & 0.498 & \\ 0 & & & 0.374 \end{bmatrix} \times \begin{bmatrix} 0.050 \\ 0.100 \\ 0.100 \\ 0.200 \end{bmatrix}$$

$$= \begin{bmatrix} 0.999 \\ 0.999 \\ 0.996 \\ 0.998 \end{bmatrix}.$$

Using equation (8), effective consumption tax rates are given by

$$\tilde{\tau}' = [0.077, 0.101, 0.178, 0.147]. \qquad (12)$$

The last column of Table 12 describes the artificial equilibrium, which is generated by applying the origin principle with the credit method and effective consumption tax rates. An important point to note is that the two counterfactual equilibria are exactly the same. From the last row it is clear that factor and consumer prices coincide. Hence, per unit factor requirements are identical in both tax regimes. Quantities demanded and total quantities produced coincide because VAT revenues are the same in both cases. To facilitate verification, we specify the interregional input-output table (evaluated in consumer prices) corresponding to the two identical counterfactual equilibria (Figure 1). All quantities can be obtained by dividing by the relevant consumer prices. Note that international capital movements occur in the counterfactual but (by chance) not in the benchmark equilibrium. Having an idea of the concept and computation of effective consumption tax rates we can now turn to the interpretation of our welfare results.

		D 1	D 2	F 1	F 2	D	F	Total
D	1	21.339	43.617	10.690	10.861	84.023	10.849	181.380
	2	32.720	22.294	21.854	11.103	66.018	35.507	189.495
F	1	10.948	22.378	43.874	55.723	10.503	75.945	219.371
	2	22.698	23.198	34.112	34.659	11.003	59.178	184.848
		4.461	7.091	9.894	12.084	VAT	Value added	
		59.476	40.524	59.368	20.140	wL		
		29.738	30.393	39.579	40.279	rK		
		181.380	189.495	219.371	184.848	Total		

Figure 1. Counterfactual input-output-table (in consumer prices)

4.4. Decomposing and Explaining Welfare Effects

The reason for introducing the somewhat intricate concept of effective consumption tax rates is that they enable welfare effects to be explained along similar lines as developed for other VAT reform variants. Effective consumption tax rates prove to be particularly helpful in determining net tax exports when the subtraction method is in use together with the origin principle. In fact, this is the only satisfactory explanation of these effects. The following figure summarizes our basic procedure.

Starting from the benchmark equilibrium we compute welfare and revenue effects when switching to the origin principle and the subtraction method. Table 10 contains the relevant numbers. Difficulties in explaining welfare effects prompted us to construct an equivalent artificial equilibrium using the tax credit method and effective consumption tax rates. The latter allows us to compute net tax exports and substitution effects, just as we did under the common market principle in Section 3.1. The main difference is that in the artificial equilibrium, trade with ROW is no longer taxed according to the destination principle. Instead, ROW is treated in exactly the same manner as the EU countries. Net tax exports and substitution effects are then used to decompose and explain the welfare effects of the VAT reform under consideration.

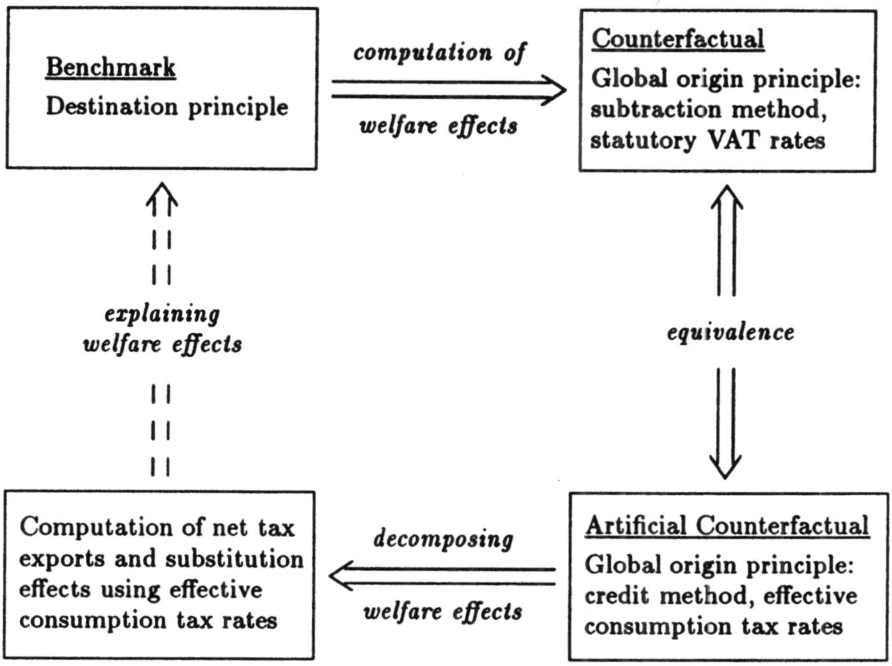

Figure 2. Explaining welfare effects under a global origin principle and the subtraction method

In Table 13 we repeat relative HEV values and decompose welfare effects into the associated substitution and net tax export effects. Let us start our exercise by elaborating on the computation of net tax exports. These effects have been defined as the difference between national VAT revenue and the tax payments attributable to domestic consumers. Country h's national tax revenue in the counterfactual equilibrium may be written alternatively as (upper index h omitted)

$$\sum_{i\in N} \tau_i(wL_i + rK_i) = \sum_{i\in N}\tilde{\tau}_i\tilde{q}_iC_i + \sum_{k\in W_h}\sum_{i\in N}\tilde{\tau}_i\tilde{q}_iC_i^{\cdot k} + \sum_{k\in W_h}\sum_{i\in N}\sum_{j\in N}\left(\tilde{\tau}_i\tilde{q}_iV_{ij}^{\cdot k} - \tilde{\tau}_i^k\tilde{q}_i^kV_{ij}^{k\cdot}\right),$$

where the left hand side of the equation states the tax revenue under the origin principle and the subtraction method, and the right hand

Table 13. Decomposing welfare effects under the origin principle and the subtraction method[a]

	HEV	Net tax exports		Subst.	Terms of trade (in %)	
		g.e.	f.r.	effect	Total	Int'l
Country	(1)	(2)	(3)	(4)	(5)	(6)
F	−2.45	−1.76	−0.29	−0.60	0.50	−1.10
B-L	−9.94	−6.48	−6.39	−3.70	−0.31	−0.33
NL	4.01	8.49	10.57	−4.00	0.25	−0.65
D	4.08	5.47	5.48	−0.50	0.38	−0.08
I	−3.53	−3.05	−3.40	−0.87	0.06	0.13
UK-IRL	−1.02	0.19	0.85	−1.12	0.48	0.11
DK	−1.22	5.82	9.11	−7.03	2.61	−3.02
ROW	0.07	−0.31	−0.55	0.34	−0.68	0.76

[a] The values in columns (1)-(4) are in per cent of the benchmark equilibrium's VAT revenues.

side the tax revenue under the artificial counterfactual equilibrium. The equality holds because the two counterfactual equilibria are completely equivalent. All quantity variables refer to their equilibrium values under the origin principle and the subtraction method. The VAT payments of domestic consumers are given by

$$\sum_{i \in N} \tilde{\tau}_i \tilde{q}_i C_i + \sum_{k \in W_h} \sum_{i \in N} \tilde{\tau}_i^k \tilde{q}_i^k C_i^{k \cdot}.$$

Replacing $\tilde{q}_i$ with $p_i/(1+\tilde{\tau}_i)$, net tax exports for country h can be calculated as

$$\sum_{k \in W_h} \sum_{i \in N} \left(\frac{\tilde{\tau}_i}{1+\tilde{\tau}_i} p_i X_i^{\cdot k} - \frac{\tilde{\tau}_i^k}{1+\tilde{\tau}_i^k} p_i^k M_i^{k \cdot} \right). \tag{13}$$

General equilibrium net tax exports are obtained if export revenues as well as import expenditures are evaluated in the counterfactual equilibrium. Column (2) in Table 13 contains the corresponding values as a percentage of each country's base year VAT revenue. It might be interesting to compare these net tax exports with those resulting from a switch to the common market principle (column (2) of Table 6). For some countries, net tax exports differ considerably. This is because the calculation of net tax exports according to equation (13) now includes commodity transactions with ROW and the countries in question have much larger trade imbalances with ROW than other countries. Again, one can compare general equilibrium with first round net tax exports, as reported in the third column of the last table. Here we have taken export and import values from the benchmark equilibrium. In addition, we have used statutory VAT rates instead of effective consumption tax rates. Thus, only observable variables entered the calculation of first round net tax exports. Columns (2) and (3) reveal that the differences are considerable. Furthermore, net tax exports no longer approximate total welfare changes. For CGE modelers this is a comforting result. The difference between total welfare changes and net tax exports is due to aggregate substitution effects to which we turn now.

After net tax exports have been neutralized by an international redistribution scheme, only substitution effects under a global clearing system remain. There are, however, two basic differences when compared with the clearing system in subsection 3.2. The first, of course, is that effective tax rates are relevant. The second and more important point to note is that these effective tax rates now also apply to EU trade with ROW. Hence, EU imports from ROW bear ROW's low effective consumption tax rates, whereas ROW's imports from EU countries are taxed according to the exporting countries' higher effective rates. This clearly shifts demand towards ROW's exportables and improves the terms of trade in favor of ROW. The last number in column (6) confirms this reasoning. The reverse side of ROW's terms of trade gains is that most EU member states are exposed to increasing terms of trade losses, as a comparison between column (5) of Table 8 and column (6) of Table 13 proves. Welfare losses due to international substitution effects may be explained along similar lines as under the clearing system in subsection 3.2., when statutory VAT rates are replaced by effective consumption tax rates. Once again, our basic hypothesis is that these international substitution effects have the same signs as the corresponding terms of trade effects in column (6).

The operation of domestic substitution effects is also readily explained. Switching from statutory VAT rates under the destination principle to the whole set of effective consumption tax rates implies lowering the lowest and raising the highest tax rates for most countries. In view of our separable and homothetic utility trees, less uniformity in the rate structure generally results in greater distortions and lower welfare. From columns (4) and (6) in Table 13 we can conclude that welfare losses due to domestic substitution effects may even be high enough to dominate possible gains from international substitution effects. Combining welfare changes from aggregate substitution and net tax exports effects yields approximately total welfare changes (in percentage form).

This concludes our computations with the central case parameter specifications. The following section contains some sensitivity analysis in order to examine the robustness of our numerical results.

5. Some Sensitivity Analysis

This section deals with the question of how much confidence to have in the numerical results of our simulation experiments. In essence, numerical results depend on the following features of CGE models:

- the choice of functional forms for utility and production functions;

  We have chosen combinations of Cobb-Douglas and CES functions. Even if the empirical implications are somewhat restrictive, we consider our choice a reasonable compromise between flexibility and tractability. One must, however, be aware that a number of results depend heavily on the properties of demand and supply functions. Deaton (1981) very clearly stresses this point in an optimal taxation framework, and the same arguments apply to the tax reform approach. Therefore, we should test the robustness of our results with respect to different specifications of functional forms. The linear expenditure system, for example, is a natural extension of homothetic utility functions. Similarly, on the production side, one could try to use translog instead of CES production functions. The problem with these more flexible functional forms is that the number of exogenous parameters increases considerably, and that we do not have reliable parameter estimates. Therefore, a sensitivity analysis with different functional forms is not included here.

- the choice of extraneously specified parameters;

  To calibrate our model to the benchmark data set, we had to specify exogenously a number of parameter values. These parameters, mostly elasticity values, were borrowed from current econometric literature whenever possible. Sometimes, however, we had no information at all and inevitably had to use best guesses obtained in "coffee table conversations" (Harrison and Vinod, 1992, p. 357). Hence, there is a large degree of uncertainty concerning the "true" values of key model parameters. The intriguing question then is how sensitive simulation results are with respect to pertubations of these unknown parameters. In the next subsection we will deal with this problem in greater detail.

- the choice of the model structure;

  Even if basic features of general equilibrium models are undisputed, CGE modelers are left with important decisions on the structure of the theoretical model. Policy conclusions from the model may, for example, depend heavily on whether it is assumed that capital is internationally mobile or immobile. Should the economic model exhibit an intertemporal structure with an explicit treatment of savings and investment decisions? Is it necessary to model distributional issues within a country? What about the modelling of unemployment and industrial organization features? All these questions have to be decided upon according to the abilities of the modelers or according to their judgement as to the importance of different model structures. Even though model preselection is a more general problem in economic theory, one should be aware that different model structures may imply different policy conclusions. Therefore, any conclusions should be regarded with a high degree of reservation.

- some aspects of the benchmark equilibrium data set;

  Construction of a micro-consistent data set is time-consuming and not very rewarding, but it is critical in the sense that the structure of the data set may heavily influence the results. It is true that most of our data were taken from the national accounts. However, in order to guarantee consistency with a Walrasian general equilibrium model, a number of adjustments are necessary, implying that benchmark data are not matched by observable data. An even more intricate problem is the choice of a base year for the benchmark equilibrium data set. Usually this is decided upon by the availability of reliable data information (for example, input-output tables) and not by economic reasoning. In subsection 5.2. we will deal with a crucial weakness of our data base and elaborate on the consequences of different data assumptions.

5.1. Varying Key Parameter Values

The exogenously determined key parameter values of our simulation model were reported in Table 5 of Chapter IV. Everything else being given, these parameter sets (uniquely) determine the numerical solution. The problem is that quantitative and qualitative model results may be sensitive to even small changes in parameter values. For example, Fullerton and Lyon (1986) have shown how the welfare ranking of different tax reform options depends on the choice of the savings elasticity. In the CGE literature, sensitivity analysis with respect to uncertain parameter values is the common answer to this problem. Basically, two different approaches have been followed. The most commonly used procedure is a limited sensitivity analysis (Wigle, 1991, p. 36), consisting of ad-hoc perturbances of single or combined parameter values. The second approach is to conduct a conditional or unconditional systematic sensitivity analysis.[88] The procedure is to attach probability distributions to each parameter. Perturbing parameters according to their probability distribution yields an implicit probability distribution for the model results.

Systematic sensitivity analysis requires a vast number of simulation runs and we do not feel that the results justify the effort. Over time, the CGE modeler should get a sound feeling for the crucial parameters of a model. Usually these are the elasticity of saving (which does not appear in our model), the labor supply elasticity, and the trade elasticities. In contrast, demand parameters or capital-labor elasticities of substitution prove to be much less important. We performed a number of ad hoc simulation experiments with the latter parameters (not reported here), varying them by 50 per cent downwards and upwards. Economic welfare as measured by the HEV did not change by more than one per cent. Hence, model results are remarkably robust with respect to these parameters.

Instead of systematically varying labor supply and trade elasticities, we simply consider some extreme parameter configurations and concentrate on explaining in economic terms the observed welfare changes. With respect to the labor supply elasticity, we consider the case of an inelastic labor supply in all countries, corresponding to an elasticity value of zero. The most important trade elasticities are the substitution elasticities between domestic and imported intermediate inputs.

[88] Key references are Pagan and Shannon (1985), Harrison, Jones, Kimbell and Wigle (1993), Harrison and Vinod (1992), and Wigle (1991).

Here we reduce all elasticity values to zero in all countries, which is equivalent to assuming a fixed coefficient technology. We consider these changes one after another.

Table 14 contains the welfare changes and their decomposition for the switching option of the transitional system, the common market principle, and the origin principle with the subtraction method. The mixed system and the clearing system are omitted because the substitution effects under these taxation principles coincide with those under the common market principle, and furthermore, net tax exports do not occur under the clearing system. For ease of reference we repeat the results from our central case simulations in the first part of the table.

Let us consider the welfare changes for the transitional system and the common market principle first. Overall, the HEV values do not change very much. The signs and orders of magnitude remain completely unchanged, and only the volume of welfare effects changes moderately. Readers should not take the precise numbers too seriously. Our limited sensitivity analysis illustrates that, on average, welfare losses and gains increase when adjustments on the supply and demand side become more sluggish. The surprising feature is that welfare changes are almost exclusively due to higher substitution effects, whereas net tax export effects remain virtually unchanged. The explanation may run as follows.

Consider the labor market diagram in Figure 3. L_0^D is the pre-change labor demand curve, L^S an elastic and $\hat{L}^S$ an inelastic labor supply curve. The initial wage rate is given by w_0. Suppose now that a change in value-added taxation shifts labor demand to L_{1f}^D. Obviously, the factor price change that is necessary to remove excess demand has to be much higher if labor supply is completely inelastic. This induces greater variations in producer and consumer prices, thereby increasing substitution effects. Higher substitution effects also result if fixed instead of variable coefficients with respect to intermediate inputs are considered.

Think of w_{1f} as the counterfactual wage rate when labor supply is inelastic and input coefficients are fixed. The wage rate increase from w_0 to w_{1f} will be accompanied by an increase in domestic producer (and consumer) prices. Now, if domestic and imported intermediate inputs were substitutes, higher domestic producer prices would induce some substitution of domestic by imported intermediates. Domestic output and, with it, domestic labor demand would fall, shifting the labor demand curve back to L_{1v}^D. Hence, the equilibrium wage rate and

Table 14: Welfare dependence on parameter variations (EU only)

	Central Case				Fixed input coefficients				Fixed Coefficients and fixed labor supply			
Country	(1)	(2)	(3)	(4)	(1)	(2)	(3)	(4)	(1)	(2)	(3)	(4)
					Transitional system with switching option							
F	−1141	−2.23	−2.03	−0.17	−1360	−2.65	−2.02	−0.27	−1796	−3.44	−1.99	−0.37
B-L	145	1.81	1.91	−0.06	155	1.94	1.90	−0.13	192	2.40	1.90	−0.18
NL	−610	−5.24	−5.19	−0.19	−711	−6.10	−5.17	−0.35	−956	−8.22	−5.17	−0.51
D	810	1.85	2.02	0.08	1075	2.45	2.02	0.19	1492	3.40	2.02	0.29
I	259	1.13	1.23	0.04	275	1.21	1.23	0.06	359	1.57	1.23	0.07
UK-IRL	554	1.91	1.56	0.39	645	2.23	1.56	0.51	907	3.13	1.56	0.73
DK	−149	−2.06	−1.71	−0.30	−187	−2.58	−1.70	−0.51	−246	−3.40	−1.70	−0.69
					Common market principle							
F	503	0.98	1.59	−0.60	435	0.85	1.58	−0.97	543	1.06	1.57	−1.32
B-L	213	2.66	3.13	−0.28	228	2.84	3.15	−0.52	289	3.60	3.15	−0.76
NL	1094	9.40	10.10	−0.36	1225	10.52	10.26	−0.66	1639	14.08	10.24	−0.98
D	−568	−1.29	−1.78	0.28	−503	−1.15	−1.75	0.88	−613	−1.40	−1.74	1.32
I	−670	−2.93	−3.34	0.04	−718	−3.14	−3.40	0.07	−942	−4.12	−3.39	0.09
UK-IRL	−891	−3.08	−3.84	0.65	−987	−3.41	−3.88	0.88	−1361	−4.70	−3.87	1.28
DK	317	4.38	5.73	−1.47	331	4.58	5.75	−2.23	432	5.97	5.73	−2.93

Origin principle and subtraction method

F	−1255	−2.45	−1.76	−0.60	397	0.77	−0.90	1.94	616	1.20	−0.88	2.70
B-L	−798	−9.94	−6.48	−3.70	−902	−11.25	−6.68	−3.53	−1108	−13.81	−6.57	−4.34
NL	467	4.01	8.49	−4.00	721	6.19	9.81	−4.06	951	8.17	9.72	−5.61
D	1793	4.08	5.47	−0.50	2555	5.82	5.68	−0.37	3499	7.97	5.62	−0.58
I	−806	−3.53	−3.05	−0.87	−944	−4.13	−3.50	−0.74	−1250	−5.48	−3.50	−1.01
UK-IRL	−294	−1.02	0.19	−1.12	210	0.73	0.90	−0.12	200	0.69	0.81	−0.41
DK	−88	−1.22	5.82	−7.03	399	5.51	7.62	−3.30	535	7.40	7.63	−4.25
ROW	386	0.07	−0.31	0.34	−1698	−0.30	−0.47	0.25	−2209	−0.39	−0.46	0.34

(1) HEV in mill. ECU (3) Net tax exports

(2) HEV in % of VAT (4) Substitution effects

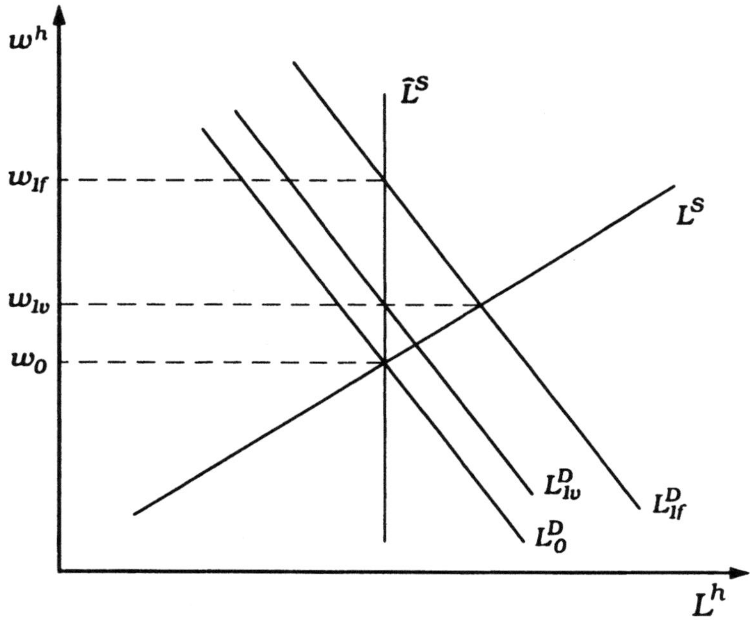

Figure 3. Wage rate changes and labor supply elasticity

the induced substitution effects will be lower when input coefficients are variable rather than fixed.

The above figure shows the case in which the labor demand curve shifts to the right following a change in value-added taxation. If the demand curve had shifted to the left, the wage rate would have fallen but substitution effects would still have increased. This explains why in Table 14 both welfare gains and welfare losses increase in absolute value.

Even if producer and consumer prices change, net tax exports remain more or less unchanged within a given international taxation principle because price and quantity reactions neutralize each other if price elasticities of import demand center around one.

When comparing variable with fixed intermediate coefficients under the origin principle and the subtraction method, it is more difficult to explain welfare changes. This difficulty becomes obvious when considering our concept of effective consumption taxes. These tax rates depend on the counterfactual's consumer prices and its value added as well as on intermediate input coefficients. Hence, effective consumption tax rates will vary in a non-trivial way with the Leontief-matrix. Without explicitly knowing effective consumption tax rates, meaningful interpretations are almost impossible.

The change in effective consumption tax rates is less dramatic when comparing the fixed versus the variable labor supply cases under the origin principle and the subtraction method in the second and third part of Table 14. Here, the matrix of intermediate input coefficients is the same in both cases, and effective consumption tax rates change only moderately. Hence, welfare changes may be explained with arguments similar to those put forward when discussing the transitional system and the common market principle.

5.2. Varying the Data Set

When constructing our microeconomic consistent data set, we used the most reliable sources we could find. Nevertheless we feel that our data set could be improved. Besides being out of date, the weakest part is the data concerning international direct consumption purchases. To account for the uncertainty surrounding these data, we performed a limited sensitivity analysis. Leaving each country's total imports and exports unchanged, we changed its composition by doubling all direct consumption purchases from abroad and diminishing intermediate imports by the same amount. This required a corresponding change in domestic production and consumption of a commodity. Table 15 presents the sensitivity results for the same three VAT reform options considered above. With respect to the parameters, computations are based on the central case parameter configuration (elastic labor supply, price dependent input coefficients). The slanted numbers give our original results from Tables 2, 6 and 13, which are once again reproduced for ease of reference.

Changing the data base as indicated above may have consequences for net tax exports as well as for substitution effects. Increasing the share of direct consumption imports in total consumption expenditures amounts to assuming better substitution possibilities between domestic and foreign consumption commodities. In fact, as Table 15 illustrates, welfare changes due to aggregate substitution effects approximately double. The change in net tax exports depends on which taxation principle is considered. As one would expect from equation (2a)

Table 15. Welfare dependence on direct consumption imports/exports

Country	Transitional system with switching option				Common market principle				Origin principle and subtraction method			
	(1)	(2)	(3)	(4)	(1)	(2)	(3)	(4)	(1)	(2)	(3)	(4)
F	−2250	−4.34	−3.98	−0.32	−13	−0.03	1.20	−1.17	−2064	−3.98	−2.77	−1.19
	−1141	*−2.23*	*−2.03*	*−0.17*	*503*	*0.98*	*1.59*	*−0.60*	*−1255*	*−2.45*	*−1.76*	*−0.60*
B-L	281	3.50	3.75	−0.11	218	2.71	3.52	−0.58	−849	−10.57	−6.71	−4.21
	145	*1.81*	*1.91*	*−0.06*	*213*	*2.66*	*3.13*	*−0.28*	*−798*	*−9.94*	*−6.48*	*−3.70*
NL	−1198	−10.02	−9.95	−0.34	990	8.27	9.37	−0.72	250	2.09	7.22	−4.69
	−610	*−5.24*	*−5.19*	*−0.19*	*1094*	*9.40*	*10.10*	*−0.36*	*467*	*4.01*	*8.49*	*−4.00*
D	1634	3.65	3.95	0.17	−219	−0.49	−1.22	0.61	1154	2.57	4.16	−0.95
	810	*1.85*	*2.02*	*0.08*	*−568*	*−1.29*	*−1.78*	*0.28*	*1793*	*4.08*	*5.47*	*−0.50*
I	510	2.22	2.41	0.08	−623	−2.71	−3.14	0.08	−955	−4.15	−3.63	−1.02
	259	*1.13*	*1.23*	*0.04*	*−670*	*−2.93*	*−3.34*	*0.04*	*−806*	*−3.53*	*−3.05*	*−0.87*
UK-IRL	1056	3.63	3.07	0.72	−619	−2.13	−3.75	1.21	−293	−1.01	0.38	−1.33
	554	*1.91*	*1.56*	*0.39*	*−891*	*−3.08*	*−3.84*	*0.65*	*−294*	*−1.02*	*0.19*	*−1.12*
DK	−287	−3.88	−3.24	−0.55	96	1.29	4.11	−2.82	−214	−2.89	4.95	−7.78
	−149	*−2.06*	*1.71*	*−0.30*	*317*	*4.38*	*5.73*	*−1.47*	*−88*	*−1.22*	*5.82*	*−7.03*
ROW	−3				−10				2490	0.45	−0.07	0.51
	5				*−4*				*386*	*0.07*	*−0.31*	*0.34*

(1) HEV in mill. ECU (3) Net tax exports
(2) HEV in % of VAT (4) Substitution effects

above, net tax exports should approximately double under the transitional system. Under this tax reform option, however, substitution effects remain rather unimportant even if doubled. Hence, it is not at all surprising that total welfare effects double in absolute value.

Under the common market principle, net tax exports are determined by total export revenues and import expenditures, which are not affected by our data base change. Column (3) in the second part of Table 15 illustrates that net tax export changes are only of minor importance. Under the CMP, only the change in substitution effects is relevant. Because they approximately double in absolute values welfare gains or losses increase whenever the aggregate substitution effects are positive or negative for a country. When using effective consumption tax rates, at least in principle, the same arguments apply to the origin principle and the subtraction method as to the common market principle. One has to consider, however, that effective consumption tax rates differ in the two counterfactual equilibria reported in the last part of Table 15. This is the reason why net tax exports differ by more than under the common market principle, and why substitution effects will increase but not double.

In summary, if someone were to quarrel with our direct consumption data our answer would be twofold. In the first place we would be happy to add more reliable data estimates into our model and restart our simulations. Perhaps more important is the fact that we have gained some intuition as to how the basic welfare determinants – net tax exports and aggregate substitution effects – will vary with a change in the central components of our data base.

Chapter VI

Summary and Conclusions

In the preceeding chapters we used a computable general equilibrium model to evaluate the welfare effects of different VAT reform proposals. When we started our project we were convinced that CGE modelling would be the most appropriate approach for an investigation of the welfare effects of tax reforms in a multi-commodity, multi-country framework. After having finished our work we still believe in the virtues of CGE analysis, but also regard rough-and-ready first round calculations much more favorably than before. The reason is not so much that CGE models have a number of serious drawbacks; these were known to us beforehand. The more disturbing fact is that in most cases first round calculations proved to be reasonable approximations for general equilibrium quantifications.

In this final chapter we will summarize our numerical results, discuss our experience with CGE modelling, and offer some tentative policy conclusions.

The drawbacks of CGE models include objections which could be raised to our specific equilibrium model and those which are inherent to the CGE approach in general. As to the former, we would stress two shortcomings which have been mentioned already in previous chapters. The first one concerns our disregard of strategic aspects of tax rate setting. This is one of the main topics to be dealt with in recent theories of international taxation but it has not yet crept into applied equilibrium models. We hope to tackle this issue in future research. The second valid objection is that our data base probably exaggerates

Table 1. Summary of welfare effects[a] of VAT reforms

Countries	F		B-L		NL	
Welfare effects	Eff.[b]	Red.[b]	Eff.	Red.	Eff.	Red.
						Switching
Transitional system	−0.17	−2.03	−0.06	1.91	−0.19	−5.19
		−1.95		*1.95*		*−5.05*
						Mixed
	−0.60	−0.33	−0.28	3.66	−0.36	−1.77
		0.17		*4.08*		*−1.53*
						Common
	−0.60	1.59	−0.28	3.13	−0.36	10.10
		2.07		*3.33*		*10.73*
						Clearing
Origin principle/ credit method	−0.60	-	−0.28	-	−0.36	-
		-		-		-
						Clearing
	−0.60	−0.24	−0.28	1.69	−0.36	−1.42
		−0.02		*1.88*		*−1.31*
Origin principle/ subtraction method	−0.60	−1.76	−3.70	−6.48	−4.00	8.49
		7.23		*1.49*		*12.48*

[a] in per cent of VAT revenue

[b] Eff.: Efficiency (substitution) effects
Red.: International redistribution (net tax export) effects

[c] EU: Proposal of the EU Commission
GER: Proposal of Germany's Country of Origin Comission

D		I		UK-IRL		DK	
Eff.	Red.	Eff.	Red.	Eff.	Red.	Eff.	Red.
option							
0.08	2.02	0.04	1.23	0.39	1.56	−0.30	−1.71
	1.90		*1.19*		*1.52*		*−1.56*
system							
0.28	−2.01	0.04	0.56	0.65	2.17	−1.47	2.96
	−2.69		*0.28*		*1.89*		*4.55*
market principle							
0.28	−1.78	0.04	−3.34	0.65	−3.84	−1.47	5.73
	−2.39		*−3.69*		*−4.19*		*7.30*
system (EU)[c]							
0.28	-	0.04	-	0.65	-	−1.47	-
	-		-		-		-
system (GER)[c]							
0.28	−0.92	0.04	0.45	0.65	1.29	−1.47	1.20
	−1.23		*0.33*		*1.16*		*1.91*
−0.50	5.47	−0.87	−3.05	−1.12	0.19	−7.03	5.82
	4.94		*−1.99*		*0.84*		*18.77*

international direct consumption purchases. Unfortunately, we have been unable to get more reliable data. For the time being, some limited sensitivity analysis with respect to the data base in section 5.2. of the last chapter is all we can offer. There are a large number of further objections which, however, do not only concern our model but CGE analysis in general.[89] This is not the place to grapple with the pros and cons of CGE methodology. Instead, we will summarize our results and point out what we have learnt from our CGE exercise.

Table 1 reproduces the quantitative substitution and net tax export effects for all the VAT reform options considered. Substitution effects describe the efficiency aspects of tax changes whereas net tax exports stand for the international redistribution effects. As to the latter, we present both general equilibrium and, in slanted numbers, first round calculations. The following broad messages emerge.

- In almost all cases, international redistribution effects due to tax exporting or importing activities clearly dominate efficiency effects.
- Efficiency losses or gains are extremely small; they hardly exceed one per cent of the benchmark equilibrium's VAT revenues.
- Except for the origin principle combined with the subtraction method, first round calculations in most cases give reasonable approximations for general equilibrium net tax exports.

From these stylized facts we draw the following conclusions:

- Economists usually stress the efficiency effects of taxation policy, whereas in the political arena redistributional considerations dominate the discussion. We are inclined to admit that politicians have a better feeling for the quantitative significance of income effects as compared to substitution effects.
- Beginning in the early 1970s, the public economics literature concentrated on the efficiency aspects of fiscal policy whereas the older literature emphasized the redistributional side of the ledger. Our numerical findings suggest that emphasizing efficiency effects may be highly misleading. We even dare to say that the time is ripe for a re-orientation, putting at least the same or even more emphasis on distributional problems than on efficiency issues.
- We are still convinced that the development of CGE models over the last two decades has made a major contribution to applied

[89] Tait (1989) lists and discusses some critical assumptions.

welfare economics. But we have learnt that the heavy machinery of computable equilibrium models should be applied with some caution. In some cases, first round calculations may give a fairly good impression of the relevant magnitudes. In fact, we had to employ a rather complicated computable general equilibrium model to learn that, at least in some cases, one could grasp the dominant quantitative features just as well without it.

- The policy conclusions concerning VAT reform after 1997 are rather clear-cut. There are two possible reform options. The most far-reaching alternative is a switch to an origin-based VAT with the subtraction method applied by EU member states and all their trading partners. This option is particularly favored by leading German economists. However, even if practical objections are put aside, welfare considerations cast serious doubts on the realistic chances of this proposal. Not only would the EU as a whole lose, but there would also be considerable welfare shifts within the EU. Of course, welfare effects would look quite different if each member state adopted a strictly uniform rate structure. But no member state is seriously considering giving up its differentiated VAT rate structure. The second VAT system under consideration is the clearing-system favored by the EU Commission. If distance sales are not too large, the proposal recently made by the German Country of Origin Commission may come close to a complete neutralization of net tax exports. In this case, welfare and terms of trade effects would be fairly small in comparison to the destination principle. But then one really wonders about the usefulness of a reform which leaves everything as before. The only benefit might be that administration and compliance costs are lower under the clearing system than under the destination principle with frontier controls or under the present transitional system. We doubt that this is the case. In 1996, at the latest, the practical difficulties which currently plague the transitional system will have been overcome. Our guess is that the transitional VAT rules will be the final ones in Europe for the rest this century.

List of Abbreviations

B-L	Belgium-Luxembourg
CES	Constant elasticity of substitution
CGE	Computable general equilibrium
CMP	Common market principle
D	Germany
DK	Denmark
DM	Deutsche Mark
DP	Destination principle
EC	European Community
ECSC	European Coal and Steel Community
ECU	European Currency Unit
ECOFIN Council	Council for Economic and Financial Affairs
EEC	European Economic Community
EU	European Union
EUROSTAT	Statistical Office of the European Communities
F	France
f.r.	first round
GATT	General Agreement on Tariffs and Trade
GDP	Gross domestic product
g.e.	general equilibrium
GNP	Gross national product
HEV	Hicksian equivalent variation
I	Italy
Int'l	International substitution effects
I-O	Input-Output
mill.	million
MITI	Ministry of International Trade and Industry, Japan

NL	the Netherlands
OECD	Organisation for Economic Co-operation and Development
OP	Origin principle
RAS	Row and column adjustment algorithm
ROW	Rest of world
ToT	Terms of trade
UK	United Kingdom
UK-IRL	United Kingdon – Ireland
US	United States of America
VAT	Value-added tax

Glossary of Notation

Production sector i in country h

First level

Q_i	production of commodity i
V_{ji}^H	intermediate use of composite input j for the production of commodity i
q_{ji}	price index of the composite input j
f_i	value-added function of commodity i
a_{0i}	(fixed) coefficient of the value-added function of commodity i
$a_{ji}^{k:}$	(fixed) coefficient of the composite input j from country k for the production of commodity i (fixed coefficient model)
$av_{ji}^{k:}$	(variable) coefficient of the input j from country k for the production of commodity i (variable coefficient model)

Second level (primary inputs)

$K_i(k_i)$	demand for composite capital (per-unit form)
$L_i(l_i)$	demand for labor (per-unit form)
ϕ_i	scale parameter of the value-added function
δ_i	share parameter of labor
σ_i	elasticity of substitution between capital and labor
ϱ_i	auxiliary parameter
$Cost_i$	primary input cost function
b_i	primary input cost per unit
w	wage rate
r	rental price of capital

Second level (intermediate inputs)

$V_{ji}^M(v_{ji}^M)$	demand for composite imported input j (per-unit form)
$V_{ji}(v_{ji})$	demand for domestically produced input j (per-unit form)

ξ_{ji}	scale parameter of the composite input production function of intermediate j
λ_{ji}	share parameter of composite imported input j
ω_{ji}	elasticity of substitution between domestic and imported intermediate j
θ_{ji}	auxiliary parameter
$Cost^H_{ji}$	cost function of composite input j
q^M_{ji}	price index of the composite imported input j
q_j	domestic producer price of commodity j
a_i	share of sector i's imports in the total imports
ρ	(auxiliary) country specific elasticity between imported and domestic intermediates
η_i	sector specific elasticity of substitution between imported and domestic intermediates
ψ	country specific elasticity of substitution between imported and domestic intermediates

Third level (intermediate inputs)

$V^{k\cdot}_{ji}(v^{k\cdot}_{ji})$	intermediate use of input j from country k (per-unit form)
ζ_{ji}	scale parameter of the composite imported input production function of intermediate j
κ^k_{ji}	share parameter of input j from country k
$Cost^M_{ji}$	cost function of the composite imported input j
q^k_j	producer price of commodity j from country k

Household sector in country h

First Level

U	utility function
C	composite consumption commodity
ℓ	leisure time
β	share parameter of leisure time
ν	elasticity of substitution between composite consumption and leisure

μ	auxiliary parameter
e	uncompensated elasticity of labor supply
$\hat{e}$	elasticity of leisure demand
s_e	share of maximal possible labor income of full disposable income
s_ℓ	share of leisure 'expenditure' of full disposable income
w_n	net wage rate
r	interest rate
E	total time endowment
$\bar{K}$	total capital stock owned by household sector
Y	full disposable income
p	price index of composite consumption

Second level

C_i^H	composite demand category i
β_i	share parameter of composite demand category i
ν_c	elasticity of substitution between composite demand categories
μ_c	auxiliary parameter
L	labor supply
Y^H	disposable income
p_i^H	price index of composite demand category i

Third level

C_i^M	composite imported consumption commodity i
C_i	consumption of domestically produced commodity i
β_i^H	share parameter of domestic consumption commodity i
ν_i	elasticity of substitution between composite imported and domestic consumption commodity i
μ_i	auxiliary parameter
ε_i	price elasticity of import demand for commodity i
Y_i^H	disposable income for commodity category i
p_i^M	price index of imported consumption commodities
p_i	consumer price of domestically produced commodity i

Fourth level

$C_i^{k\cdot}$	consumption of commodity i produced in country k
β_i^k	share parameter of consumption commodity i from country k
ν_i^M	elasticity of substitution between imports of commodity i from different source countries
μ_i^M	auxiliary parameter
Y_i^M	disposable income for direct imports of commodity i
$p_i^{k\cdot}$	consumer price of commodity i from country k
q_i^k	producer price of commodity i from country k

Government sector

τ_{qi}	production tax in the production sector i
t_j^{hk}	tariff rate of country h for commodity j from country k
τ_y	marginal income tax rate
τ_i^k	consumption tax rate of country k for commodity i
T_C	value-added tax revenue of the government sector
T_C^H	value-added tax payment of the household sector
T_Y	income tax revenue
All	income tax allowance
$T_Q(T_{Q_i})$	production tax revenue (from sector i)
TAR^H	tariff payment of the household sector
TAR^Q	tariff payment of the production sector
TAR_i^Q	tariff payment of production sector i
TAR	total tariff revenue
Tr	transfer payments received by household sector
G	quantity of public good
q_g	producer price of the public good

Foreign sector

TB	trade balance
SB	service balance

BP	balance of payments
TRB	transaction account
p_m	price index for imports
p_x	price index for exports
ToT	net-barter terms-of-trade
M_i^{kh}	total imports of commodity i from country k
X_i^{hk}	total exports of commodity i to country k

The Debate about Value-added Taxation in the European Union:

Timetable of Events since 1985

June 14, 1985	"White Paper on the Completion of the Internal Market" is issued by the Commission of the European Communities
June 28 to June 29, 1985	European Council meets in Mailand, Italy
December 2 to December 3, 1985	European Council meets in Luxembourg
February 28, 1986	"Single European Act" is adopted
August 7, 1987	Draft Proposals concerning an intra-Community clearing system (COM (87) 320 final to COM (87) 324 final) are issued by the Commission of the European Communities
September, 18, 1988	EC Ministers of Finance meet in Crete, Greece
December 3 to December 4, 1988	European Council meets in Rhodes, Greece
May, 1989	New Draft Proposal (COM (89) 260 final) is issued by the Commission of the European Communities
June 19, 1989	Ad hoc study group to examine the Commission's proposals is established by the ECOFIN Council

June 26 to June 27, 1989	European Council meets in Madrid, Spain
October 9 and November 13, 1989	Transitional system is in principle agreed upon by the ECOFIN Council
May 17, 1990	Draft Proposal concerning the transitional system (COM (90) 182 final and COM (90) 183 final) is issued by the Commission of the European Communities
June 15 to June 16, 1990	European Council meets in Dublin; once again, an ad hoc study group is put into place
December 3, 1990	ECOFIN Council decides in principle to introduce the transitional system
December 14 to December 15, 1990	European Council meets in Rome, Italy
March 18 and June 24, 1991	ECOFIN Council decides on the details of the transitional system
December 16, 1991 and January 27, 1992	ECOFIN Council finally adopts the transitional system
January 1, 1993	Single European Market becomes effective; the transitional system is introduced

References

Abe, K., Okamura, M. (1989): The Welfare Effects of International Tax Harmonization. Economic Studies Quarterly 40, 203-211.

Ahlheim, M., Rose, M. (1989): Messung individueller Wohlfahrt. Berlin Heidelberg New York.

Allen, R., Ely, J.E. (1953): International Trade Statistics. New York.

Andel, N. (1985): Kommentar zu den Artikeln 95 bis 99 EWGV. In: H. von der Groeben, J. Thiesing, C.-D. Ehlermann (Eds.): Handbuch des Europäischen Rechts. Systematische Sammlung mit Erläuterungen, I A 51, 217. Lieferung (June 1985). Baden-Baden, 1-44.

Andel, N. (1986): Sollte man in der EG im Rahmen der Mehrwertsteuer zum Ursprungsland übergehen? Finanzarchiv N.F. 44, 484-488.

Armington, P.S. (1969): A Theory of Demand for Products Distinguished by Place of Production. IMF Staff Papers 16, 159-176.

Atkinson, A.B., Stiglitz, J.E. (1980): Lectures on Public Economics. London New York etc.

Aujean, M., Vis, P. (1992): VAT in the Single Market: the Transitional Arrangements Explained. EC Tax Review , 117-137.

Bacharach, M. (1970): Biproportional Matrices and Input-Output Change. Cambridge.

Ballard, Ch., Fullerton, D., Shoven, J.B., Whalley, J. (1985): A General Equilibrium Model for Tax Policy Evaluation. Chicago.

Berglas, E. (1981): Harmonization of Commodity Taxes. Journal of Public Economics 16, 377-387.

Bergstrom, T.C. (1976): Toward a Deeper Economics of Sleeping. Journal of Political Economy 84, 411-412.

Bhagwati, J.N., Srinivasan, T.N. (1983): Lectures in International Trade. Cambridge London.

Biehl, D. (1969): Ausfuhrland-Prinzip, Einfuhrland-Prinzip und Gemeinsamer-Markt-Prinzip. Ein Beitrag zur Theorie der Steuerharmonisierung. Köln.

Biehl, D. (1982): Towards a General Theory of Taxing International Transactions - A Taxonomy of International Taxation Principles. Public Finance 37, 189-205.

Biehl, D. (1988): On Maximal Versus Optimal Tax Harmonization. In: R. Bieber, R. Dehousse, J. Pinder, J. Weiler (Eds.): 1992: One European Market? Baden-Baden, 261-282.

Boadway, R.W. (1974): The Welfare Foundations of Cost-Benefit Analysis. Economic Journal 84, 926-939.

Boadway, R.W., Bruce, N. (1984): Welfare Economics. Oxford New York.

Boomsma, P., van der Linden, J., Oosterhaven J. (1991): Note on the Comparability of Export and Import Data from E.C. Input-Output Tables and Trade Statistics. Unpublished, Department of Economics, University of Groningen.

Borges, A. (1986): Applied General Equilibrium Models: An Assessment of their Usefulness for Policy Analysis. OECD Economic Studies 7, 7-43.

Bosi, P., Golinelli, R., Stagni, A. (1988): Effetti Macroeconomici e Settoriali dell'Armonizzazione dell'Iva e delle Accise: La Valutazione del Modello Hermes-Italia. Politica Economica 4, 361-384.

Boss, A. (1989): Steuerharmonisierung und Realisierung des EG-Binnenmarktes. Wirtschaftsdienst 69, 249-251.

Bovenberg, A.L. (1987): The General Equilibrium Approach: Relevant for Public Policy? In: H.M. van de Kar, B.L. Wolfe (Eds.): The Relevance of Public Finance for Policy-Making. Detroit, 33-43.

Bovenberg, A.L., Horne, J.L. (1992): Taxes on Commodities: A Survey. In: G. Kopits (Ed.): Tax Harmonization in the European Community. Policy Issues and Analysis. Washington D.C., 22-51.

Brugiavini, A., Weber, G. (1988): Welfare Effects of Indirect Tax Harmonisation: The Italian Case. Politica Economica 4, 385-408.

Clemens, R., Paulini, M. (1991): Harmonisierung der indirekten Steuern im Europäischen Binnenmarkt. Stuttgart.

Cnossen, S. (1982): What Rate Structure for a Value-Added Tax? National Tax Journal 35, 205-214.

COM (85) 310 final (1985): Completing the Internal Market. White Paper from the Commission to the European Council. Luxembourg.

COM (87) 320 final (1987): Completion of the Internal Market: Approximation of Indirect Tax Rates and Harmonization of Indirect Tax Structure. Global Communication from the Commission. Brussels, 5.8.1987.

COM (87) 321 final (1987): Proposal for a Council Directive Completing the Common System of Value-Added Tax and Amending Directive 77/388/EEC – Approximation of VAT Rates. Brussels, 5.8.1987.

COM (87) 322 final (1987): Proposal for a Council Directive Completing and Amending Directive 77/388/EEC – Removal of Fiscal Frontiers. Brussels 5.8.1987.

COM (87) 323 final/2 (1987): Completing the Internal Market – The Introduction of a VAT Clearing Mechanism for Intra-Community Sales – Working Paper of the Commission. Brussels, 25.8.1987.

COM (87) 324 final (1987): Proposal for a Council Directive Instituting a Process of Convergence of Rates of Value-Added Tax and Excise Duties. Brussels, 25.8.1987.

COM (88) 810 final (1988): Proposal for a Council Regulation (EEC) on the Statistics Relating to the Trading of Goods between Member States. Brussels, 11.1.1989.

COM (89) 260 final (1989): Completion of the Internal Market and Approximation of Indirect Taxes. Communication from the Commission to the Council and the European Parliament. Brussels, 14.6.1989.

COM (90) 177 final (1990): Amended Proposal for a Council Regulation (EEC) on the Statistics Relating to the Trading of Goods between Member States (Submitted by the Commission Pursuant to Article 149(3) of the EEC Treaty). Brussels, 27.6.1990.

COM (90) 182 final/2 (1990): Amendment to the Proposal for a Council Directive Supplementing the Common System of Value Added Tax and Amending Directive 77/388/EEC. Transitional Arrangements for Taxation with a View to Establishment of the Internal Market. Brussels, 18.10.1990.

COM (90) 183 final (1990): Proposal for a Council Regulation (EEC) Concerning Administrative Cooperation in the Field of Indirect Taxation. Brussels, 19.6.1990.

Cornilleau, G. (1988): L'harmonisation de la TVA dans la perspective du grand marché européen. Observations et diagnostics économiques 22, 109-129.

Council of Economic Advisors to the German Ministry of Economics (1986): Stellungnahme zum Weißbuch der EG-Kommission über den Binnenmarkt. Studienreihe des Bundesministeriums für Wirtschaft, Heft 51. Bonn.

Country of Origin Commission (1994): Ausarbeitung der endgültigen Regelung für die Umsatzbesteuerung des innergemeinschaftlichen Waren- und Dienstleistungsverkehrs und für ein funktionsfähiges Clearing-Verfahren. BMF-Schriftenreihe 52. Bonn.

Crombrugghe, A. de, Tulkens, H. (1990): On Pareto Improving Commodity Tax Changes under Fiscal Competition. Journal of Public Economics 41, 335-350.

Deaton, A. (1981): Optimal Taxes and the Structure of Preferences. Econometrica 49, 1245-1260.

Dewald, W.G., Thursby, J.G., Anderson, R.G. (1986): Replication in Empirical Economics: The Journal of Money, Credit and Banking Project. American Economic Review 76, 587-603.

Donges, J. (1989): Die EG auf dem Weg zum Binnenmarkt? Erwartungen, Konsequenzen, Probleme. Kiel Institute of World Economics, Discussion Paper 360 . Kiel.

Ebert, U. (1985): On the Relationship between the Hicksian Measures of Change in Welfare and the Pareto Principle. Social Choice and Welfare 1, 263-272.

Ernst & Young (1993): VAT & Excise. A Taxpayer's Guide to Indirect Taxation in the Single Market. London.

EUROSTAT-Statistical Office of the European Communities (1982): Monthly Trade Bulletin 12. Luxembourg.

EUROSTAT-Statistical Office of the European Communities (1983): Statistische Grundzahlen der Gemeinschaft. Luxembourg.

EUROSTAT-Statistical Office of the European Communities (1986): National Accounts ESA: Input-Output Tables 1980. Luxembourg.

EUROSTAT-Statistical Office of the European Communities (1987): Balance of Payments: Geographical Breakdown 1981-1985. Luxembourg.

Fane, G. (1991): Piecemeal Tax Reforms and the Compensated Radial Elasticities of Tax Bases. Journal of Public Economics 45, 263-270.

Fehr, H., Rosenberg, Ch., Wiegard, W. (1991): A Multi-Country Applied General Equilibrium Model for the Examination of VAT-Harmonization Proposals in the European Community. Modelling, Calibration and Construction of a Microconsistent Dataset. University of Regensburg, Discussion Paper 236. Regensburg.

Fehr, H., Rosenberg, Ch., Wiegard, W. (1993): Value-added Taxation in the EC after 1992. Some Applied General Equilibrium Calculations. European Economic Review 37, 1483-1506.

Fehr, H., Rosenberg, Ch., Wiegard, W. (1994): Should the EU Adopt the Origin Principle for VAT after 1997? Finanzarchiv N.F. 51, 1-27.

Fratianni, M., Christie, H. (1981): Abolishing Fiscal Frontiers within the EEC. Public Finance 36, 411-429.

Frenkel, J., Razin, A., Symansky, S. (1991): International VAT Harmonization – Macroeconomic Effects. IMF Staff Papers 38, 789-827.

Frenkel, J.A., Razin, A., Sadka, E. (1991): International Taxation in an Integrated World. Cambridge (Mass.) London.

Fullerton, D., Lyon, A.B. (1986): Uncertain Parameter Values and the Choice among Policy Options. Journal of Public Economics 30, 109-116.

Georgakopoulos, Th. (1974): The Excess Burden Controversy in a Trading World: A Case for Special Indirect Taxes. Public Finance 29, 152-167.

Georgakopoulos, Th. (1989): Harmonization of Commodity Taxes. Journal of Public Economics 39, 137-139.

Georgakopoulos, Th. (1992): Trade Deflection, Trade Distortions, and Pareto Inefficiencies under the Restricted Origin Principle. Journal of Public Economics 47, 381-390.

Georgakopoulos, Th., Hitiris, T. (1991): The Equivalence of the Destination and the Restricted Origin Principles of Taxation in the Case of Non-General Taxes. Osaka Economic Papers 40, 331-335.

Georgakopoulos, Th., Hitiris, T. (1992): On the Superiority of the Destination over the Origin Principle of Taxation for Intra-Union Trade. Economic Journal 102, 117-126.

German Ministry of Finance (1981): Informationsdienst zur Finanzpolitik des Auslandes 1. Bonn, 9-10.

Gillis, M. (1990): The VAT and Financial Services. In: M. Gillis, C.S. Shoup, G.P. Sicat (Eds.). 83-94.

Gillis, M., Shoup, C.S., Sicat, G.P., Eds. (1990): Value Added Taxation in Developing Countries. The World Bank, Washington D.C.

Gordon, J.P.F. (1991): Tax Reform and Uniformity: Explaining the Hatta Result. Journal of Public Economics 45, 257-261.

Gottfried, P., Wiegard, W. (1991): Exemption Versus Zero Rating: A Hidden Problem of VAT. Journal of Public Economics 46, 307-328.

Grossman, G. (1980): Border Tax Adjustments, Do they Distort Trade? Journal of International Economics 10, 117-128.

Hahn, W. (1988): Steuerpolitische Willensbildungsprozesse in der Europäischen Gemeinschaft. Das Beispiel der Umsatzsteuer-Harmonisierung. Frankfurt a.M.

Hamilton, B., Whalley, J. (1986): Border Tax Adjustments and U.S. Trade. Journal of International Economics 20, 377-383.

Harberger, A.C. (1962): The Incidence of the Corporation Income Tax. Journal of Political Economy 70, 215-240.

Harberger, A.C. (1966): Efficiency Effects of Taxes on Income from Capital. In: M. Krzyzaniak (Ed.): Effects of Corporation Income Tax. Detroit, 107-117.

Harrison, G., Jones, R., Kimbell, L., Wigle, R. (1993): How Robust is Applied General Equilibrium Analysis? Journal of Policy Modeling 15, 99-115.

Harrison, G., Rutherford, T., Wooton, I. (1991): An Empirical Database for a General Equilibrium Model of the European Communities. In: J. Piggott, J. Whalley (Eds.): Applied General Equilibrium. Heidelberg, 95-120.

Harrison, G., Vinod, H. (1992): The Sensivity Analysis of Applied General Equilibrium Models: Completely Randomized Factorial Sampling Designs. Review of Economis and Statistics 74, 357-362.

Hatta, T. (1986): Welfare Effects of Changing Commodity Tax Rates Toward Uniformity. Journal of Public Economics 29, 99-112.

Haufler, A. (1993): Commodity Tax Harmonization in the European Community. A General Equilibrium Analysis of Tax Policy Options in the Internal Market. Heidelberg.

Hemming, R., Kay, J.A. (1981): The United Kingdom. In: H.J. Aaron (Ed.): The Value-Added Tax. Lessons from Europe. Brookings Institution, Washington D.C., 75-89.

Hoffman, E.P. (1977): The Deeper Economics of Sleeping: Important Clues toward the Discovery of Activity X. Journal of Political Economy 85, 647-649.

Ishi, H. (1993): The Japanese Tax System. 2nd Edition. Oxford.

Johansson, P.-O. (1987): The Economic Theory and Mearsurement of Environmental Benefits. Cambridge etc.

Jorgenson, D.W. (1984): Econometric Methods for Applied General Equilibrium Analysis. In: H.E. Scarf, J.B. Shoven (Eds.) . 139-204.

Kaiser, H., Wiegard, W., Zimmermann, H.G. (1990): Testing the Reliability of Optimal Tax Calculations. Finanzarchiv N.F. 48, 77-96.

Kanbur, R., Keen, M. (1993): Jeux Sans Frontièrs: Tax Competition and Tax Coordination When Countries Differ in Size. American Economic Review 83. 877-892.

Kay, J.A., Warren, N.A. (1980): Effective Rates of Value Added Tax. Working Paper No. 16. Institute for Fiscal Studies, London.

Kay, J. A., Davis, E. (1990): The VAT on Services, In: M. Gillis, C.S. Shoup, G.P. Sicat (Eds.). 70-82.

Keen, M. (1987): Welfare Effects of Commodity Tax Harmonisation. Journal of Public Economics 33, 107-114.

Keen, M. (1989): Pareto-Improving Indirect Tax Harmonisation. European Economic Review 33, 1-12.

Keller, W. (1976): A Nested CES-Type Utility Function and its Demand and Price-Index Functions. European Economic Review 7, 175-186.

Kemp, M. (1968): Terms of Trade. In: D.L. Sills (Ed.): International Encyclopedia of the Social Siences, Vol. 8, 105-108.

Krause-Junk, G. (1990): Ein Plädoyer für das Ursprungslandprinzip. In: W. Kitterer, F.-X. Bea (Eds.): Finanzwissenschaft im Dienste der Wirtschaftspolitik. Festschrift für Dieter Pohmer. Tübingen, 253-266.

Langer, Ch. (1987): Produktionsverflechtung in der EG. Ein interregionales Input-Output Modell für die Staaten der Europäischen Gemeinschaft. Hamburg.

Lau, L.J. (1984): Comments. In: H.E. Scarf, J.B. Shoven (Eds.). 127-137.

Lee, C., Pearson, M., Smith, S. (1988): Fiscal Harmonization: An Analysis of the Commission's Proposal. Institute for Fiscal Studies, London.

Lookwood, B. (1993): Commodity Tax Competition under Destination and Origin Principles. Journal of Public Economics 52, 141-162.

McKee, M., Visser, J., Saunders, P. (1986): Marginal Tax on the Use of Labor and Capital in OECD Countries. OECD Economic Studies 7, 45-101.

McKenzie, G.W. (1983): Measuring Economic Welfare. Cambridge etc.

McLure, Ch. (1972): The Tax on Value Added. In: McLure, Ch., N.B. Ture (Eds.): Value Added Tax: Two Views. American Enterprise Institute for Public Policy Research, Washington D.C., 1-68.

McLure, Ch. (1987): The Value-Added Tax - Key to Deficit Reduction? American Enterprise Institute for Public Policy Research, Washington D.C.

McLure, Ch. (1990): Income Distribution and Tax Incidence under the VAT. In: M. Gillis, C.S. Shoup, G.P. Sicat (Eds.). 32-40.

MITI-Ministry of International Trade and Industry (1989): The 1985 Japan-US Input Output Table. Research and Statistics Department Minister's Secretariat, Tokyo.

Mintz, J., Tulkens, H. (1986): Commodity Tax Competition between Member States of a Federation: Equilibrium and Efficiency. Journal of Public Economics 29, 133-172.

Neumark Report (1963): The EEC Reports on Tax Harmonization. The Report of the Fiscal and Financial Committee and the Reports of the Subgroups A, B and C. International Bureau of Fiscal Documentation, Amsterdam.

Nguyen, T., Perroni, C., Wigle, R. (1993): An Evaluation of the Draft Final Act of the Uruguay Round. Economic Journal 103, 1540-1549.

Nicoll, W., Salmon, T.C. (1994): Understanding the New European Community. New York London etc.

Norman, V. (1990): Assessing Trade and Welfare Effects of Trade Liberalization: A Comparison of Alternative Approaches to CGE Modelling with Imperfect Competition. European Economic Review 34, 725-745.

OECD-Organisation for Economic Co-Operation and Development (1988): Taxing Consumption. Paris.

OECD-Organisation for Economic Co-Operation and Development (1989): Revenue Statistics of OECD Member Countries 1965-1988. Paris.

OECD-Organisation for Economic Co-Operation and Development (1990): Modelling the Effects of Agricultural Politics. OECD Economic Studies, Special Issue 13. Paris.

OECD-Organisation for Economic Co-operation and Development (1993): Assessing the Effects of the Uruguay Round. Paris.

Pagan, A., Shannon, J. (1985): Sensitivity Analysis for Linearized Computable General Equilibrium Models. In: J. Piggott, J. Whalley (Eds.): New Developments in Applied General Equilibrium Analysis. Cambridge, 104-118.

Parsche, R. (1991): Europäische Umsatzsteuerharmonisierung und Clearing-Verfahren. Ifo Studien zur Finanzpolitik 49, München.

Parsche, R., Seidel, B., Teichmann, D. (1988): Die Beseitigung von Steuergrenzen in der Europäischen Gemeinschaft. DIW Sonderheft 145, Berlin.

Patrizi, V., Rossi, N. (1991): The European Internal Market and the Welfare of Italian Consumers. Public Finance 46, 111-122.

Perraudin, W., Pujol, T. (1990): Tax Efficiency in an Open Economy. IMF Working Paper No. 94, Washington D.C.

Piggott, J. (1988): General Equilibrium Computation Applied to Public Sector Issues. In: P. Hare (Ed.): Surveys in Public Sector Economics. Oxford, 248-298.

Pohmer, D. (1981): Germany. In: H.J. Aaron (Ed.): Value-Added Tax. Lessons from Europe. Washington D.C., 91-101.

Rose, M. (1987): Optimal Tax Perspective on Tax Coordination. In: S. Cnossen (Ed.): Tax Coordination in the European Community. Deventer Antwerp etc., 113-138.

Sandmo, A. (1974): A Note on the Structure of Optimal Taxation. American Economic Review 64, 701-706.

Scailteur, C. (1974): L'influence de l'Integration et de la Coopération Economique Internationale dans la Domaine de la Taxation. Chronique de Politique Etrangère 27, 455-478.

Scarf, H. (1967): On the Computation of Equilibrium Prices. In: W.J. Fellner (Ed.): Ten Economic Studies in the Tradition of Irvin Fischer. New York, 207-230.

Scarf, H. (1969): An Example of an Algorithm for Calculating General Equilibrium Prices. American Economic Review 59, 669-677.

Scarf, H. (1973): The Computation of Economic Equilibria. New Haven London.

Scarf, H., Shoven, J.B., Eds. (1984): Applied General Equilibrium Analysis. Cambridge etc.

Scrivener, C. (1990): Harmonization of Tax Law within the Community. European Taxation 30, 355-358.

Shibata, H. (1967): The Theory of Economic Unions: A Comparative Analysis of Customs Unions, Free Trade Areas and Tax Unions. In: C.S. Shoup (Ed.): Fiscal Harmonization in Common Markets 1: Theory. New York London, 145-264.

Shoup, C.S. (1969): Public Finance. Chicago.

Shoup, C.S. (1990): Choosing among Types of VATs. In: M. Gillis, C.S. Shoup, G.P. Sicat (Eds.). 3-16.

Shoven, J.B. (1983): Applied General Equilibrium Tax Modeling. IMF Staff Papers 30, 394-420.

Shoven, J.B., Whalley, J. (1972): A General Equilibrium Calculation of the Effects of Differential Taxation of Income from Capital in the U.S. Journal of Public Economics 1, 281-321.

Shoven J.B., Whalley, J. (1984): Applied General Equilibrium Models of Taxation and International Trade. Journal of Economic Literature 22, 1007-1051.

Shoven, J.B., Whalley, J. (1992): Applying General Equilibrium. Cambridge.

Siebert, H. (1989a): Harmonisierung der Mehrwertsteuer oder Anpassung der Wechselkurse? Kiel Institute of World Economics, Discussion Paper 156. Kiel.

Siebert, H. (1989b): Perspektiven zur Vollendung des europäischen Binnenmarktes. Kyklos 42, 181-201.

Sinn, H.-W. (1987): Capital Income Taxation and Resource Allocation. Amsterdam New York Oxford Tokyo.

Sinn, H.-W. (1990): Tax Harmonization and Tax Competition in Europe. European Economic Review 34, 489-504.

Spahn, B., Kaiser, H. (1991): Tax Harmonization or Tax Competition as Means to Integrate Western Europe. Konjunkturpolitik 37, 1-44.

Statistical Office (1984): Fachserie 18: Volkswirtschaftliche Gesamtrechnungen. Reihe 2: Input-Output-Tabellen 1980. Stuttgart Mainz.

Stern, R., Francis, J., Schumacher, B. (1976): Price Elasticities in International Trade. An Annotated Bibliography. London.

St-Hilaire, F., Whalley, J. (1983): A Microconsistent Equilibrium Data Set for Canada for Use in Tax Policy Analysis. Review of Income and Wealth 29, 175-204.

St-Hilaire, F., Whalley, J. (1987): A Microconsistent Data Set for Use in Regional General Equilibrium Policy Analysis. Review of Income and Wealth 33, 327-343.

Sullivan, C.K. (1965): The Tax on Value Added. New York London.

Symons, E., Walker, I. (1988): The Revenue and Welfare Effects of Fiscal Harmonisation for the U.K. Institute for Fiscal Studies Working Paper Series 8/88, London.

Tait, A. (1988): Value Added Tax, International Practice and Problems. International Monetary Fund, Washington D.C.

Tait, A. (1989): Not so General Equilibrium and Not so Optimal Taxation. Public Finance 44, 169-182.

Terra, B.J.L. (1988): Sales Taxation: The Case of Value Added Tax in the European Community. Series on International Taxation No. 8, Boston.

Terra, B.J.M., Kajus, J. (1992): Introduction to Value-added Tax in the EC after 1992. Boston.

Tinbergen Report (1953): Report on the Problems Raised by the Different Turnover Tax Systems Applied within the Common Market. European Coal and Steel Community.

Tower, E. (1984): Effective Protection, Domestic Resource Costs, and Shadow Prices. A General Equilibrium Perspective. The World Bank, Washington D.C.

Turunen-Red, A.H., Woodland, A.D. (1990): Multilateral Reforms of Domestic Taxes. Oxford Economic Papers 42, 160-186.

United Nations (1985): National Account Statistics: Analysis of Main Aggregates. New York.

U.S. Treasury Department (1984): Tax Reform for Fairness, Simplicity and Economic Growth. Vol. 3: Value Added Tax. Washington D.C.

Vandendorpe, A. (1972): Optimal Tax Structures in a Model with Traded and Non-Traded Goods. Journal of International Economics 2, 235-256.

Whalley, J. (1976): Some General Equilibrium Analysis Applied to Fiscal Harmonization in the European Community. European Economic Review 8, 291-312.

Whalley, J. (1979): Uniform Domestic Tax Rates, Trade Distortions and Economic Integration. Journal of Public Economics 11, 213-221.

Whalley, J. (1981): Border Adjustments and Tax Harmonization: Comments on Berglas. Journal of Public Economics 16, 389-390.

Whalley, J. (1985): Trade Liberalization among Major World Trading Areas. Cambridge.

Wigle, R. (1991): The Pagan-Shannon Approximation: Unconditional Systematic Sensivity in Minutes. In: J. Piggott, J. Whalley (Eds.): Applied General Equilibrium. Heidelberg, 35-49.

Zanden, J. van der, Terra, B.J.M. (1987): EC: The Removal of Trade Barriers: the White Paper from the Commission to the European Council. Intertax 6/1987, 130-142.

MIX
Papier aus verantwortungsvollen Quellen
Paper from responsible sources
FSC® C105338

If you have any concerns about our products,
you can contact us on
ProductSafety@springernature.com

In case Publisher is established outside the EU,
the EU authorized representative is:
Springer Nature Customer Service Center GmbH
Europaplatz 3, 69115 Heidelberg, Germany

Printed by Libri Plureos GmbH
in Hamburg, Germany